Community Learning & Libraries

Cymuned Ddysgu a

SUNFLOWERS AND SNIPERS

'Come on' cried Selma, 'Hurry up!'

Furtively checking to make sure that their parents were not watching, Mirza followed his sister through the doorway. They were not supposed to go outside but there was always a lull in the fighting around this time. Mirza still remembered life before the war, when he and Selma played on the banks of the Neretva, watching in awe as the older boys dived off the bridge across the turquoise river. Croatian propaganda echoed across the front line but the children barely noticed, the sound was more common than birdsong within the besieged city. Shielding his eyes from the brightness of the midday sun, Mirza looked around for his ball.

There was a deafening blast as a mortar exploded close to the house, scattering shards of shrapnel in all directions. Unable to see through the billowing smoke, Mirza could hear Selma screaming. He tried to stand but it hurt and he saw that part of his right foot was missing. Determined to reach his sister he began crawling through the rubble, tears streaming down his blackened face as he desperately called out her name.

★★★

Dear Sally,

It was with great sadness and a feeling of shame that I received the news of the terrible deed of those who threatened your life, the life of the 'angel'. The greatness of your work seems to be that nothing can stop you. Wishing you a speedy recovery I look forward to seeing you soon.

Sincerely yours,

Dr Bujar Bukoshi

Prime Minister of Kosovo (in exile in Tirana)

★★★

SUNFLOWERS AND SNIPERS

SAVING CHILDREN IN THE BALKAN WAR

SALLY BECKER

For Billie.

Whom shall I send and who will go for us?
Then said I, Here am I; send me.

Isaiah, chapter 6, verse 8

First published 2012

The History Press
The Mill, Brimscombe Port
Stroud, Gloucestershire, GL5 2QG
www.thehistorypress.co.uk

British Library Cataloguing in Publication Data.
A catalogue record for this book is available from the British Library.

ISBN 978 0 7524 8309 2

Typesetting and origination by The History Press
Printed in Great Britain

CONTENTS

Acknowledgements		7
Foreword by Professor Tom Gallagher		9
Introduction		10

Part I

1	From Brighton to the Balkans	12
2	'You Can Do So Much More'	20
3	Crescent, Cross and Star	24
4	'I'm Sure You Mean Well'	31
5	The Baby Brigadier	35
6	'Stick to Helping the Jews'	42
7	Handouts and Holdups	49
8	Crossing the Line	55
9	An Unlikely Angel	65
10	The East Side	72
11	Incoming	78
12	Collette	83
13	Operaton Angel	89
14	Jinxed	100
15	'You Have Put People's Lives at Risk!'	110
16	'They Could Have Done This Without You'	115
17	Nova Bila	121
18	The Promise Kept	127

Part II

19	Kosovo and the Queen	135
20	To Bajram Curri	144
21	Dangerous Crossing	154
22	'Welcome to Kosovo'	160
23	The Pied Piper	166
24	The Accursed Mountains	171
25	Under Arrest	178
26	The Interrogation	183
27	A 'Confession'	188

28 Lipljan Prison   194
29 An Unexpected Visitor   206
30 Another Mission   211
31 Blood and Rain   223
32 Nobody's Angel   228
33 Bajram Bill   233
34 'I am the Baby You Rescued'   240

    Epilogue   250
    Index   252

ACKNOWLEDGEMENTS

My thanks to Shaun Barrington at The History Press for believing my story should be told. Professor Tom Gallagher, Mark S. Smith and Leslie Woodhead for their guidance and encouragement and Edward Becker for his literary contribution.

To all my family and friends, most especially my mother Carol for her eternal faith in me, and Heather James for her constant support.

Brigadier Dr Ivan Bagarić and his colleagues at Bijeli Brijeg for enabling me to help the 'other side', and Vava (Vladimir Mikulić), my great friend and protector.

Lynne Gillete without whom I might not have stayed, and my colleagues Tim Clancy, Paul, Tim, Thierry, Domi and Paddy. To Collette Webster who will never be forgotten, and Sean Vatcher for loving her.

Thanks to Stipe, Erna and Damir who took such good care of me and to the Bosnian officer who risked his life to help me reach the hospital. To Hafid Konjihoddzic, Jovan Rajkov, Dragan Malović and the staff at Higijenski; true heroes who will hopefully receive the recognition they deserve.

To all those who helped to organise Operation Angel, especially Mike and Jennifer Mendoza, Val Young, Justine, Stewart Weir, Brian Charig and Alicia. Those who gave their support to the mission; Andrew Popkeiwicz, Brian Lee, Barbara Hayward, John Dyer, Ron Waight, Harold Pinter, Lady Antonia Fraser, Bob Marshall Andrews QC and Andrew Bowden MP.

To JACS, UKJAID ICJW and the 35s; with special thanks to Michael Harris, Ansel Harris, Joyce Simpson, June Jacobs, Eva Mitchell and Rita Eker. Eli Benson, Rabbi Dr Jeremy Collick, Lana Kaye and the Hove Reform Synagogue and Rabbi Pesach Effune. The Immam of Hove, Molly Brandl-Bowen and Dr T. Scarlett Epstein OBE.

Dr Duncan Stewart, my 'knight in a flak jacket' and the Sir Halley Stewart Trust.

The *Sunday Mirror*, Sally Line Ferries, Nissan, Trailblazers, Teddies for Tragedies, the AA and the BRS, the Life Foundation, the Brighton Collective Group of Hotels and the Celebrity Guild of Great Britain. To everyone involved with *Hear the Children*, especially Gloria Macari, Roger Ferris, Yolanda Beeny, Graham Boyd and the children of St Christopher's and The Torah Academy.

To the great British public who helped raise funds and aid for the convoy and to all the brave volunteers, in particular Mick Fegan, Lawrence Le Carré, David and Ashley Rose, the truck drivers, nurses, doctors, paramedics, ambulance technicians, firemen, police and members of the Territorial Army.

I would also like to thank the UNPROFOR soldiers who risked their lives to help with the evacuation of the wounded and the officers who took part in what was a very complicated mission. In particular Colonel Peter Williams, Major Tohler, Major Need, Sonja Thompson (UN), Jerry Hulme (UNHCR) and members of the US Air Force, the British Army and Royal Navy.

My thanks to Norris McWhirter, Sir John Major, Baroness Margaret Thatcher, George Urban and Sir Paddy Ashdown.

Tony Redmond and his team from the Staffordshire Hospital in Stoke, the Heartlands Hospital Trust in east Birmingham, the Walsgrave Hospital, Coventry; the Midland Centre for Neurosurgery, Smethwick and the Groby Road Hospital, Leicester. A special thank you to the Veterans for Peace (US) for taking such good care of the children.

To all those in the media who reported with fairness and accuracy, in particular Emma Daly, (the *Independent*) Richard Beeston and Anthony Lloyd (*The Times*) Mark Downdney, (the *Daily Mirror*) Christopher Morris (Sky News) Brent Sadler (CNN) Anne Diamond and Nick Owen (BBC) Eamonn Holmes (GMTV) Robin White (ITV) Fred Dinenage (Meridian) Mark Longhurst, Mark Norman and Sally Taylor (BBC South) Lorraine Kelly (Talk Radio) BBC World Service and BBC Radio 4. And award-winning photo journalist Tim Hetherington, who was tragically killed whilst highlighting victims of war.

Thanks also to Her Royal Highness The Duchess of Gloucester, Anne Wood CBE and the myriad charities, organisations and individuals who made donations, raised funds or collected aid for the various missions to Kosovo and Albania and to all the volunteers who took part in the convoys, especially Karen Turner, Mary McDermott, Bernard Sullivan and John Cox.

Isa Zymberi (Kosovo Information Centre), Jak Mita and Marta (Mother Theresa Charity), Ismet Shamolli, Riza Laha, Abedin (Rambo), Chamed and Sadedin (Dino), Gani Shehu and Lum Haxihu. Colonel John Crosland, Ambassador Brian Donnelly, Bob Gordon, David Slinn and Bukurie Gjonbalaj.

Prime Minister Bukoshi of Kosovo, President Meidani of Albania and Demetrios Plaits, the Greek Chargé d'Affaires in Tirana. And special thanks to the Courtlands Hotel, the Nuffield Group of Hospitals, Christopher Lui and the Sussex Eye Hospital and to Keith Carney and all the medical staff who helped our patients in the States.

A special thank you to Liz Dack who was with me through the worst of times and to the brave members of the OSCE in northern Albania, especially Pierre Maurer MEP, Phil Figgins, Andrea Shulz, Artan and Beni.

And to my dear friend Bill Foxton OBE, who I believe is somewhere on the Accursed Mountains … laughing.

FOREWORD

Sally Becker partly redeemed the good name of Western Europe by the heroic work that she carried out in Bosnia at the height of the war in the early 1990s, fought mainly against defenceless civilians. She brushed aside often cold-hearted international bureaucrats and soldiers from the United Nations to bring relief to wounded and hungry victims of a brutal conflict. The bravery and determination of this unassuming English woman earned her the epithet of the 'Angel of Mostar'. Her memoir of her years delivering aid and helping children in Bosnia and later Kosovo has many of the ingredients of a classic war memoir. She displays impressive narrative skills and powers of description, revealing the depths human beings could sink to and the ability of bureaucracies to insulate themselves from horrors they were supposedly meant to overcome. Her vivid and often beautifully-told memoir is sure to keep alive memories of a low-point in the European story and perhaps motivate others to try and mitigate the effects of wars in which civilians find themselves the chief victims.

Tom Gallagher
24 February 2012

Tom Gallagher is Professor of the Study of Ethnic Conflict and Peace in the Department of Peace Studies at the University of Bradford in northern England. His books include *Outcast Europe: The Balkans, 1789–1999* (Routledge, 2001); *The Balkans after the Cold War* (Routledge (2003); *The Balkans in the New Millennium: In the Shadow of War and Peace* (Routledge, 2007); and *Romania and the European Union: How the Weak Conquered the Strong* (Manchester University Press, 2009).

INTRODUCTION

Before setting off to Bosnia-Herzegovina, I was determined to learn as much as possible about the Balkans conflict, not an easy task considering the enormous complexity of the region.

Following the end of the Second World War, a Communist regime was established in Yugoslavia headed by Josef Broz Tito. The federation was comprised of six Socialist Republics: Serbia, Slovenia, Montenegro, Bosnia-Herzegovina, Croatia and Macedonia and included the autonomous provinces of Vojvodina and Kosovo. The communist doctrine of 'brotherhood and unity' had helped to bind the diverse and multi-ethnic society of Bosnia-Herzegovina, which was made up of three main groups; Serbs Muslims and Croats. Tito's death in 1980, however, created an opportunity for nationalist elements in the society to spread their influence. This was hastened by the rise of Serb Nationalist Slobodan Milošević, who was intent on creating a Greater Serbia.

After the collapse of the Soviet Union, democratic movements swept across much of Eastern Europe, including Yugoslavia. Each of the republics held multiparty elections and on 25 June 1991, Slovenia and Croatia became the first to declare their independence. Because of its military strength and small population of Serbs, Milosevic allowed Slovenia to secede with little resistance – but Croatia's declaration of independence was met with a declaration of war.

As fighting broke out in neighbouring Croatia, Alijah Izetbegović, the Muslim leader of the multi-ethnic government party, was concerned that Bosnia would soon become embroiled in the conflict. He initially proposed a loose confederation to preserve a unitary Bosnian state but with its parliament fragmented along ethnic lines, tensions continued to rise. Radovan Karadžić, leader of the SDP, the largest Serb faction in the Bosnian parliament, gave a warning to Izetbegović on the fate of the Muslims should Bosnia try to separate from the federation:

'Don't think that you won't take Bosnia and Herzegovina to Hell and the Bosnian Muslim people perhaps to annihilation; because the Muslim people would not be able to defend themselves if there were a war here.'

On 9 January 1992, the Bosnian Serb assembly proclaimed a separate Republic for the Serbian people of Bosnia and Herzegovina, and proceeded to form autonomous regions throughout the state. Milošević vowed to defend his people from what he described as 'Croatian genocide' and 'Islamic fundamentalism'.

Fearing the drive for a Greater Serbia, the Muslims and Croats called for a referendum for Bosnian independence and the Serbs responded by launching an offensive. Towns and villages were surrounded and those who did not manage to escape were burned along with their homes. Men were detained in camps and women were systematically raped. This was the infamous 'ethnic cleansing', which led to the horrors shown on television. Muslim enclaves in central Bosnia were crowded with refugees but access was blocked by Serb forces, leading to acute shortages of food, fuel and medicines.

An arms embargo imposed by the UN Security Council affected Bosnia's Muslims the most. The Serbs had inherited the lion's share of the JNA arsenal and the Croats were able to smuggle arms from the coast but just as Karadžić predicted, the Bosnian Muslims were unable to defend themselves and thousands were killed. The International community viewed the conflict with detachment and Secretary of State Warren Christopher stated: 'Since the conflict in Bosnia does not affect our vital national interests, America will not intervene.'

During that first year of the conflict the predominantly Catholic Croats fought alongside the Bosnian Muslims but by the time I arrived in May 1993, the situation had started to change. Disillusioned with the Sarajevo government and supported militarily and financially by Croatia, the Bosnian Croats were planning to establish their own ethnically-based state. The armed forces of the Croatian Defence Council known as the HVO began their own 'ethnic cleansing' campaign in an attempt to create a homogenous Croatian population in parts of Herzegovina. This included the strategic city of Mostar, which they intended to appoint as their capital. As with all civil wars, people found themselves fighting those who had once been their friends; neighbours who had always lived in harmony were now bitter adversaries and families were being divided according to ethnic origins.

In Mostar, where the joint Muslim-Croat army had successfully defended the city against the Serbs, thousands of Muslims were being rounded up by the Croats and driven into camps or forced across the river to the east. The city was divided along ethnic and religious lines and Mostar soon became a haunting symbol of the war. At the same time 200,000 Croats had been 'cleansed' from central Bosnia by Serbs and Muslims. Neither side seemed to know who started the conflict, though inevitably each blamed the other.

PART ONE

1 | FROM BRIGHTON TO THE BALKANS

'YOU CAN'T GET INSURANCE for dismemberment!' called my father from the hall. I ignored him and continued to place the last few items in my hold all, wondering if I had overlooked anything of vital importance; it isn't easy packing for a war zone. Dog tags, engraved with my name and blood group and given to me for luck by a friend, were the last items to enter the bag. We would be travelling by road across Europe without any overnight stops so I was advised to bring a sleeping bag.

When my parents learned that I planned to go to Bosnia they reacted in different ways. My mother, although concerned about the danger, accepted my decision whilst my father insisted I had 'lost my marbles' and tried to dissuade me from going. He would describe in great detail the horrific injuries caused by anti-personnel mines, which ultimately resulted in the loss of a limb.

When it was time to say goodbye I found him in the sitting-room watching a rerun of Laurel and Hardy. He held up a dark object, opening it to reveal a wicked looking blade. 'It's a killing knife,' he stated sombrely and proceeded to demonstrate its locking device.

'Carry it with you always; you never know when you might need it'.

'I couldn't kill anyone,' I said.

'You might need to use it in self defence' he persisted. 'There's a lot of fascists out there!'

I agreed to take it with me though I was sure it would never be used.

A friend had offered to drive me to the rendezvous point in Godstone, Surrey, and I accepted her offer gratefully. Karen wasn't fazed when I told her of my plans; we had known each other for some time and nothing I did surprised her. My mother insisted on coming to see me off and as we drove into the car park, my sense of adventure mounted when I saw ten white trucks and a bus with red crosses painted on the sides

Convoys left the warehouse every month funded by the Medjugorje Appeal, a Catholic organisation run by Bernard Ellis, a local businessman. The charity was named after a small village in Bosnia-Herzegovina which had become a famous place of pilgrimage since 1981 when a group of children claimed to have seen visions of the Virgin Mary.

A Croatian organisation called *Suncokret*, (Sunflowers), had accepted me as a volunteer for one of the refugee camps based in Bosnia-Herzegovina and they had arranged for me to travel with the convoy.

One of the rare occasions when Sally wore a dress.

Sally aged ten.

Jack Becker as a young man.

We entered a very large, dimly lit warehouse packed from floor to ceiling with humanitarian aid: boxes of tinned food, flour, medical supplies, mattresses, blankets and clothes of all kinds. My mother became somewhat tearful as she stared at the army stretchers stacked to the ceiling, for the scene brought back memories of the wounded in the Second World War. I reminded her that the initial length of stay for a Suncokret volunteer was only about three weeks.

Although the work would be unpaid, food and board would be provided by the camp; which was fortunate as I had very little money. Smiling and waving as they drove off, I tried hard to conceal the doubts and fears lurking beneath my excitement. That night as I lay on one of the stretchers unable to sleep, I thought about the past and the events that culminated in this journey to the war-torn region of Bosnia.

My family moved to Brighton on the south coast of England when I was four and on the day we arrived, a boy called Greg Lester came to check me out. He and his friends were teasing me about something and in the end I marched over and sang 'Sticks and stones may break my bones but names will never hurt me!' Greg was obviously very impressed because he invited me to join his 'gang'.

I had two sisters and a brother and plenty of cousins who lived near by, so my childhood was fun. There were no computers, iPods or play stations but somehow we got by. The holidays were spent riding our bikes to the local park and we would rarely be home before dark; in spite of having no mobile phones to keep in touch with our parents. My mother was a warm and generous person but my father was quite different. He found it hard to show affection, especially to me and the only time he displayed real emotion was when he was angry.

Fortunately, I was very close to my maternal grandmother, whom I loved dearly. She was the only person who did not fear my father and would defend me when we argued, which was often. He used to say that if she found me standing over a body with a smoking gun, she would swear I hadn't done it.

My best friend, Heather James, was my complete opposite. She was very pretty with curly blond hair and a pert little nose and she looked like a fairy princess. My hair, on the other hand was black and very straight and I looked more like Mowgli. We both attended Knoll County Secondary School for girls, having failed the eleven plus, an exam upon which a child's future depended. Although extremely bright, Heather didn't pass because on the day of the exam she was very ill. According to the Headmaster I failed simply because I didn't bother to read the exam paper properly. Although I got every question right, I occasionally wrote feet instead of inches or ounces instead of pounds.

We were both good at art but the school had a strange attitude to learning. During one of the lessons we weren't happy with our drawings and decided to start again. The teacher caught us taking a new sheet of paper and sent us both to the Headmistress, a real disciplinarian. For the rest of that term, instead of attending our favourite lesson in which we both always came top, we were forced to sit outside her door and copy every word from a random book.

My parents split up when I was about fourteen and at the same time I moved schools. The new school was a mixed comprehensive and learning soon became secondary to boys. Until then I had always wanted to be a doctor but the thought of having to study for a further seven years no longer appealed. I eventually left school at seventeen with five O levels and a couple of A levels and no desire for a nine-to-five job.

Like most Jewish children, I learned about the Holocaust at a very early age and how from the ashes of six million Jews, the State of Israel was born. As an avid reader, inspired by stories of Moses and the Exodus, I decided to visit Israel as soon as I left school. The country was only 30 years old and one of the few places where men and women were regarded as equal. I spent the first few months living on a kibbutz and it was there that I encountered my first experience of war.

Kibbutz Hanita was situated in Western Galilee close to the Lebanon border, just two kilometres from the village of Alma-a-shaab. Originally an ancient Jewish settlement, the kibbutz had been founded when Israel was still known as Palestine. During its first year of existence, ten of its residents were killed by Arab snipers and the kibbutz came to demarcate Israel's border with Lebanon.

On 11 March 1978, a PLO guerrilla raid from Lebanon led to the Coastal Road Massacre, in which 35 Israeli civilians were killed and 75 injured. Israel responded by launching an invasion of southern Lebanon to destroy the PLO bases south of the Litani River. That night the kibbutz came under attack from a barrage of katyushas fired from positions close to the border and we were told to get to the underground shelters. In the morning someone was needed to bring back food and water from the communal kitchen and I volunteered for the job. As I ran across the wide expanse of lawn between the shelter and the dining room, two Katyusha rockets landed close by but I made it.

My first love was an Israeli called Uri Eshkoli from Kfar Giladi on the Golan Heights. He was a good looking man with a great sense of humour, a hero of the Arab-Israeli 'War of Attrition'. Wounded during the fighting near Cantara on the Suez Canal, his spine was damaged causing partial paralysis. Somehow in spite of his injuries he still managed to live a full and active life and was always surrounded by women.

After seven months I left the kibbutz and moved to Tel Aviv, where I started work at the Hilton Hotel art gallery, selling paintings by Chagall and other renowned artists. To supplement my income I worked as a manager at the Omar Khayam, a night club in Old Jaffa.

When I was almost nineteen my grandmother became very ill, and by the time I found out it was too late. According to Jewish tradition, she would be buried within 24 hours and I rushed to get a flight, hoping to make it in time for her funeral. The cemetery was on the outskirts of Brighton and after battling up the hill through the wind and rain, I entered the small, cold chapel, where I stared at the coffin and cried. I berated myself for having left Britain and desperately wished I had been there when she died. The guilt overwhelmed me and as a result I went off the rails for a while.

I travelled a lot throughout my twenties, living in Austria for a year and then the south of France. For a while I worked for a property developer and was expected to deal with bankers, planning officers, architects and the local Mayor. In the process I gained valuable negotiating experience and the confidence to face up to powerful men, which would later stand me in good stead.

In Austria I lived in one room and earned a small living from my paintings. In France when there was money I would buy a decent meal but when there wasn't I would search through my flat collecting loose change to buy a loaf of bread. An eternal optimist, I believed that no matter how bad things were it would all turn out right in the end.

People assume I must be a rugged, stoical person who doesn't mind roughing it but I much prefer to be comfortable and am essentially quite lazy; I used to say that if I'd had to walk across the front line in Bosnia I might never have gone; but that was before I trekked across the mountains into Kosovo. I have never been very practical and climbing Ben Nevis on a school trip I decided not to wear

Queen Noor visiting the Gulf Peace Team in Amman.

Sally was living on the Costa del Sol when she heard about the conflict in Bosnia.

hiking boots because they didn't look cool. Twenty years later I would be trudging through the snow in Central Bosnia wearing sneakers. I also dislike extremes; whereas someone else might feel cold, I am freezing and instead of simply being hungry I am starving. Tough I am not.

In January 1991 there was an item on the news about the peace protesters who were demonstrating against the planned invasion of Iraq. Having always thought that war was something beyond the ordinary individual's influence, I was filled with admiration, for these were ordinary people attempting to do something extraordinary. I found their headquarters in London, packed my bags and two days later was flying to the Middle East.

Being Jewish, it was thought that my presence might put the other volunteers at risk; I could be seen as a spy or used as a hostage, so instead of travelling with them to Iraq, I was asked to remain in Amman with a member of the team called Marnie Johnson and deal with their PR.

When the air strikes began, the volunteers from the Gulf Peace Team were moved to the El Rashid Hotel in Baghdad. The press had commandeered all the vehicles, leaving them stranded, so Marnie and I decided to send a message to Queen Noor, the wife of King Hussein. We had no computers at that time so I wrote a letter and faxed it to the Palace in Amman. To my surprise the Queen responded and the following day two buses and a car arrived at our hotel. I was taken to the Iraqi border to collect the volunteers and although I was a little

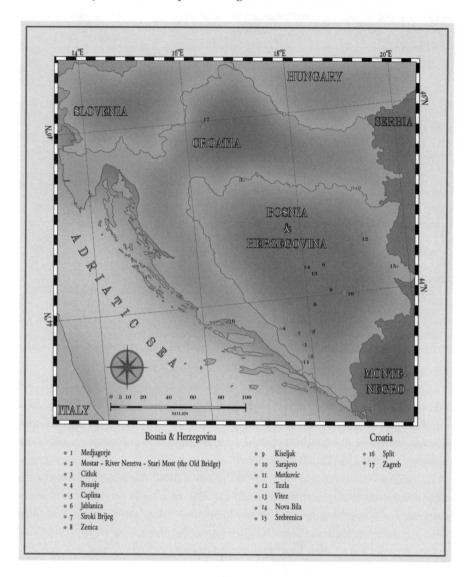

Bosnia & Herzegovina

- 1 Medjugorje
- 2 Mostar - River Neretva - Stari Most (the Old Bridge)
- 3 Citluk
- 4 Posusje
- 5 Caplina
- 6 Jablanica
- 7 Siroki Brijeg
- 8 Zenica

- 9   Kiseljak
- 10 Sarajevo
- 11 Metkovic
- 12 Tuzla
- 13 Vitez
- 14 Nova Bila
- 15 Srebrenica

Croatia

- 16 Split
- 17 Zagreb

nervous, the only time I felt in any real danger was when my driver disappeared and an Iraqi soldier climbed into my vehicle. My passport was new, having just been issued before I left Britain and he was obviously suspicious. I couldn't speak Arabic so when he mentioned Saddam Hussein I smiled and nodded and when he asked about George Bush I simply frowned. Fortunately this seemed to do the trick and when the driver returned I was permitted to continue.

I spent the rest of the First Gulf War in Israel where the Israeli government had agreed to refrain from any action against Iraq. The region was being targeted by Scud missiles and upon my arrival at Ben Gurion airport I was issued with a kit containing a gas mask and an atropine injection against chemical warfare. Most of my time was spent in the air raid shelters helping children with their battery-operated masks. Although the patriot missiles weren't very accurate, the Scuds were even worse, usually landing harmlessly in the desert.

I was working as an artist on the Costa del Sol when I first became aware of the conflict in the former Yugoslavia. Terms such as 'genocide' and 'ethnic cleansing' became commonplace, something I had only heard before in relation to the Holocaust. Night after night the television news would be full of harrowing pictures and I watched with mounting concern.

I cared little about the soldiers; they at least had some choice in the matter; it was the innocent victims, particularly the children, who so distressed me. In April 1993, I was watching the latest news reports from Bosnia when I decided to go there and try to help.

2 | 'YOU CAN DO SO MUCH MORE'

HAVING SPENT A RESTLESS night on a mattress in the warehouse I drank a quick coffee before helping to load the aid onto the trucks via a human chain. As a passenger, I would travel in an old single-decker bus together with some pilgrims who were on their way to visit Medjugorje. The Catholics said Mass before we set off and the vehicles were blessed.

After crossing the Channel to France we drove through Italy to the port of Ancona. The journey was long and arduous but once we boarded the ferry to Split we were able to get some sleep and by the time we sailed into the beautiful Adriatic seaport, I was feeling refreshed and eager to get ashore.

The dock was crowded with refugees, mostly elderly women dressed in black, their heads covered with scarves leaving only their eyes to reveal the horrors they had witnessed. Many had lost their husbands and children either through separation or death. These were the displaced and dispossessed whose homes had been burned to the ground, their cherished belongings gone forever.

We drove around the glorious Croatian coastline, passing through a succession of idyllic resorts. The sea was calm and reflected the deep blue of the sky and it seemed inconceivable that battles were raging just a few miles away; though once we crossed the border into Bosnia-Herzegovina we passed trucks filled with soldiers and a road sign to Medjugorje was peppered with bullet holes.

We parked the vehicles in a compound not far from the main street, which was overlooked by the Hill of Crosses; a place pilgrims would climb barefoot, or even on their knees, stopping to pray at each way station until they reached the top. It was dominated by a large church and the way was lined with souvenir shops selling crosses, rosaries and postcards. The local *pension* where we all would be staying was built in the style of a Swiss chalet. It was immaculate and the landlord and his wife made a great effort to make us feel welcome.

The following day we travelled in convoy to Posušje, a dusty town 26 miles northwest of Medjugorje. The bulk of the aid was delivered to a school housing hundreds of Muslim refugees from Central Bosnia. A few women and children were huddled together on pieces of cardboard beneath the trees in the schoolyard, trying to escape from the musty stench that pervaded the air inside.

The building was dirty and rundown and most of the refugees were lice-ridden. There had recently been an outbreak of hepatitis A that the Red Cross had only just managed to contain. The camp was run by a small and dedicated group of Italian volunteers who were dishing out a meal of pasta from a large metal vat when we arrived. The refugees sat down to eat at long wooden tables in a large, dimly lit room. There was no electricity or running water and people slept side by side on mattresses; crammed in shoulder to shoulder.

I was introduced to an old woman and her brother who were known as Mama and Babo by the residents of the camp. Mama made me a cup of sweet syrupy Turkish coffee that she heated in an *ibrik,* a small copper pot with a long handle, while I listened in horror as she told me her story.

When the 'Chetniks' (originally a word that described nationalist monarchist Serbian paramilitary organisations of the first half of the 20th century, in the later conflict a name proudly assumed by Serbian national extremists) reached her village, they systematically began to force out the residents at gunpoint or flush them out by setting fire to their homes. Many had been burned alive, trapped in the basements where they had sought refuge. Some of the men were arrested and taken off to camps but Mama's husband and son had been shot in front of her. Tears welled up in her eyes and spilled down her wrinkled cheeks as she described what had happened.

I wanted so much to help her, to offer her a glimmer of hope for the future but there was nothing I could do apart from show her that I cared. The only thing I had of any worth was a ring with a small heart-shaped ruby in the centre, which I placed in her hand. She seemed delighted with it but when she tried to put the ring onto her finger it wouldn't slide over her swollen joints. She looked so disappointed that I removed my gold necklace and threaded the ring through the chain and fastened it around her neck. When it was time to leave, there were tears in my eyes and frustration and rage in my heart.

I was appalled that an innocent old woman had been forced to witness the murder of her loved ones who were guilty of nothing. How could human beings be capable of such brutality? It was my first question when I learned about the Holocaust and one that I would ask again many times throughout the coming years.

Across the road from the camp I found some of the other volunteers drinking beer at a drab little bar. They were sitting with a dark haired boy who grinned at me from behind his hand; trying to conceal the fact that all his teeth were missing. A volunteer called Collette explained that Seemo, who was sixteen, had been captured and taken to a Serb concentration camp along with his parents; his brother and sister had disappeared and he hadn't seen them again. She told me he had been tortured by his captors who broke both his arms and then hit him in the mouth with a rifle, smashing all his teeth.

Someone suggested I draw his portrait so I went to search through my belongings for a pad and a pencil. A thin and scrawny little boy with fair hair and blue eyes stood watching as I climbed inside the van and he continued to stare at me, his eyes filled with fear and mistrust. Aldo was eight years old though he looked much younger; having witnessed the murder of his entire family, he rarely spoke and never smiled. Apart from my sketch book and pencils, I had some toys and a guitar. I offered him a teddy bear but he shook his head and tried to back away.

On impulse I reached for the guitar and to my surprise the fearful expression in his eyes was replaced by a look of sheer delight. He tentatively reached out and began to stroke the varnished wood and so I gently placed it in his hands. All of a sudden he raced off in the direction of the camp, clutching the cumbersome instrument in his frail little arms.

I returned to the bar and proceeded to draw Seemo's portrait. He could barely sit still, so excited was he by the prospect of seeing himself on paper. When the drawing was finished I handed it over and he beamed with pride, holding it aloft for all to see.

The two young men who had travelled with me would be staying on at Posušje. One of them, a carpenter, was a devout Catholic and had spent the previous afternoon climbing the Hill of Crosses. The other was a fair-haired youth who had travelled to the Balkans on the advice of his parents; he had been in some trouble back home and they thought the experience might change his attitude. I thought this was a bit extreme. On the plus side, he had brought a football and cricket bat with him and being quite gentle and shy, he seemed to be the right type of person to work with the traumatised children. Before we left, I wished them both luck.

Late that afternoon we drove back to the guest house in Medjugorje and when night fell, I stood on the balcony and watched the tracers streaking across the surrounding hills. It was an incredible firework display but I could hear the distant thump of explosions, causing me to shiver in spite of the warm night air.

Early in the morning I started work at the Pax Hotel where part of the building had been set aside for refugees. Most of them were Catholic and had fled either from a Serbian offensive or from the recent conflict between Muslims and Croats in Mostar. Marina, a woman who seemed to be their unofficial leader, was a typical example. She had left Mostar with her two young children in 1992 but after spending five months with relatives in Croatia, she had decided to return home.

Within minutes of their arrival in the city there was an air raid and the neighbour's children were killed. They were the same age as her own children and she immediately decided to leave. Her husband was responsible for the city's water supply and would remain there. (He was paid around $100 per month.) He would try to visit his family at least once every fortnight, as did the soldiers of the HVO whose wives were also living at Pax. Some of the women were less fortunate; either their husbands were dead or their whereabouts unknown.

There were 63 children living in the camp at this time, three of whom had been born in the past few months. On the whole the women were friendly and helpful to each other but the atmosphere was often uneasy, especially for the one Muslim amongst them. She told me that she had begun to sense their hostility as news of fighting between Muslim and Croat began filtering back to the camp. Each of the families had one small room; not bad for a mother and child but very cramped for those with big families. Compared to Posušje though, the Pax camp was luxurious.

Foreign aid supplied one main meal each day but they were short of the every-day items that most of us take for granted. Sanitary towels, nappies, feeding bottles, toiletries, clothes and vitamins could only be obtained with money. As I looked around the well equipped kindergarten I realised that art therapy for the children was less essential than making life a little easier for their mothers. The children certainly weren't showing any signs of trauma, unlike those in Posušje.

Marina took me downstairs to drink coffee in the hotel reception and I was introduced to the receptionist's brother, a young soldier who should have been studying for his exams but instead was fighting for his life and that of his family. As we sat and discussed the war, he grew angry, shouting about the plight of his people and the lack of interest from the West; in particular the US and Britain. Almost weeping with frustration he began to hurl figures at me; the numbers of Croatian deaths, the amount of Croats ethnically cleansed from Central Bosnia. To him, I represented the nations who had abandoned his country. I had no answers for him and could only suggest that the West might soon intervene.

'It's too late,' he cried. 'Two years too late!'

We were joined by a smartly dressed woman in her late forties and Marina explained that she was the hotel owner. I expressed my admiration for the fact that she had foregone most of her income to house the refugees but she just shrugged.

'What else could I do,' she said 'leave my own people to sleep on the streets?' When Marina explained that I had come to work at Pax she startled me by sud-denly leaning forward and seizing my arm.

'This is not for you,' she said. 'You can do so much more.'

As it happens, I had already decided that Pax indeed wasn't for me. I was plan-ning to continue bringing aid to the region instead and suggested Marina made of list of the items the women needed most.

As I began to pack my bag, Marina noticed I had some Tarot cards and she asked me to read them for her. I was reluctant to do so, having really only used them for fun but she continued trying to persuade me until I gave in; we locked the door, not wanting to offend anyone who might not approve. Marina's reading was pretty basic, indicating hard work and a great deal of responsibility. Renata, one of my room mates, also wanted a reading. Her cards foretold of a wonderful surprise; happiness, romance and love. She smiled ruefully when I told her; 'No chance of that' she said, 'I haven't seen my husband for five months. He has been fighting with the HVO in Mostar but he's a Muslim, so I'm beginning to doubt whether I'll ever see him again.'

Later that day as I was preparing to leave, a man knocked on our door. He was dressed in uniform and asked for Renata. She was outside with her children so I called to her from the window. When she saw him she squealed with delight and threw her arms around his neck. 'This is my husband!' she cried, tears streaming down her face.

3 | CRESCENT, CROSS AND STAR

MARTIN OFFERED ME A lift and we shared the driving of the eight-ton truck. Apart from the bus, the other vehicles were left in Medjugorje so we were able to travel much faster. Another convoy was scheduled to depart from Godstone in two weeks and I planned to spend the time collecting aid.

Duncan Stewart, our local GP, gave me some boxes of medical equipment and I made an appeal on BBC Radio Sussex on behalf of the refugees. People brought blankets, feeding bottles, nappies and anything else they thought might be useful.

When I arrived at the warehouse I was introduced to Sean Vatcher, who would be my co-driver on the bus. Sean was in his mid-twenties, tall and slim with brooding good looks, olive skin and short black hair. He aspired to be a war photographer and he planned to use this mission to add to his portfolio.

Before heading off Sean suggested I drive the bus around the car park. It was hard to judge the length of the vehicle but he assured me I would soon get the hang of it. Some of the vehicles would normally have required an HGV or PSV licence but as they were all painted white with red crosses, they were classified as ambulances. I was driving by the seat of my pants for a while but by the time we reached France I was used to it.

The volunteers were all men apart from Lynne Gillette. She had travelled down from Manchester where she worked as a temp whilst also running a collection point for the Medjugorje Appeal. Lynne was 26 years old. She was dressed in a flared skirt and flat pumps and had curly brown hair and brown eyes. I liked her immediately for she was bright and bubbly and had a great sense of humour.

On the dashboard of the bus was a large portrait photo of Collette, the volunteer Sean had met on a previous trip. The photo was displayed so that he could see it throughout our journey to Bosnia, where he hoped she would be waiting. I teased him mercilessly whenever I caught him gazing adoringly at her photograph instead of the road.

The journey through Europe was tiring and I was relieved when we finally reached Croatia. We were waiting to cross the border into Bosnia when I noticed a crowd of people at the roadside. A young man was jumping up and down and I realised that he was trying to attract my attention. To my surprise I saw that it was Seemo, the refugee from Posušje.

'Sally,' he shouted in excitement, 'I go to Italy!'

Dr Duncan Stewart.

He was with some of the refugees from the camp so I leapt off the bus and quickly unloaded the things I had bought them. They were accompanied by one of the Italian volunteers who looked pale and exhausted as she recounted what had happened.

Following our visit to Posušje, two soldiers from a local HVO (Bosnian Croat Army) unit had entered the school and beaten some of the refugees. The volunteers tried to intervene but were also hurt and then a group of soldiers fired guns into the building, albeit over the heads of the inhabitants. The volunteers had persuaded the Red Cross to transfer the refugees to Italy and most, like Seemo, were thrilled; others though were devastated, convinced they might never return to their beloved country.

The volunteer believed that the attack had been a deliberate attempt to frighten them into leaving; seven Croats originally from Posušje had been killed by Muslim soldiers and this could have been retaliation. There were also 400 Croatian refugees moving into the school who had recently been forced from their homes in Central Bosnia. Regardless of the cause, I was glad that these people would now be safe. I gave Seemo some clothes and handed Mama a navy blue skirt, white blouse and a beautiful hand crocheted shawl sent by my mother. For the other women I had brought cosmetics, perfumes and toiletries; frivolous perhaps but I hoped the items would raise their morale. We hugged each other at the roadside until the Croatian police angrily signalled for us to move on.

As the conflict continued to escalate, the Croats seemed less willing to allow the Muslims their fair share of aid and Lynne and I grew increasingly frustrated. We were told that we would not be able to distribute any of the aid to the Muslim camp at Capljina, just a few kilometres away; instead it would be left in a warehouse. Bernard Ellis had recently flown out with his wife so we broached the subject with him and he arranged a meeting with the local Mayor. We pointed out that the aid had been raised for those most in need, regardless of their religion and eventually despite their reluctance; they agreed to let us proceed.

Once again it seemed that most of the vehicles we had brought from Britain were earmarked for the priests in Medjugorje. This would not have mattered if it weren't for the fact that we saw one of the Land Rovers being driven by HVO soldiers; the whitewash having been removed to reveal the camouflage paint underneath. Lynne was especially angry because that particular vehicle had been paid for by funds she raised in Manchester.

The following day we delivered some aid to the West side of Mostar, which was now under Croat control. On our way back to Medjugorje a large red fire truck came up behind us flashing its lights. I assumed the truck was trying to overtake but we were driving along a narrow ridge and there wasn't enough space for the vehicle to pass. As we came around a bend I saw a gap and quickly pulled in but instead of passing us, the truck pulled up alongside, blocking the road completely. Two HVO soldiers jumped out and aimed their machine guns at us, causing some of the pilgrims to panic. They were told to hand over their cameras and most of the passengers complied except for one man who was clutching his camcorder, begging them not to take it. One of the soldiers cocked his weapon and aimed it at his head and the camera was swiftly handed over.

Upon our arrival in Medjugorje we recounted the story to the Mayor who told us that some of the HVO soldiers were undisciplined and ran around in gangs. He apologised for their behaviour and much to our astonishment, the cameras were returned.

When all the aid had been distributed, I suggested we make use of the vehicles before they disappeared. We decided to take the Pax refugees on a picnic, their first outing in almost a year. There was a river nearby and the children splashed and played in the water, their faces beaming. Lunch was an improvised barbecue and the women, who hadn't left the camp for so long, seemed to enjoy the trip as much as the children.

Following our visit to Capljina, Lynne decided that she wanted to do something more hands-on. Although she had done a brilliant job of gathering and sorting literally tons of humanitarian aid, she had reached the conclusion that the charity was too biased in favour of the Croats. I felt the same way; for although we had managed to make some deliveries to Muslim refugee camps it would soon become dangerous, if not impossible.

Lynne applied for a place at Capljina while I decided to focus on helping the Jewish community in Mostar. It made sense to direct my efforts towards a small neutral group rather than choosing between Muslim or Croat. The Jews of Sarajevo took care of their Muslim neighbours and I was hoping the same might be the case in Mostar. I had little idea what form my help should take or even how I would be able to afford to continue without the umbrella of a charity, but I was determined to find a way. The people of Bosnia, a place I had never heard of prior to the conflict, had really got under my skin.

The third convoy arranged by the Medjugorje Appeal consisted of 38 women; half of them from Britain and the others from the States. Between us we drove ten vehicles, including the bus. Some were on a pilgrimage to Medjugorje, while others had simply volunteered to help. Each of the women had raised funds towards the costs of the journey.

We bonded quickly and the atmosphere was full of excitement and expectation as well as a little fear. Because it was a women's convoy we were warned there might be trouble. In fact the women were much more easy going and less inclined to whinge than some of the men I had travelled with; even when we broke down on Mont Blanc and had to freewheel the bus down the mountain without any lights.

Although most of the aid was unloaded into the Medjugorje warehouse, I had warned some of the volunteers that supplies were badly needed elsewhere. Four American nurses had brought with them some vital medical equipment, which they gave me to distribute whereever I thought best.

We arranged another outing for some of the Pax refugees and some of the children rode with me in an old Bedford ambulance. On the way back I turned on the siren, causing the children to squeal with delight. Miranda told me they were singing a song about me: 'Our Sally accelerates and no one overtakes her.'

We were preparing to take the ambulance to a hospital in Mostar when I received a message from Bernard Ellis. He had arranged for me to meet with a Jewish doctor who worked at the hospital. Built on a hillside overlooking the city, the hospital at Bijeli Brijeg-White Hill had been targeted during the Serb offensive and there was a hole in the roof.

Dr Vladlena Atijus was an anesthetist from Zagreb who had been assigned to work in the hospital as part of the war effort. She was a robust looking woman in her late forties with a mass of black hair flattened beneath a green surgical cap. Although she had not been at the hospital for long she was already taking charge; but the staff seemed to like her demonstrative, no-nonsense approach.

Between operations to remove bullets and shrapnel from a never-ending stream of wounded soldiers, she found time to talk. Vladlena was Jewish so she was able to give me information about the community I was aiming to help. She

'The Boys'.

told me that since the war first broke out in 1992, many of Bosnia's Jews had gone to live abroad. Only about 70 people still remained in Mostar and having managed to survive the horrors of the Second World War, they were determined to stay. Only one or two families still remained on the east side of Mostar but no one had heard from them for several weeks. She told me that the Jews were regarded as neutral by both the Muslims and the Croats and were respected by both sides.

Vladlena returned to the staff room after a particularly long operation and told me that a man had just died. Her face was flushed and tears rolled down her cheeks. 'You see what they do to us?' she cried. 'These Muslims whom you so pity? They kill us! Our parents, our husbands, even our children. Come with me.' She led me through wards filled with scarred and bandaged victims of the war raging in the city centre, less than a mile away. She showed me the well equipped casualty and first aid room and the two operating theatres. She told me that they were short of medicines and equipment; the aid organisations donated several tons of medicines but most were out of date.

'We only use them if we really have no choice,' she said, 'because there are times when something, even if it is a year out of date, is better than nothing at all.' Before I left she gave me a long list of what was needed.

Sean and Collette were inseparable and seemed to be more in love with each passing day. They were staying in Citluk just three kilometres from Medjugorje on the outskirts of Mostar and invited Lynne and me to join them. The hotel was used as a base for soldiers from various units as well as doctors who had been given military status at the outbreak of war. It was quite disconcerting at mealtimes when we would find ourselves surrounded by men in uniform but the hotel had the only functioning kitchen in town; the others were without electricity.

The room was a little shabby with just enough space for two single beds, a small couch and a table. There was a shower and toilet en suite but the water only came on for two hours each day and always at different times. Fortunately, our room was quite cheap, at 200 deutschmarks per month, a major consideration since neither Lynne nor I had much money.

Amongst the guests were a group of mercenaries from a unit of foreign nationals known as *Grdani* – The Crazy Ones. They were a curious bunch who had originally joined not for financial gain, which was negligible, but to defend the Muslims and Croats against the Serbs. Thierry was a former Legionnaire who had originally fought with ARBiH (army of the Republic of Bosnia-Herzegovina) but when the situation began to change, he was assigned to a unit within the HVO. Slightly built with close cropped hair parted by a long scar, he had bright twinkling eyes and dimples in his cheeks and spoke English with a sexy French accent. His best friend Dommie, with dark hair and brooding good looks, was also French but much more reserved.

Dave, their leader, had served with the British Army. He was short and squat, with arms and shoulders like martello towers that made him appear very tough and the effect was enhanced by an old bullet wound in his jaw. There was also a young man called Paul, a real 'Jack the lad' and an Irishman called Paddy with the requisite birthright sense of humour who harboured a desire to become a game warden in Tanzania.

Having never encountered a mercenary before, I found the boys intriguing. In some ways they seemed so ordinary – laughing, joking, flirting and talking of home – yet I knew that Thierry, who detested cruelty to women, children or old people, was nonetheless a sniper who could target his victims with deadly accuracy and each of his fellow soldiers was equally ready to kill.

At first we found it difficult to sleep for the sound of missiles being fired from a rocket launcher a couple of miles up the road and the crowing of a cockerel at dawn. The boys occasionally took pot shots at it from their windows but that only seemed to make it worse.

Sean, who was a member of the Territorial Army in Britain, was training with Grdani, convinced that any experience alongside the boys would be good for his portfolio. He wore combats and carried a Klashnikov rifle along with his camera.

Collette was able to strip down a gun faster than most men and she was a crack shot who played a mean game of cards. With sun-streaked hair and startling green eyes, she was popular with most of the residents, especially Thierry and the 'boys', who lived just down the hall.

Despite her aptitude with guns, Collette was a peacenik by conviction who wanted to see an end to the violence. Originally a grocer from Michigan, she had come over as a Suncokret volunteer to help the refugees. When the Muslim camps began to close, she started working for the Croat Health Authority, transporting patients to Split where the facilities were much better. Collette was a Catholic and very spiritual. One of the patients didn't make it and he died in her arms. She told me that a few moments later she saw a shooting star and wondered whether it was the dead man's soul, on its way to heaven.

4 | 'I'M SURE YOU MEAN WELL'

WE HAD ONLY BEEN IN Čitluk for a couple of days when I received a message from Zoran Mandlebaum, President of the Jewish Community in Mostar. He would be sending someone to see me who was in urgent need of help.

Damir Rozic had a thin, angular face, a mop of thick curly black hair and big brown eyes. He was only fifteen but he had hitchhiked through a highly dangerous area to come and find me. His grandfather had been wounded. He asked me to come with him to Mostar and Lynne offered to join us, though we were not sure how we would get there. The boys had a one-ton army truck from the Medjugorje appeal and they offered to let us use it; the vehicle was still painted white with a red cross so I figured we would be safe.

Mostar, which is 60 kilometres from the Adriatic coast, is one of the largest cities in Herzegovina. Built on the banks of the River Neretva between Hum Hill and the Velez mountains, it was popular with tourists prior to the war. As we drove along the winding road leading down into the valley, Damir suggested we keep our heads down as the area was exposed to snipers. The west side of the city was a geometric mass of modern high-rise blocks and abandoned shopping malls. Some of the buildings were damaged and we passed a church with a gaping hole in the roof.

The old city hospital was situated downtown, only 200m from the front line. The walls were pockmarked with shrapnel and ribbons of UN tape were flapping around in the breeze. The patients were housed in the basement – above ground was too dangerous – and as we went down the stairs we had to adjust our eyes to the dim light. We passed the pale, haunted faces of young soldiers, many of whom were prisoners of war, Damir explained that they had been injured whilst being forced to dig trenches on the front line. I must have looked shocked for he immediately assured me that this was common practice for all sides. 'But surely it's against the Geneva Convention?' I said. Damir laughed wryly.

'The Geneva convention means nothing out here.'

His grandfather Haim Romano was lying on a bed at the far end of the ward. Sitting beside him was Damir's mother, Erna, a striking looking woman in her early forties with dark curly hair and big brown eyes. In broken English she told me that her father, who was 83 years old and quite deaf, had been taking a walk outside his apartment when he was shot in the leg. Somehow he managed to roll

Erna and Damir.

beneath a car but it was several hours before he was found and taken to hospital.

The bullet had shattered the bone, causing an infection. He had lain there in the basement of the hospital for several weeks and each day Erna braved the snipers and rocket-propelled grenades to visit him. Her mother was crippled with arthritis and unable to walk so she hadn't seen her husband since the shooting. She remained at home, the windows boarded up to protect her from the elements and the constant artillery fire.

I approached the bed and in the gloom I could see rheumy eyes staring out from a wrinkled, weathered face. Haim was so gaunt that his skin looked almost translucent and he was covered in bed sores, there was no rubbing alcohol available. His leg was propped up on a pillow and metal pins protruded from the external fixator on his shin, holding together the festering wound.

'He needs a special antibiotic which they cannot get here, and without it he'll die,' said Erna, her eyes filling with tears. I was shocked to find a hospital so desperately short of medicine when there were so many aid agencies based in the region and I wondered where it was going. Rumours of aid being sold on the black market were rife and although evidence emerged of the UN's involvement, the charges were routinely dismissed, a seemingly common occurrence no matter what the crime. When soldiers were accused of using local brothels, Sylvana Foa, spokesperson for the UN, was quoted as saying that it was no surprise that 'out of 1400 pimply 18-year-olds, a bunch of them should get up to hanky-panky'. One of these so called 'brothels' was a Serb-run concentration camp where Bosnian women were routinely raped. When the UN finally investigated, a special commission confirmed that some terrible but 'limited' misdeeds had occurred.

After promising that I would try to get the antibiotics and other things that were needed I bent to kiss the old man goodbye. He seemed to be trying to say something but each time he tried to speak he immediately started coughing. When he eventually fell back, exhausted, he took my hand and asked for a cigarette.

On the way to Erna's apartment I held my breath as we crossed a small intersection that left us exposed to snipers. The building overlooked the front line which ran along the main boulevard parallel to the river. It had been hit several times and their balcony was damaged; nevertheless their home was clean and tidy with simple furniture and a small television. Damir's bedroom faced the front line so he slept on a mattress in his parent's room.

We sat around a large wooden coffee table and drank squash; coffee was only available through the black market and was therefore too expensive. Erna apologised for not serving tea but they only had electricity for a couple of hours each day. Damir's jeans were old and worn because they hadn't been able to buy him any clothes for almost a year.

Bella, their little dog, jumped onto my lap but the cat spent most of the time in the bathroom, terrified by the noises outside. Erna explained that the dog had been born after the war began so she was used to the noise of battle but the poor cat was older and remained in a constant state of anxiety. The homeliness of the place felt disorientating, as we were chatting against a background of machine-gun fire and explosions. Lynne and I would flinch when the noises were particularly loud but Erna and Damir hardly seemed to notice.

There was a knock at the door and a man of about 50 entered the apartment. He had a round face, ruddy cheeks and a broad smile and was sweating so profusely that his shirt was soaked. and he was mopping his forehead. 'Zoran Mandlebaum,' he said, shaking my hand until it hurt.

Zoran was an engineer who had helped construct many of the bridges that were now being systematically destroyed. Speaking in German, a language that Lynne and I could both understand, he described the problems facing the elderly Jewish community in Mostar. He spoke animatedly, his words accentuated with an occasional prod or thump as he told us that over 100 packages had been sent out from Britain last year. Only half of them had actually arrived in Mostar and there hadn't been anything since then. Each family received 50 deutschmarks a month from the authorities but this wasn't enough to provide even the basics, let alone fruit and vegetables. Only 20 per cent of Bosnia's Jewish population had survived the Second World War. Those still living in Mostar were mostly the elderly who suffered badly with their nerves but there were no sedatives available. Some were diabetic or asthmatic but it was hard to find medication.

Zoran took us to see the Jewish warehouse which was based in the front room of an old lady's house. It was empty; just a few sprouting potatoes lying on the floor. As we prepared to leave, I assured him that we would try to get some aid. Damir guided us back to the road that would take us out of the city and then headed back alone through the dangerous streets.

While Lynne began phoning around for the antibiotics I went to see Albert Benabou, a UN civil affairs officer who was based in Medjugorje. Being Israeli I assumed he would do his very best to help. I handed him a list with the names and addresses of all the Jewish people still residing in Mostar and he seemed surprised there were so many. He asked me to make a list of those who might wish to leave the area and he allowed me to use his phone to call the Central British Fund for World Jewish Relief.

Despite my insistence to the contrary, the person I spoke to was adamant that the warehouse in Mostar had been filled on a regular basis; a conviction repeated to me again in a phone call to my hotel later that evening. Eventually the exchange became heated as the woman in charge accused me of packing a suitcase and arriving in the region with no fore-knowledge and no previous experience. Although this was true, it was irrelevant, I had seen the situation with my own eyes, but she was not interested. 'This organisation is responsible for the Jewish community in the former Yugoslavia and we certainly don't need your help.' She said firmly. 'I'm sure you mean well but your information is completely wrong. We transport aid to Croatia every month and Mr Mandlebaum knows that he can collect whatever the community requires from the warehouse in Split.'

'He tried that recently,' I told her, 'but he was turned away and returned to Mostar empty handed; in any case he doesn't have suitable transport, just a very small car, and the petrol is rationed.' There was silence at the other end and I drummed my fingers impatiently on the table as I waited for her to reply. 'I suggest you pack up your bags and go home,' she said and hung up.

Throughout the war, the Jewish community maintained relatively good relations with both Muslims and Serbs and were therefore able to move around more freely than most. During the siege of Sarajevo, the organisation known as La Benevolencia saved many lives. They operated a free pharmacy; opened the city's only clinic where multi-ethnic staff tended thousands of patients; gave away many tons of food, served hot meals from the soup kitchen and were the main carrier of mail in and out the city. They also organised several convoys to bring people to safety, less than half of them Jews; people were helped according to need, not creed. None of this would have been possible without the help of the American Jewish Joint Distribution Committee and the Central British Fund for World Jewish Relief. Somehow though, Mostar was being sidelined and I could not seem to get this across.

The *Brighton Argus* ran an appeal on my behalf. They sent a truck filled with medical aid and equipment but it would be another three months before any official aid reached the Jewish warehouse; and that was solely due to Mike Mendoza, a presenter on Spectrum, a radio station in London. Apart from raising funds for the Jewish community, Mike continued to support and defend my actions as I advanced ever deeper into the chaos of the Bosnian conflict.

5 | THE BABY BRIGADIER

LYNNE HAD CONTACTED ALL the local aid agencies but only one replied; a German organisation based in Zagreb. The man she spoke to assured her that he would drive down to Čitluk with everything we needed. He arrived within a few hours and amongst the aid he brought were the antibiotics that would save the old man. Soon after this we heard that the camp at Caplina had been closed so Lynne decided to work with me instead.

On our next visit to the White Hill medical centre we were introduced to some of the other members of staff. Dr Sefo, a surgeon, had heard that I was trying to rent a vehicle and offered to lend me his white Renault Four. We agreed to a rate of 100 marks per week and I gave him 200 in advance. I asked Vladlena if it would be possible to secure a document that would validate my right to drive the car. She told me to wait and marched off down the corridor, returning a few minutes later with a young man in uniform.

'Brigadier Dr Ivan Bagarić, Head of the Croatian Military Health Authorities,' she announced with pride. The Brigadier was only about 30, tall and broad with thick wavy black hair, olive skin and glittering dark eyes. He could not speak English but Vladlena translated and to my surprise, he beamed when she told him that I was Jewish. He spoke of his admiration for Vladlena and his affection for Zoran Mandlebaum, whom he had obviously known for some time. I told him about the lack of aid in their warehouse and he immediately offered to arrange for Zoran to obtain whatever he needed from the priests at Medjugorje. When I tentatively mentioned Damir's grandfather, he offered to have him transferred to the White Hill medical centre where he would receive better care.

I told him we had hired a car and would need permission to enter the city; following a recent offensive the HVO controlled all roads leading into Mostar and the International aid organisations were being denied access. Within an hour we had a letter signed by him and stamped by the Ministry of Defence that would enable me to pass through all the checkpoints within Croat-controlled areas. We left Mostar shortly before the 6.00pm curfew; our work could begin the next day.

Before my next visit to Mostar, I bought some food, heaters, fans and blankets for the elderly members of the Jewish community. I drove to Damir's apartment where I had been invited to stay for the weekend and as I began to unload the car, Erna leaned over the balcony, too excited to wait. She told me that since he got the right medication, her father's leg was beginning to heal. Damir helped to carry two large boxes up the stairs that I had bought from a grocer in Ćitluk and I watched with great satisfaction as Erna's eyes widened as she started unloading the supplies. She happily filled her shelves with all the things they had been denied for a very long time.

She also took pleasure in sharing some of it with her neighbours, especially a Muslim family who were desperately trying to keep a low profile in order to avoid eviction or arrest. Erna and her family did not discriminate between race or religion, indeed her husband Stipe, a Croat who worked for the police administration department, had helped many people caught up in the war.

Zoran came to visit, mopping his brow as usual as he sweated in the heat. We talked for a while and before he left he announced that he would return the next morning to take me to his office on the front line. I wasn't sure what to say, but by the time I had decided to forego his invitation, he had already gone.

That evening Erna cooked a delicious meal of roast meat and potatoes served with a fresh salad. The meal tasted particularly good after the greasy fried food served at the Citluk Hotel and it was great to see the undernourished family eating well. Damir was a gangly teenager so it was hard to tell what his natural build would have been but Erna was so thin that her shoulder blades jutted out and her clothes seemed to swamp her. Even Stipe seemed lost in his sweater. I had shed a few kilos myself since arriving in the Balkans but compared to them I looked chunky.

Lynne with Vladlena (left) and a colleague at the White Hill Hospital.

Sally and Lynne with the Renault 4. (Courtesy Simon Dack)

Whilst we were having dinner there was a series of loud explosions overhead. I prepared to dive for cover beneath the table but no one else moved; they just carried on eating. We learned later that four rocket propelled grenades had landed on the roof of the apartment block but no one was hurt.

Whilst there was electricity we watched a news item about Operation *Irma*, the airlift of wounded children from Sarajevo, which had been inspired by the plight of one little girl. The evacuation, instigated by PM John Major, resulted in an offer of hospital beds from around the world. To my surprise, it made Stipe angry.

'It is obviously just a publicity stunt for political gain,' he said, 'Otherwise why would they choose Sarajevo? The city was in a terrible state for a long time but now the situation has improved. Aid is reaching the people and they even have electricity and water, but most importantly of all, they have the attention of the media!' He stood up and began to pace around the room. 'What about Mostar? Nobody knows or cares what is happening here. This remarkable city is being destroyed yet nothing is being done to prevent it. Why?'

I had no answer for him though I understood his frustration. 55,000 people were trapped in East Mostar and no one was able to get in or out. They had not received any aid for months and the area was constantly targeted by heavy artillery and sniper fire.

That night I could hear the soldiers in the street below, their voices drifting through the open window and punctuated by erratic bursts of machine-gun fire and the occasional explosion of a rocket propelled grenade. Unable to sleep, I went to the kitchen where I found Damir standing at the window in the dark. He stopped me thoughtlessly lighting a cigarette, which would have drawn sniper fire from across the street. As we watched the tracers trailing through the night sky, I shuddered as I realised that for Damir, just fifteen years old, this was normal. He had witnessed two years of fighting on his doorstep, and his school had been blasted by shells from Serbian tanks. Many of his friends had been wounded and some of them killed. He had comforted his mother when his grandfather was shot and he often risked his own life to visit his grandmother just a few streets away. He had no social life, there was nowhere he could go, no clubs, coffee bars or football games, none of the pleasures that most young people take for granted. For Damir, life in Mostar meant the odd snatched conversation on an empty rubble-strewn street, with friends who barely flinched as a shell exploded close by; the terrifying dash across the junctions to avoid being targeted by a sniper; the anxious wait for his mother to return from the hospital and the knowledge that if the war continued, he would soon be called to fight against his former friends and neighbours.

If ever a teenager could be forgiven for getting into trouble, for using drugs or escaping into a life of crime, it was him. But he did none of these things. Instead he risked his life for others, delivering messages – hardly anyone had cars or telephone lines any more – and in between he taught himself English from old books and magazines.

I was proud to be considered his friend and as I watched him standing there in the flickering light, I was determined that somehow I would help him leave this nightmare; something his parents wanted most. Erna could not go with him because she would not leave her parents or her husband; but she desperately wanted her son to be able to live a normal life.

Zoran came to collect me the following morning and I was surprised when Erna suddenly gave me a hug. She was not a particularly demonstrative person but she knew that Zoran's office was situated in a very dangerous area. 'Take good care of her,' she called to Zoran as we left.

Following his directions we drove across the boulevard where an overturned truck was the only defence against ground attacks. We passed HIT Square named after a former department store and a machine gun seemed to be aiming at the car. I tried not to panic, as Zoran directed me towards Aleksa Santica Street, named after a famous Christian poet who fell in love with a Muslim woman. Ironically, this was the scene of some of the most intensive battles, where the soldiers fought from room to room and could hear each other creeping around through the walls.

We stopped outside the Hotel Ero, a large concrete building blackened by smoke. Zoran explained that his office was inside and we hurried past a group of soldiers who were lounging in the doorway. Part of the building had been a rest home for the elderly and some were still there, together with some refugees with nowhere else to go. Zoran pointed out that this was one of the few places where Serbs, Muslims and Croats lived together in peace. The Hotel was also headquarters for the HVO and had sustained a lot of damage caused by the constant grenades and sniper fire from the Bosnian side of the street. Most of the windows were shattered and glass and shell casings littered the floor.

Each time we passed a window that faced the front line, we had to crouch down low in order to avoid the snipers. One or two old people muttered a greeting while others ignored us and just shuffled past. Most of them were old enough to have been through the Second World War and had survived atrocities the world had vowed would never be repeated. Bloodshed and cruelty had returned for them.

Zoran's office was situated at the front of the building facing the east side but with only one small window in the corner, it was relatively safe. I glanced across the street and saw the once handsome sixteenth-century buildings now charred and pockmarked with shrapnel or missing their roofs and upper floors. The scene of devastation contrasted with the clear blue sky above and sunlight glinted on the broken glass scattered around my feet.

The shelves were piled high with books, some of them from Israel, where Zoran's wife and daughter were now living. A large famed photograph of Tito dominated the room. We sat down and Zoran offered me a glass of schnapps but I wanted to keep a clear head as we were so close to the fighting. Each time a mortar exploded I jumped but like most of the residents of Mostar, Zoran did not seem to notice.

We spent an hour sitting in the tiny room as Zoran recounted the history of his people and the city of which he was so proud. Afterwards we went down to the basement where two old women had made their home beneath the stairs. One of them had been living on the upper floor but her room had been destroyed by an explosion just a few days earlier. Everything she owned had been lost, so I offered to bring her some new clothes.

'It's kind of you' she said, 'but I have no need of anything now.'

The other woman, a Serb, had been forced to leave her home and was now a refugee. She had become separated from her family in the confusion and she wept constantly and flinched at every sound, obviously traumatised.

Zoran took me to an apartment building close by and as we climbed the stairs he warned me to keep quiet about what I was about to see. When he knocked there was the sound of panic from inside the apartment but eventually the door was opened by a middle-aged woman. The fear in her eyes turned to relief when she saw that it was Zoran and she quickly ushered us inside. The walls of the sitting room were lined with books and there were antiques displayed in a handsome oak cabinet. A small boy was sitting on the couch between his mother and grandmother. While the woman left the room to bring us some water, Zoran explained that she was a Croatian High Court Judge, forced to resign because her husband was a Muslim. He had recently escaped to Austria and she planned to join him shortly, leaving behind her spacious apartment and most of her belongings.

I sipped the water while the women talked with Zoran, occasionally glancing in my direction. He must have convinced them that I could be trusted for they soon revealed that the boy's father was living in the apartment, hidden in a concealed cupboard in the hallway. Every time somebody knocked at the door, they were thrown into a panic, afraid that he might be discovered. I was immediately reminded of *The Diary of Anne Frank*.

The reason for our visit soon became clear. The man was a civil engineer who had worked alongside Zoran for many years. As a Muslim he was listed for internment and in order to flee the country, he would have to be smuggled across the border. I was not expected to risk the journey with him. If we were caught I would be arrested and deported, forced to abandon those I had come to help. Instead, they wanted me to take his mother to Makarska in Croatia where her other two sons would be waiting. From there, they would all travel to Austria. Without a visa she would be unable to cross the border at Metković but I told them I would try to think of some way to help. Before we left, the man came out of his hiding place to meet me. As he clasped my hand I noticed how pale and drawn he looked from the months spent in hiding.

The next day I went to see Ivan Bagarić and asked him tentatively for his advice. I gave him no details, saying only that I knew an old Muslim woman who wanted to leave the country. He said that a visa would be difficult to obtain because thousands of refugees, mainly the elderly and the very young, had been fleeing from Bosnia into Croatia, putting enormous strain on the country's resources. The government had therefore decided to refuse all visas except for those who could prove they were going abroad or were already self -ufficient. I assured him that she really was leaving the country and asked him to consider her case.

He looked thoughtful for a while and then asked me for the woman's name. I hesitated until he took my hand and looked into my eyes. 'Do not worry,' he said and I knew he meant it. When he returned with the transit visa he warned me that it might not be enough, that if it were discovered that she was a Muslim she might be sent back and I would be in a great deal of trouble, as would he. I only had to think of the man living in a twilight world of terror whilst his mother looked on and I knew that the risk was worth taking. I arranged to meet Zoran later in the week when we would come to collect her.

When the day came, I waited outside the apartment block while Zoran went upstairs to collect her. I did not want to intrude as she said goodbye to her loved ones. I thought of her grandson who would be left there to continuing living with the fear that his father might be discovered. I carried a few items in a hold-all given to me by one of the soldiers at the hotel. The bag was standard HVO issue, which I hoped might indicate a connection to the Croats.

The old woman shuffled across the street carrying two small carrier bags. Tears pricked my eyes as I wondered how she had chosen the few possessions she would take. She hesitated before getting in the car, obviously reluctant to leave, but Zoran hurried her up. I could see that he was worried, his usual broad smile replaced by an anxious frown.

I drove along Mostar's tree-lined avenues, deserted streets lined with bombed-out buildings, towards the mountain road that led to the first military checkpoint. To our surprise we were not even stopped; perhaps the soldiers had grown used to seeing the Renault travelling back and forth from Citluk.

It took about an hour to reach Metković. We would then have to pass through another two checkpoints before reaching the border. The tension in the car was palpable but the policeman on duty at the first barrier barely glanced our way as he waved us through. The second checkpoint was manned by the Croatian police and it was here that I had been warned to expect trouble. As I was directed to pull over, I could feel Zoran tensing beside me and glancing in the rear-view mirror I saw fear in the old lady's eyes.

'Is she alright?' I asked Zoran, as she didn't speak English. He said something to her but she didn't answer. A policeman approached and I gave him my documents, including Ivan's letter of authorisation allowing me to travel freely throughout Herzegovina. He waved us on without even asking for the woman's papers and as I pulled away she leaned forward and squeezed my shoulder. This time when I looked in the mirror, she was smiling.

We sped along the Croatian coast in high spirits and finally reached the once-popular resort of Makarska. On Zoran's instructions, I parked outside a small guesthouse on the sea front where three large men were anxiously awaiting our arrival. One of them opened the back door, shouted 'Mama!' and half lifted her out of her seat. As he gently put her down on the pavement the others gathered round her and I could see she was crying. Zoran got out of the car but I stayed where I was, content just to watch.

Suddenly they descended on the car and hauled me out, kissing and hugging me before marching me into the bar for a drink. The judge was waiting inside. 'You have given them back their mother,' she said smiling. 'Thank you so much.' Before we left, the old lady took my face in her hands and kissed me, tears streaming down her wrinkled cheeks. I didn't feel that I deserved her thanks. Her son was still trapped in Mostar, living in a cupboard in fear of his life and my country was letting it happen.

6 | 'STICK TO HELPING THE JEWS'

LYNNE WAS VERY RELIEVED when I returned to the hotel. Thierry had been told by his commander that due to my 'interference' with the distribution of aid from the Medjugorje Appeal, I was going to be deported. We found out later that the order had been countermanded due to my 'connections'. I could only assume that the baby Brigadier had somehow intervened.

The doctors indulged in much banter and teasing with Ivan but it was clear that they held him in great esteem. Although he was still single, he had adopted his niece and nephew when their father had been killed during an attack by Serb tanks. Bagarić, a staunch Catholic who blamed the war, not the Serbs, for his brother's death, was devoted to his 'little family'.

There were three main hospitals in Bosnia: Sarajevo, Tuzla and Banja Luka. The first two were in Muslim-held territory and the third was under Serb control. The only other hospital was the White Hill hospital in Mostar. Bagarić and his colleagues had established a network of military hospitals, including a Franciscan monastery in Nova Bila, a chapel in Orasje, a school in Zepca, a tobacco factory in Grude, a hotel in Neum, and a computer company in Rama. 40,000 wounded people were treated in these makeshift hospitals, mostly Croats, but also many Muslims and Serbs. They were trying to include the hospitals in East Mostar and other Muslim enclaves but getting messages through the front lines was almost impossible. Ivan had written to the UNPROFOR battalion in Medjugorje to request their support and his letter was published in the *Lancet*.

Hereby we are kindly asking you to be the interface in our offer to the Muslim side for the accommodation and medical treatment of civilians – especially women and children – in the war hospital of Mostar as well as the other HVO hospitals. To the ill and wounded persons of Muslim nationality we guarantee the same treatment and healing as for our civilians and wounded persons. We propose that our work is controlled by the International Committee of the Red Cross, European Community, and UN observers. We are doing this for only one reason, which is a humanitarian reason, so we kindly ask you not to read anything political into this request. With respect, Assistant to the Chief of Defence, Department of Medicine and Health Care, Dr Ivan Bagarić.

UNPROFOR did not reply.

One afternoon Ivan showed me a fax headed *Top Secret* that he had received from his colleagues in Nova Bila, an area approximately twelve kilometres long and up to six kilometres wide. Of the 70,000 residents, over half were women and children. The enclave was besieged by Muslim fighters who controlled the mountains surrounding the valley of Lašva. Within this area were two small Muslim enclaves, the old town of Vitez and the village of Kruščica. Food and medicines were short and there were dozens of wounded, including many children. The local authorities made numerous appeals to Croatia and the international community but they were ignored.

The fax contained an urgent request for help because no aid had reached the area for months. When I asked whether the UN had been informed he replied, 'They are well aware of the situation but they do nothing. They have a base in that area but they have no interest in helping the Bosnian Croats.'

It was the same criticism I had heard from Vladlena and the other doctors and I was somewhat sympathetic. After a particularly brutal massacre of civilians by local Muslim forces, a human rights organisation had called a press conference but few had attended and even fewer reported it. I offered to take the fax to the UN base in Medjugorje but it was only after I told him that Albert Benabou was Israeli that he agreed to let me try.

As I drove towards the base I kept a close eye on my rear view mirror. The UN was so unpopular within Herzegovina that I feared my visit might be regarded as suspicious, especially as I lived in a military hotel. The gates were manned by a couple of Spanish soldiers from UNPROFOR who were watching the road from behind a pile of sandbags. I gave them my name and asked for the Civil Affairs Officer but he was not there. I was taken to see a Spanish Captain who offered me some coffee and asked how he could help.

I told him of the problems the doctors were facing in Nova Bila and that children as well as adults were dying for lack of medical supplies. The officer rested his chin on his hands and looked at me coldly. 'What, may I ask, is your interest in the matter?'

'I just want to try and help them,' I said, surprised by his question.

'Miss Becker,' he said, sitting up straight, 'Nova Bila is close to Vitez where the British Army is based so I am sure that they can survive without your help.'

Irritated by his patronising tone, I was tempted to show him the fax but I remembered that it was marked Top Secret owing to the detailed statistics that it contained.

'They really seem desperate,' I said. 'The hospital is responsible for the health of thousands. The letter was marked for the attention of the Health Authorities in Mostar. I just want to help.' He smiled condescendingly.

'The Croats produce propaganda like this all the time. Take no notice.'

I was confused. Could he be right? Was I just being used? I decided that the only way to find out was to go there and see for myself.

'Would it be possible for me to tag on to one of your convoys?' He looked at me as though I were deranged.

'We cannot allow you to travel with a UN convoy. You have no authorisation and anyway there are no convoys planned at present. We use helicopters to access central Bosnia.'

'Would there be room for me on a flight?' The Captain just laughed.

'Believe me, all the Croats want is an aerial view of the Bosnian and Serb positions in order to assist their military operations.' I tried another tack.

'I would take the supplies in myself but I only have a small car which isn't armoured and of course it can't carry much. Would it be possible to borrow one of your armoured trucks?' He stood up indicating that I should leave.

'I've told you,' he said, ushering me towards the door. 'It's all propaganda, they don't need a thing. Stick to helping the Jews.'

Parked at the entrance to the compound was a Land Rover marked UNICEF. On impulse, I approached the vehicle and spoke to a young woman who was sitting beside the driver. I told her that I had been tasked with getting medical aid sent to Nova Bila hospital in central Bosnia and she suggested I talk to her boss. She led me to a large apartment block on the main street and I followed her upstairs.

Danielle was an attractive blonde with big blue eyes. She invited me inside and over drinks she told me that her mission in life was to help children in need. My impression was of a sincere and caring woman who was also very brave. She was interested in the fact that I was able to travel freely in and around West Mostar; very few aid workers were afforded this privilege.

Danielle told me that the UN were planning a convoy into East Mostar, the first to enter the area since the siege began. She planned to go with them but she assured me that once she got back she would try to arrange a visit to Nova Bila. As we chatted, she suddenly let out an ear piercing scream.

'Mon Dieu!' she cried. 'Get eet out of ere, kill eet!' I had to laugh. Here was an extraordinarily courageous woman, unfazed by shot and shell, yet reduced to a gibbering wreck at the sight of a spider meandering across the floor.

One evening we were sitting with the boys in the room shared by Sean and Collette and Thierry asked me to read his Tarot. The cards indicated a bright future with love on the horizon and when I finished, Dommie and Paul wanted their own cards read too. Each spread produced similar readings with nothing untoward revealed.

'Well you may as well read my cards 'n'all' said Paddy, shuffling the deck. I lay them face down on the table and asked him to pick ten. One by one I turned them over, explaining what each symbol represented. The final card, which depicts the outcome of the question, was the ten of swords; an ominous card, foretelling violence or disaster.

I asked him what had been on his mind when he chose the cards and he said that he had asked about a mission that would take place the following day. He was due to return home to Ireland very soon and although still sceptical about such things, I warned him not to go. He laughed, insisting that this would be his last mission with the boys so he didn't want to let them down. There was nothing I could do to convince him otherwise and by the time we came downstairs the next morning, he had already gone.

Upon our return to the hotel later that morning Collette appeared looking distraught. In hushed tones she explained that Paddy was with his unit in Gornji Vackuf when he stepped on a mine. Despite losing both of his legs in the explosion he had managed to survive long enough for his colleagues to get him out. He was now in Split undergoing an emergency operation.

Trying hard to contain our emotions, we entered the hotel and saw Thierry and the others sitting around a table mute with shock. Paddy was a very special person, kind and considerate and very funny. He could always be relied upon to lighten the atmosphere when things were going badly. To make matters worse, he was not even a professional soldier, having come to the Balkans in search of adventure. When he left Ireland, he had not told his mother where he was going.

When Lynne and the others went to visit him in hospital, I remained behind. Although the reading was probably a tragic coincidence, I felt guilty for not having tried harder to stop him. To my surprise they all seemed much brighter when they returned and I was amazed to hear how resilient he was. The loss of a limb was one of my greatest fears yet Paddy was apparently laughing and joking despite losing both of his legs. 'Well look on the bright side,' he told them, looking round at the sombre faces of his friends. 'You know I've always hated being short and now the doctors tell me they can add a few inches to my prosthetic limbs!'

The squad commander was making arrangements for Paddy to be flown home once he was fit enough to travel and as we helped to pack his things. I was very aware of how fragile we all were in this war-torn country.

During my next visit to West Mostar Zoran took me to meet Vinko Martinović, a Bosnian Croat known as 'Stela'. Vinko acquired Croatian citizenship and became a commander of HOS, the Croatian Defence Force militia that operated in Mostar in 1992. He later joined the KB where he became the commander of the sub-unit ATG 'Mrmak', later named 'Vinko Skrobo'. It was rumoured that Stela operated a black van with tinted windows which was used to round up Muslim men of fighting age. He would later be tried for war crimes at The Hague and served fifteen years in prison.

Zoran hoped the introduction might afford me some protection as I carried out my work in West Mostar, although for some reason he told him I was a journalist rather than an aid worker. Damir came with us to translate and he and I were both nervous as we were shown into Stela's office.

He asked Zoran a couple of questions and then proceeded to stare at me in silence as he played with a small model of a tank displayed on his desk. Slowly he twisted the turret around towards me until it was pointing at my chest. In order to avoid his eyes I glanced around the room and noticed some bullet holes in the door.

'Have you been attacked?' I asked, hoping to dispel some of the tension in the air. There was silence as he looked at me coldly and then with a slight sneer on his face he pulled out a pistol from the drawer in his desk.

'When I am bored I like to practise my shooting skills,' he replied.

A few days later Thierry asked if I would consider talking to a journalist he knew. This did not come as a surprise, for Mostar was becoming 'hot' news and a number of journalists and TV crews had begun to descend upon the area. From an initial interview with a local newspaper, interest in our work had grown and the fact that we seemed to be the only aid workers with access to the city had attracted the attention of the international press. I had already been interviewed by the BBC, giving me a chance to highlight the worsening situation; but it was all a little nerve wracking, knowing that the broadcast would be monitored by all sides.

When we were introduced to the tall, sun-tanned stranger from Denmark, I suggested that Lynne spoke to him first. She had been the unsung heroine in the back room and much of her hard work had gone unnoticed. He began to ask a series of questions but after a few minutes I got the feeling that something was awry. It was more like an interrogation than a press interview and I challenged him.

'You're not really a journalist are you?'

He looked a little shame-faced and seemed to blush beneath his tan.

'Actually I am with UNCIPOL, the UN Civil Police.' He explained that the interview had been a device to gain an insight into my character.

'My name is Leo Bang Sorensen. And I need your help.'

We both stared in amazement.

'What kind of help?' I asked. 'And why me?' He stood up.

'I'm afraid I don't have time to explain but I'll return this evening. And if you don't mind,' he said, glancing at Lynne, 'I would prefer to speak with Sally on her own.'

I shrugged. 'I'll be here' I said, 'but I want Lynne to hear what you have to say.'

As he hurried from the room, Lynne gave me a rueful smile.

'Isn't that typical' she said,' the first time I get asked to do an interview and the reporter turns out to be a policeman.'

Leo returned that evening wearing his uniform. I felt a little concerned when I saw him for these were tense times and the sight of a UN officer in what was in effect, Croat military headquarters, could lead to trouble. There was also a soldier staying in a room just along the corridor who had a pathological hatred of the United Nations. He was convinced that they were directly responsible for the death of his wife and child and he was obsessed with vengeance. I quickly ushered Leo inside and closed the door, motioning him to sit on the small couch. He removed his blue helmet and placed it on the table and as he began to talk, Lynne discreetly pressed a button on my tape recorder.

'There is a three-year-old Muslim boy called Azem Droce living in East Mostar,' he said, unaware that the tape was running. 'He has a serious heart problem and is in desperate need of an operation. As you know, the area has been sealed off for months but if this child remains there any longer he'll probably die.' I glanced at Lynne who shook her head in wonderment.

'Sorry if I appear a little ignorant but what exactly does this have to do with me?'

He shifted slightly before answering. 'As the only aid worker with free access to West Mostar, you obviously have some influence with the Croats. I am therefore hoping that you will agree to use your connections in order to get permission for an evacuation from the east side of the city.'

East Mostar was probably one of the most dangerous areas in Bosnia at that time.

'I suppose there's no harm in asking Ivan,' I said, thinking aloud.

'I saw him earlier,' said Lynne, 'so he may still be in his room.'

Excusing myself I went along the corridor and knocked on Ivan's door. I was nervous, having only ever met him at the hospital. The door was opened by his colleague who immediately invited me inside. Ivan was lying on a bed, his hair tousled and I had to stifle a smile as he was dressed in army issue camouflage pyjamas.

'Would it be possible,' I ventured, deciding to get straight to the point, 'to arrange for the evacuation of a sick Muslim child from East Mostar?' My question was greeted with a long silence before he launched into a history of the Balkans. Ivan was a skilled politician who could see beyond the day-to-day crises but unfortunately, he also had the politicians' knack of skirting around an issue before getting to the point.

With his colleague translating, he gave me a lecture on the war and he described the massacres that had been ignored by the international community. He reminded me of the terrible conditions at the hospital in Nova Bila and though I assured him that I would do my best to draw attention to the area, it seemed highly unlikely that he would agree to help. About ten minutes passed while he and his colleague discussed the matter between them and at last they both turned to me.

'How do you intend to rescue this child?' he asked.

I told him about Leo and suggested that he would arrange something through the UN who were planning a convoy to the area within a few days. His eyes darkened.

'We do not trust the United Nations,' said Ivan. 'They are biased against the Croats and choose to ignore the suffering of our people.'

I was disappointed, convinced that he was about to tell me to leave but instead he said something that would influence the rest of my life.

'Sally Becker,' he said, 'we will give *you* permission to carry out the evacuation. Not for one child but for *all* the sick and wounded children and their mothers. You must travel with the convoy of course, for it would be too dangerous for you to go there alone.'

I was astounded, knowing that his words marked a significant development in the war. If successful, the evacuation would be the first to happen in this area since the siege began. For a moment I was speechless.

'Thank you, thank you very much,' I said, hurrying back to my room where Leo and Lynne were anxiously waiting. When I told them the news Leo seemed quite shocked but he said he would speak to his colleagues and make some arrangements.

'I assume we'll go in with UNPROFOR?' I said, as he stood up to leave.

'Oh I don't think that UNPROFOR needs to be involved,' he replied whilst securing his helmet. 'It would make a change for UNCIPOL to get some recognition for their work. They certainly do a better job.' I stared at him in surprise.

'We can't drive across the front line without protection. We have to have an escort, if only for the sake of the children.' Leo was becoming impatient.

'The Croats will arrange a ceasefire so I'm sure it'll be fine.'

When he had gone I thought about what had just taken place and I wondered why Ivan had agreed to my request. Many years later when he was asked that very question by a BBC reporter, he replied, 'We were both there for the same reason – to help people.'

I was filled with apprehension about crossing the front line but I would have risked my life to save just one child. Ivan was giving me a chance to save them all.

7 | HANDOUTS AND HOLDUPS

WHEN I MET WITH Leo the following day he told me that he would be travelling to East Mostar with the UN aid convoy. The evacuation could not take place at that stage but he would make all the necessary arrangements whilst he was there. I could not see the sense in this, especially as he had told me how desperate the situation was. Why couldn't I simply join the convoy as Ivan suggested and evacuate the children under UN protection?

I decided to call the base and found myself speaking to the Spanish Captain I had met on my previous visit. He was no more helpful than before, saying that I would need special permission to join their convoy. I asked whether he could arrange protection for me to carry out the mission alone but he repeated what Leo had already said. 'If you have official permission for the evacuation, then there will also be a ceasefire arranged, so you need not fear an attack.'

I was surprised and disappointed by his response. The UN was a multi-billion dollar organisation with thousands of soldiers, yet they were not prepared to support the evacuation of wounded children from an area that had been under siege for months. It was my first real experience of UN intransigence and it would not be the last.

I had another major problem; we were almost out of deutschmarks. We had been promised funds from a British charity but so far nothing had been forthcoming. Without money to pay for our food and accommodation we would have to go home; the prospect of leaving when so many people were still in need of help was unbearable.

Hearing that representatives from the charity had arrived at the Pax hotel, we drove there to see what was happening. Their press officer was in the middle of a photo shoot with a little boy who suffered from asthma. After watching her record the children singing the Pax song of Peace for her local radio station, I managed to get her attention and showed her the permit that had been issued for the evacuation of wounded children. She told me that the charity had raised £1000 for the refugees but it was to be given to the local priest.

We were in despair, but as was often to be the case, whenever it seemed there was no way forward, a helping hand would be offered from the most unlikely source. A woman who had overheard the exchange invited us to meet a friend of hers. Peter Kates was born a Jew but later he converted to Catholicism; a quiet, unassuming man who had come to Medjugorje on a pilgrimage with his wife and daughter. We told him of our problems; the lack of funds to continue our work with the Jewish community and give us time to arrange the evacuation of wounded children. His daughter had been listening to the conversation and she suddenly spoke up; we could have the savings that she had brought with her. Peter told her that wouldn't be necessary; he would give us the money himself.

We calculated that we would need around £400 in order to survive a few more weeks and that's exactly what he gave us. I thanked them both and assured him that he would be reimbursed as soon as I got home. Peter Kates was not a rich man by any means; he had used his savings to pay for the pilgrimage of his family and for others to come along with them. That evening we returned to Citluk with a renewed faith in human nature.

Waiting at the hotel was a film crew from ITN. They wanted to film us delivering aid to West Mostar and we agreed, knowing it would provide another opportunity to highlight the situation. I had to get special permission for them to accompany us but Ivan came through, as usual. Sean and a friend of his who worked with the Croatian army had offered to act as an escort. They were both in uniform and carried guns, which I hoped might serve as a deterrent should anyone be tempted to harm the journalists. The British press were extremely unpopular and therefore prone to attack from angry individuals convinced of their bias.

Damir's grandfather had refused to be transferred to the White Hill hospital, wishing to remain close to his family instead. He had agreed to be filmed so we arranged to meet Damir and Erna at the hospital. As the reporter questioned the old man beneath the bright lights, I could see he was getting upset and I asked them to stop filming. They insisted it was necessary to emphasise the situation but I felt he was being exploited and was relieved when they agreed to talk to a member of staff instead.

The surgeon told them that the hospital's policy was to treat all patients equally. The war ceased for them, he said, the moment they entered the ward regardless of whether they were Muslim, Croat or Serb. Lying in one of the beds was a young Bosnian soldier who had been taken prisoner by the HVO. He told the reporter that whilst he was forced to build trenches for the Croats, he was shot in the leg by a sniper from his own side. Although Damir had explained that it was common practice for all sides to use their prisoners in this way, I was surprised that the Croats would allow him to discuss it openly and on camera.

As we were leaving Mostar, I stopped off at the main hospital to pay Dr Sefo for the car but Vladlena told me that he was no longer there. She believed that he may have saved the deutschmarks I'd been paying him in order to escape. He was a Muslim and either through fear or because he no longer wished to work with the Croats, he had fled with his wife and children during his weekend leave. Whatever the reason, he had left me with the papers for his car.

That evening we were watching the news on satellite television and saw the piece by ITN. Lynne was not included in the broadcast, which seemed unfair for she had been a tower of strength over the past two months. Where I was impulsive, she was practical and she was always supportive, sympathetic and kind. While I was dashing around, she would beaver away back at the hotel, not only struggling with endless faxes and phone calls but also having to deal with some of the dangerous characters who hung around the place.

There was a particularly strange individual called Eddo who would hassle her each time I was away. He was a German mercenary, a psychopath who had joined the HVO for the sheer pleasure of killing. Tall and thin with greasy blond hair and very few teeth, he carried a knife as well as two guns. He was nearly always drunk, which exacerbated his aggression.

We first met when he lurched towards our table during dinner one evening and began spouting insults against Muslims. As we attempted to eat our greasy eggs and chips, he described in guttural German the vile ways he used to kill his victims. We were both disgusted and hastily pushed our plates away, having lost our appetites. We did not dare leave yet for fear of provoking him but he soon got around to the subject of Jews; how Hitler was right and they all should have died in the gas chambers.

Staring at me with cold blue eyes, he ran his forefinger along the edge of the long thin blade of his knife. It glinted menacingly as he described in detail what it was used for but I met his gaze steadily, though I was trembling inside. 'I'm Jewish,' I said slowly 'So what do you intend to do about that? Kill me?'

I heard Lynne's intake of breath but to my surprise Eddo just seemed shocked.

'But you cannot possibly be Jewish.' He said, 'You are much too attractive.' I shook my head in disbelief as he continued.

'Anyway I've got nothing against the Jews, so long as they stay in Israel.'

Unable to stand his psychotic ramblings any longer I pushed back my chair and stood up, aware that the rest of diners were watching; 'Come on Lynne,' I said, 'we've got work to do.'

As far as I was concerned, Eddo was an ignorant fool but he terrified Lynne and it didn't help that his room was very close to ours. I was given a small can of tear gas by one of the boys and we decided Lynne should keep it with her whenever I wasn't around.

On 25 August 1993 the UN convoy was finally assembled and nineteen ODA (Overseas Development Administration) trucks were lined up on the main street in Medjugorje. Behind them were the representatives of the major aid organisations including UNICEF and the IRC, their 4x4s slowly baking in the midday sun. There were twelve armoured personnel carriers belonging to the Spanish contingent of UNPROFOR (Tactical Group Canarias) plus several vehicles belonging to the press.

We approached some of the aid personnel and showed them the documents, one of which was signed by General Praljak, commander of the HVO. I also had a letter from Dr Sarić, the Minister of Health, but no one seemed willing to get involved. An official from the Red Cross told me that they had no evacuation policy in place outside of Sarajevo.

The heat was intolerable so eventually we gave up and returned to our hotel feeling despondent. It seemed that nobody was interested in what we were trying to do and we were both growing increasingly frustrated. As time went by however, we discovered that this attitude was almost integral to the major organisations. They all had their own well established way of doing things and resented outsiders rocking the boat. Apparently strangled by bureaucracy, they were incapable of swift and decisive action in emergencies. Everything had to be done through the 'proper channels' regardless of the desperation of those in urgent need. I was frustrated that we were so dependent on Leo, concerned that any delay could jeopardise the mission but I could hardly carry out an evacuation of the sick and injured in a Renault Four.

The convoy arrived in Citluk that afternoon and Leo was standing on an APC directly outside our hotel. Waving the documents at him I asked what we should do.

'Wait until I get back,' he shouted, leaving me standing by the roadside. I threw up my hands in despair and returned to the hotel. The convoy remained there for hours, surrounded by a menacing crowd of people, most of them refugees. They were angry for they felt they had been forgotten. All the recent press reports were focused on the Muslims; the conditions of the camps, the siege of East Mostar and the desperation of those who were trapped there. These people were victims too. They had been separated from their loved ones; driven from their homes with nothing but the clothes on their backs; they too were suffering from a shortage of food and other essentials. Their plight was not nearly as desperate as those under siege but they also needed help. Eventually the UN agreed to make a separate delivery to a local warehouse.

A deal had also been struck whereby both sides could exchange their dead, for one of the dreadful aspects of this war were the number of bodies, civilian and military, which had been left where they fell. Sometimes the bodies would remain there for weeks, until an exchange could be negotiated and the dead laid to rest amongst their own kind.

A few hours later the convoy still had not moved. I found one of Ivan's colleagues and asked what was happening. He told me that BBC journalist Jeremy Bowen had managed to reach East Mostar and was broadcasting shocking images of the wounded children. The Croats were concerned about the effects of further broadcasts once the rest of the media entered Mostar with the convoy. I explained that I was intending to carry out an evacuation of those very same children in co-ordination with the Croat Health Authorities.

'In that case,' he said, lowering his voice, 'it might be better if we prevent the convoy from leaving until they agree to take you with them.' It seemed incredible that a UN convoy could be detained on my say-so.

Women and children prevent the UN convoy from leaving East Mostar. (© Gilles Perres/ Magnum)

'Nothing can justify withholding the aid,' I said firmly. 'Media attention is already focused on this convoy and if it's delayed any longer, you'll make matters even worse.'

He seemed to think for a moment and then hurried away. Half an hour later General Praljak arrived and gave a speech. The crowd was then dispersed and the convoy prepared to depart and I breathed a great sigh of relief. Although the Croats had allowed the mission to continue, they had confiscated some of the mobile satellite dishes carried by the television crews, hoping this would limit the information coming out of the area.

The following day we were in the dining room watching a report by Brent Sadler on CNN. The convoy had finally reached East Mostar at 3am but once the aid had been unloaded they were prevented from leaving. A few Bosnian soldiers had apparently surrounded the convoy and they were soon joined by a crowd of women and children. Brent Sadler was making a live report.

'Following the delivery of aid to East Mostar last night, the convoy is unable to leave as desperate Muslims fear an attack by their enemies, the Croats. Apart from the danger and discomfort faced by nearly 200 Spanish UN Peacekeepers, truck drivers and aid workers, they also have to deal with the embarrassment of being held hostage by women and children.'

The image of a tall grey-haired man wearing a blue UN helmet appeared on the screen. Beneath his image were the words:

CEDRIC THORNBERRY, DEPUTY CHIEF OF MISSION IN BOSNIA

'Unfortunately … those whom we came to help have been holding us hostage here,' he said. The camera then focused on Colonel Angel Morales, commander of the Spanish Battalion. He began to shout at the camera from beneath his blue helmet;

'Not hostage – prisoner!' he cried.

His image was then replaced by a shot of the interior of a hospital. A child was lying on blood-stained sheets, her head swathed in bandages and her face badly burned. I stared at Lynne in horror. The situation meant further delays for without Leo Sorensen I could not proceed. I chain-smoked and drank endless cups of coffee as we waited for further news. Ivan appeared and told me that he had arranged for me to borrow an ambulance from the hospital but he still could not authorise my departure until we had confirmation from the other side.

All we could do was wait. When the electricity was off there was no television but I kept one ear to my radio, listening intently to the BBC World Service. Despite pressure from the international community, the position remained unchanged. The presence of the UN convoy had brought a ceasefire and the Bosnians were terrified that as soon as it left, the shelling would recommence.

By late afternoon our table was littered with empty coffee cups and overflowing ashtrays. Lynne was called to the phone and I saw by her face that she had good news. Leo had managed to send a message through his colleagues in Medjugorje using a satellite phone; it was now safe for me to enter East Mostar and carry out the evacuation; the mission had been approved by the Bosnian authorities but I would have to leave at once.

We were immediately plunged into a frenzy of activity. A slightly built Englishman called Paul had been hanging around the hotel lobby and hearing that I was about to enter East Mostar, he offered to come along, claiming that he spoke the language and knew the route well.

Ivan had come to see me off and as we were leaving, he hugged me and said, 'I will pray for you.' I could see both fear and concern in his eyes; he was worried about my safety but he was also fearful for his own reputation. He had authorised a rescue mission from enemy territory and in the bitter battle for Mostar, a city emotionally and strategically important to both sides, there were many who did not distinguish between combatants and civilians.

8 | CROSSING THE LINE

26 AUGUST 1993; THIS WAS as far as the police escort would go and I stared anxiously across the disused airfield that crossed No Man's Land. Having previously been confined to driving on the west side of Mostar, the route was unfamiliar to me and I was alarmed when Paul announced that he had never been this way before either. One of the policemen scrawled the directions on a scrap of paper but he could not guarantee its accuracy; he had not been beyond this point since hostilities began.

I carried spare clothing and a torch in case we should be forced to remain in the area like the UN convoy. The rear of the vehicle was filled with antibiotics, dressings and some medical equipment. I had also bought coffee, cigarettes and cheese for the hospital staff – items that were impossible to obtain on the besieged side of the city.

According to Ivan, the ceasefire would last until 1 pm the following day. There remained, however, the question of snipers positioned within a four-mile radius around the city. The thought that some of these maverick marksmen might not have heard of the arrangement did little for my confidence.

I drove as fast as I could across the deserted runway. It was late afternoon and the air was still hot and humid, so I slid back the door. We were the only thing moving for miles and I knew that we were within sight and gunsight of both sides. I cringed at the thought of how many eyes might be watching us but hoped that an ambulance would not be targeted by snipers. As we passed the main road that leads to Sarajevo I wondered what it must have been like before the war, when the road was teeming with traffic.

The area was eerily quiet apart from the distant thump of shells and the road was empty except for the mines, whose deadly spikes protruded from the tarmac. Steering carefully around them, I followed the directions drawn on the crude map and drove towards the first checkpoint, where three soldiers stood watching us approach. They were dressed in shabby uniforms displaying the insignia of the Bosnian army and wore sneakers instead of boots; each of them carried a rifle.

'It seems they weren't expecting you,' said Paul.

Reaching beneath my seat I handed the soldiers a carton of cigarettes, which immediately brought a smile to their faces.

'Ask them how we get to the hospital,' I said to Paul.

Without waiting for a translation one of the men pointed towards some buildings in the distance.

'Follow the road,' he said in English. I glanced across at Paul.

'Toto, we're not in Kansas anymore.' He was clearly not amused.

Passing through a village on the outskirts of the city, people began to appear on the roadside asking for food. We stopped to hand out some packages but were immediately surrounded and I decided we had better press on.

The road soon narrowed onto a track filled with potholes and as we drove towards the divided city I caught a glimpse of our destination. Nestling at the foot of the mountains, small, quaint houses with terracotta roofs and moss-covered grey stone walls led down to the River Neretva. The city looked relatively peaceful beneath the setting sun, with only the odd puff of smoke in the distance to remind us of the war. Mostar had once been regarded as one of the jewels of central Europe and was a favourite haunt of tourists who would pay the local children to dive off the old sixteenth-century bridge. Originally commissioned by Suleiman the Magnificent, construction began in 1557 and took nine years. The architect, Mimar Hayruddin was ordered (under pain of death) to construct a bridge of such unprecedented dimensions that he is supposed to have prepared for his own funeral on the day the scaffolding was finally removed from the finished structure. Upon its completion it was the widest man-made arch in the world and certain associated technical issues remain a mystery: how the scaffolding was erected, how the stone was transported from one bank to the other, how the scaffolding remained sound during the long building period. As a result, the bridge is considered one of the greatest architectural works of its time.

Suddenly a shot was fired across the roof of the ambulance and when I realised what it was, I wondered what had happened to the promise of a ceasefire.

'Sniper!' shouted Paul as he dived into the back and buried himself beneath a pile of boxes. I slid down in my seat while trying to slide the door closed and change gear, all at the same time.

'This is a nightmare!' I cried, 'I don't know what to do!'

'Just keep driving,' he shouted, 'we need to reach the cover of the buildings.'

'Thanks for the tip,' I called, unable to see where I was going, 'you just stay there nice and safe; back-seat bloody driver.'

I desperately tried to stem the panic that threatened to engulf me but my heart seemed to be somewhere in my throat and I debated leaping from the vehicle and running for my life. Instead, I jammed the accelerator to the floor and with the engine roaring in protest, I weaved the lumbering vehicle to and fro, hoping to confuse the snipers.

The shots came one after the other and I was convinced that we would both be killed. I was sure that the gunman would not be shooting if he knew we had come to help the children. I had never stared death in the face before and it was the most terrifying experience of my life.

I kept my head down most of the way, only popping up when absolutely necessary to see where I was going. My heart thumped loudly in my chest, the sound reverberating in my ears and in the background I could hear Paul's muffled voice issuing instructions. It must have taken about ten or fifteen minutes to reach the cover of the buildings but each of those minutes felt like an hour.

I am often asked whether I get a 'buzz' from such experiences and the answer is no – not for a moment. I was filled with dread, believing that my life was about to end on that dusty road. The fear never left me and in fact it got worse.

As we approached the main street I saw that the way ahead was blocked by an overturned vehicle. This was Marshal Tito Street, which runs the full length of the city. Behind the makeshift barrier stood the nineteen ODA trucks that brought in the first consignment of aid to reach the city since the siege had begun. Alongside them were the UNPROFOR armoured vehicles, there to protect the truck drivers, the representatives of the aid organisations and members of the press. The position of the convoy was precarious, constantly exposed to the threat of shelling or sniper fire and some of the soldiers looked worried; having already lost half a dozen members of their battalion since their deployment in Bosnia.

I parked the ambulance and climbed out, my hands and legs shaking from the tension of the journey. Paul announced that he was going to visit some friends, so I locked the vehicle, as once again I was surrounded by desperate looking people. They were quite thin but did not seem to be starving as we had feared, though the children were pale and sickly.

UN soldiers with their heavy flak jackets and steel blue helmets stared in surprise as I strolled past them dressed in my white T-shirt and jeans. Albert and Leo appeared and to my surprise Albert clapped me on the back.

'I knew you would come,' he said smiling. Unable to think of a suitable response I ignored him and turned to confront Leo.

'You assured me that everything had been arranged, meanwhile we were almost killed!'

He looked a little shamefaced. 'Sorry but I couldn't tell them you were coming because I wasn't able to leave my APC.'

'Well, what about Azem Droce, the child in need of surgery?' I asked.

'I'm afraid he died about three weeks ago.'

Of course I was shocked and saddened by the news, as well as a little confused – but I had been granted permission to evacuate *all* the children in need of medical treatment so I decided to get moving.

A Spanish officer accompanied me back to my vehicle and offered to drive me to Higijenski where the wounded were being treated. The walls of the makeshift hospital were painted red and pockmarked by shrapnel and bullets, the windows blocked with sandbags and wood. The building had suffered constant shelling and artillery fire and part of the upper floor was missing. I had to use a torch to negotiate my way down the stairs and as soon as I entered the basement I became aware

The staff at Higijenski, East Mostar.

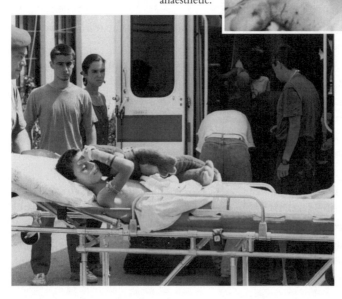

Sally takes in the appalling conditions of the children's ward. In the background is Nermina, a thirteen-year-old girl in need of surgery. (© Popperfoto)

Selma's arm is amputated without anaesthetic.

Mirza is carried from the ambulance on a stretcher.

of a terrible smell; sweet and cloying and overwhelming, the stench of blood and putrefaction. I had never smelt anything like it before but I knew that it was the smell of death.

The floor was slippery with blood that squelched beneath my feet as I picked my way along the dimly lit corridor. The building had once been a public health laboratory in a thriving city but was now a makeshift hospital in a devastated war zone. Around me there was a frenzy of movement and noise as doctors and nurses, their eyes red and their faces slack with exhaustion, struggled to deal with the constant flow of sick and wounded. Patients were lined up on stretchers, trolleys and tables, anything that could be pressed into service as they awaited emergency surgery. Drip lines dangled from hat stands and some of the patients were moaning or crying out in pain; while others lay still with frightening resignation. It was a production line in hell.

A reporter approached me from ITN and told me she had permission to film me with the evacuees.

'It's a wonderful story,' she enthused. 'A UN convoy trapped in a war zone and you come in to rescue the children.'

Following her into a small room, I was met by a sight that would forever haunt me. This was the children's ward, crowded with the innocent victims of a conflict beyond their comprehension. They had been wounded by shrapnel or sniper fire, mines or rocket-propelled grenades, either in their own homes or whilst running a desperate errand for their families. The oldest was sixteen, the youngest a toddler.

Lying in one of the beds was Selma Handzar, the ten-year-old girl I had seen on TV. Her face was burned and pitted with shrapnel and beside her on the blood-stained pillow was a yellow teddy bear with a large pink nose. Next to her was Mirza, her brother, who was also wounded; an enormous bandage swelling his right leg. Their mother, Nermana, was crying.

'My Selma was so beautiful. Why her?'

'The doctors will make her beautiful again,' I said.

I sat down carefully beside the little girl. 'I've come to take you away from here, to somewhere safe and quiet. There will be no more bullets, no more shelling, just a peaceful place where doctors can make you well again.'

The nurse translated my words and Selma smiled. She then threw back the sheet to reveal a small stump where her right arm used to be. The horror must have shown on my face for she tried to reassure me.

'Don't worry,' she said, 'it's nothing.' A nurse explained that when the children were brought into the hospital there was only enough anaesthetic for one operation and Selma insisted that her brother should have it. Her arm was then amputated with only the teddy to bite on for relief from the pain.

I recalled all the times I had moaned about a toothache, headache or some other trivial complaint and was filled shame. I realised that for her, this tragedy was part of her normal life; she had seen friends suffer similar trauma and probably worse. To me, this was a living nightmare but for her it had become an everyday reality. Her brother called out, 'Kiki-riki,' and a nurse translated.

'He's asking for peanuts, they are his favourite.'

'Tell him he'll have peanuts, chocolate and anything else he wants,' I said, fighting back the tears.

Nermina Omeragić, who was just thirteen, had been preparing medical supplies for distribution to the wounded in Mostar when she was hit by mortar shrapnel. Her lower right leg was shattered and several inches of the tibia destroyed. The wound was badly infected and she would need extensive treatment if she was to survive.

A sixteen-year-old girl called Maja Kazazić was lying on a bed close by. She had been wounded several weeks earlier when a mortar exploded outside her apartment, killing five of her friends. Due to the heat and lack of antibiotics, she had developed infections in both of her legs and one of them had to be amputated. Her father, who had also been wounded, was sitting beside her. He told his daughter what was happening and explained that she would be leaving with her aunt.

The doctors were grateful for the supplies we had brought, even the simplest items were scarce. Prior to this latest convoy there had only been one delivery of humanitarian aid and that had been 67 days ago; even the 200 tonnes brought in by the ODA would only relieve the situation for a very short time. Word of my arrival spread quickly and upon my return to the main street, Albert Benabou drew me to one side: 'We are trying to arrange the release of the convoy in return for the evacuation of the children.' Still shaken by the scenes at the hospital, I rounded on him.

'When I requested UN assistance for this mission no one wanted to know, yet now that you're in trouble you're prepared to use me to get you out !'

'Don't you understand!' he said, beginning to get angry. 'We are all in danger here. There has been a great deal of shelling and there is no food or water. The locals are desperate and could turn on us at any time. Your evacuation may be the only chance we have of getting out.' He then tried another tack.

'In any case it would be impossible to take all the children and their mothers in your own vehicle but we can lend you an ambulance. We also have helicopters on standby in Medjugorje to fly the patients to the field hospital in Zagreb.'

I thought for a moment. He was right about the lack of space in my ambulance and in any case it was too dark to move the patients now. If we had to leave without the protection of the convoy, it would certainly be better to wait until daylight.

'Ok,' I said finally, 'Go ahead and negotiate but we will have to leave tomorrow morning regardless.'

I went to sit in the ambulance and was joined by Brent Sadler and his camerawoman. They had entered Mostar by trekking through the mountains from Sarajevo, carrying their equipment on the back of a donkey. Brent stretched out on the floor, oblivious to the thuds and bangs around us, not even waking when a shell exploded in the car park.

Taking my torch I returned to the basement where the doctors sat talking and smoking their precious cigarettes. Hafid Konjihoddzic, a neurosurgeon, was a slightly built man in his forties, serious and sad with intense dark eyes and a nervous manner. He had come to work as usual on the night of 8 May and became trapped when the Croats began their offensive against the East side. He and his colleague, Jovan Rajkov, a Serb, were averaging 20 to 30 operations per day in the appalling conditions. They were only two sets of clothes between the two surgical teams so as soon as they had carried out two procedures they had nothing left to wear and had to work stripped to the waist.

Many of the patients had come from West Mostar, evicted from their homes by the Croats and forced across the front line at gunpoint, putting extra strain on the scant resources. The city lay in ruins and of the seventeen mosques only two remained standing. There was no running water or electricity and people were using their furniture for fuel to cook and boil water. The front lines were no more than ten metres apart in some places, so the enemy was half a street away. Fortunately, the houses were built very close together so those brave enough to venture out would use each other's kitchens and living rooms as cut-through routes to avoid the snipers.

Hafid's wife, who was still living in West Mostar, was pregnant with their first child. Being a Muslim, she was in danger and he was desperately worried. She also had endometriosis, hazardous in childbirth when it can cause complications such as abscess or rupture. He asked me to deliver a letter to her. Some of the other doctors wanted me to do the same for them. When the letters had been written, they put the names and addresses inside the envelopes in case they should be discovered. One doctor asked me to phone his brother in Germany and tell him that his wife had been killed. I broached the subject of the UN convoy with the hospital director, Dr Dragan Malović, a tall muscular man dressed in surgical greens with dark hair and a beard. He was an anaesthetist who had founded the makeshift hospital at the start of the conflict between the Croats and Muslims. Malović pointed out that I had come in alone and if I wanted to help the children that was fine, but stay out of the politics. Only the journalists would be allowed to leave with me so they could highlight the situation in Mostar.

The Spanish officer joined me at the entrance to the hospital and offered me a cigarette. We talked against the background hum of the oil-fired generator, the building's only source of power. He told me that the doctors had insisted they were not able to release the UN convoy without permission from the Bosnian army.

'My ceasefire ends at lunchtime,' I said, ' so I can wait until mid-morning to give you more time but then we really must leave.'

As dawn broke, Jeremy Bowen sent a report to the BBC's *Today* programme.

'There has been an amazing turn of events' he announced. 'Sally Becker, an independent aid worker from Britain, has entered East Mostar to rescue wounded children and the UN is planning to use the evacuation to come out on her tail.'

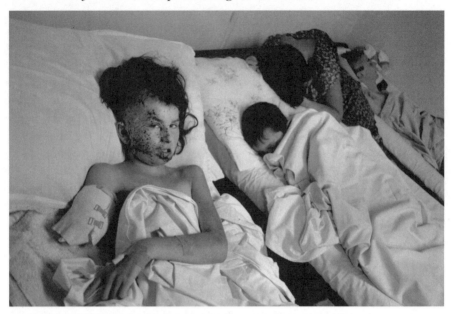

Selma with her younger brother Mirza. (© Gilles Perres/Magnum)

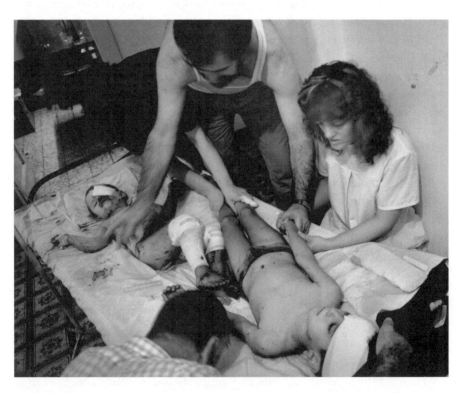

Elmir and Damir are rushed to the hospital when an anti-tank missile hits their apartment. (© Gilles Peress/Magnum)

At 11.00am the second ambulance drew up outside the hospital. There was still no sign of movement from the convoy so we began to bring the children up the stairs. As they were lifted into the vehicles, Selma's mother wept as she kissed her husband goodbye.

Suddenly a car screeched into the compound. There was no glass in the windows, the bodywork was scarred with bullet holes and a crude red cross was daubed on the side. I watched in horror as two little boys aged three and five were carried from the back of the vehicle. Their small bodies were covered in blood and they writhed and screamed in agony. Behind them their mother was led from the car in a state of shock. She was carrying a new-born baby girl with shrapnel wounds to her legs and face.

The scenes in the basement were bad enough, but the sight of those small bodies with their appalling injuries was even worse. A doctor grabbed my arm and asked me to help them. He told me that the older boy had a serious injury to his head while the younger child had shrapnel in his eyes and damage to his kidneys. He told me that they would need to be stabilised before they could be moved but he hoped I would come back in two or three days to get them and I promised that I would.

'Of course,' I said, knowing that I might regret it.

Outside the hospital the young father was leaning against the vehicle with his head in his hands. To see a child in pain is hard for any parent but he had three injured children, two of them with horrifying wounds. We tried to make the patients as comfortable as possible in the back of my ambulance while Brent Sadler and his camerawoman squeezed into the passenger seat beside me. Paul turned up just as we were leaving and he climbed in the back.

I pulled out of the hospital compound and waited on the main street for the other vehicle to join us. Five, ten minutes ticked by and still there was no sign of them. Brent offered to find out what was happening and we waited with the sun beating down on the roof. The intense heat was causing the children to moan in discomfort but I had brought some water along and handed it around. At last Brent reappeared with Albert and Leo.

'We cannot allow you to leave without the convoy,' said Albert, as I climbed out of the vehicle.

'What do they intend to do' I asked, 'Hold us hostage?'

It seemed incredible that the United Nations should consider delaying the evacuation of seriously injured children as a means of breaking their own deadlock. I was outraged and told him so.

'You have to have coordination,' he insisted.

The second vehicle pulled up behind us and Albert said it might now be needed by the UN soldiers; we would either have to carry all the patients in my ambulance, or return some of them to the hospital. I couldn't decide which was worse; to endanger the children by crowding them together or to tell them that they couldn't leave at all. He alarmed me still further when he announced that the UN helicopters would no longer be waiting to transport the patients to Zagreb: they had been cancelled.

My head was spinning. The ambulances were parked in the blazing heat filled with wounded children and the ceasefire would end in 40 minutes. I couldn't believe that United Nations personnel were prepared to endanger lives in this way. The local people were equally desperate, knowing that as soon as the UN convoy left the area, they would be bombarded with rockets and shells. They wanted the UN to establish a permanent presence in Mostar and this was the only way they believed they could get it. The hospital director had made it quite clear that my mission was a separate issue and therefore the army would not release the convoy in return for the lives of five children. 55,000 people were trapped in East Mostar, all of whom would be at risk from the moment the UN departed, the shelling and sniper fire providing a never-ending staccato accompaniment to relentless hunger and deprivation.

Cedric Thornberry appeared with Colonel Morales and as I got back behind the wheel I was accosted by the UNPROFOR commander. He demanded that I hand over the keys to the ambulance and I tried to explain that it did not belong to the UN but was in fact on loan from the hospital in West Mostar. He ignored me and started shouting as he tried to drag me from my seat. The children looked frightened and I told Paul to reassure them, though I felt far from reassured myself.

As I left the vehicle prepared for a confrontation with Thornberry, the TV cameras began closing in. Before I could say anything, Albert took me aside.

'It's ok, you can take the other vehicle after all. There has been a misunderstanding.'

I received no explanation for the sudden change of plan but at that moment I didn't care. As we made our way through the ruined streets followed by some press vehicles, a man appeared, hobbling along on crutches in front of my vehicle. It was Selma's father, Mirsad Handzar, on point, determined to ensure that nothing else would impede our departure.

9 | AN UNLIKELY ANGEL

27 AUGUST 1993; I was feeling euphoric as, mission accomplished, I headed towards Medjugorje with my precious cargo. When we reached the UN base a crowd of photographers and film cameramen were waiting at the gates. We drove into the compound and while the children were carried from my ambulance the press began to clamber onto the gates in order to get pictures.

An officer suggested I should leave but first I asked to see the patients. He refused my request and as I turned towards the gates and the flashing cameras, Christopher Morris from Sky News suddenly intervened. He had overheard the exchange and began talking to the officer in Spanish. To my delight I was suddenly called back. I rushed into the clinic where each child had been allocated a bed and those that were able were sitting up and eating. I just had time to kiss each of them goodbye before being hurried from the room.

Once outside the compound, Brent Sadler asked if I would agree to an interview. I had never been on live television before and was feeling nervous but he stood beside me and looking directly into the camera he declared, 'This woman got us out!' Between interviews with the press, Lynne and Ivan arrived, having both waited anxiously for my return. I clasped Ivan's hand in mine and thanked him, for it was he who had made it all possible.

The mission made headlines around the world and appeared on the front page of the *Independent*, *The Times* and the *Daily Telegraph*. Silvana Foa issued a statement to the press on behalf of the UN saying 'Becker has helped to raise the profile of medical evacuations but we don't want every granny with a bus turning up in Bosnia.' I was only 33 at the time – perhaps the war had aged me.

I was dubbed 'The Angel of Mostar' but with my short black hair I was an unlikely looking angel. I have never felt I warranted such attention, especially when there were people throughout the region risking their lives on a daily basis. The name seemed to stick though and other versions developed over time: 'Angel of Mercy', 'Angel of Bosnia' and even 'Angel in Blue Jeans'. The press love that sort of thing.

A few days later I prepared to return to East Mostar to evacuate the children who had been injured during our departure. I had no desire to make the journey again but I had given my word and the image of the two blood-stained little boys had haunted me ever since.

Before setting off, I visited the UN base to inform them of my intentions and to make sure they would be ready to receive the children. Following negotiations between Boutros Boutros Ghali and Izetbegovic, the UN aid convoy was finally being released. It had been agreed that two armoured personnel carriers would remain behind as insurance and I asked the Spanish Captain to send a message to his colleagues to ensure that the Bosnian army would be expecting me. In the meantime, Liz had been visiting various organisations in the area to request help for the children once they were out.

Sky had set up a live link through a satellite dish and I was able to speak to my mother and father on television. It had been several weeks since they had seen me and my mother was thrilled. Even my father, not given to emotional outbursts, declared how proud and pleased he was with what I had achieved. The television crew had a whip round and gave me £50 to buy cigarettes for the doctors in East Mostar.

Unfortunately, Lynne had not had much success. None of the aid agencies, including the Red Cross, would agree to take responsibility for the children. I was not overly concerned though, as these children were wounded during the original evacuation, so I assumed the UN would transfer them to the MASH hospital in Zagreb with the others.

Ivan turned up with the new documents authorising the mission and once again he agreed that I could take along a colleague. This time I chose Tim, an American Suncokret volunteer who also spoke the language.

Helping me load the aid into the back of the ambulance was Ivan's friend, Vladimir Mikulić, a 37-year-old Bosnian Croat known as Vava. He was a teacher, painter and poet, and was currently working for the local radio station in Široki Brijeg. Tall and lean, with fair skin and an open, friendly face, he had short hair that sprang up in cartoon tufts. Ivan had appointed him to help us and he would soon become my great friend and protector.

Our departure was filmed by a local television crew and it occurred to me that unlike the last time, millions of people would know about this mission, which might help ensure our safety.

Once again we were escorted to the front line by the Bosnian Croat police. The airport was bathed in sunshine and it all seemed very quiet as we crossed No Man's Land. The first checkpoint seemed to be abandoned, so Tim climbed out and was about to lift the barrier when a group of Bosnian soldiers suddenly appeared.

Tim did his best to explain who we were but the soldiers kept shaking their heads, unable to comprehend what he was saying. One of them spoke German and I understood that he wanted to take us to his commander. Obviously they had not been informed of our mission and I cursed the UN for their intransigence. I refused to leave the ambulance, afraid they might take it and to their annoyance I clung stubbornly to the keys. Eventually they agreed to let us follow behind with the vehicle.

We began to make our way down an old railway siding but halfway down I stopped, afraid that we might get stuck. The soldiers insisted we press on but a few minutes later my fears were realised; the wheels were buried in the shingle and we were unable to move.

I was startled by a burst of machine-gun fire which sounded close by and the soldiers immediately ran to take cover behind an old railway carriage. They gestured for us to join them and as bullets ricocheted against the train, we crouched behind the rusting wheels for what seemed like an eternity.

'Why are they doing this? There's supposed to be a ceasefire!' Tim shrugged and shook his head, no wiser than me. We had no idea who was shooting at us. After a while one of the soldiers raced off down the hill, returning a few minutes later with an older man, who seemed to be in charge.

He could not speak English but I handed him my documents, which were written in Croatian. As he read Ivan's letter, he started to nod. He pointed towards the ambulance and mimed the rocking of a baby. Yes, yes, I nodded; relieved that at last someone understood the purpose of our mission. Ducking and weaving to avoid the bullets he ran over to the ambulance and started the engine. His head was in full view and I feared he might be killed at any moment. The engine roared for he was unfamiliar with the vehicle and I had no choice but to leave the cover of the train.

Fearful that a bullet could penetrate the windscreen at any moment, I leaned inside and pulled the lever into reverse but the vehicle was still well and truly stuck. The officer shouted to one of his men who disappeared into a small outbuilding. He returned a few moments later carrying a spade and I watched anxiously as he courageously began to dig away the gravel from beneath each of the wheels. The officer released the handbrake and gunned the engine while the other two soldiers pushed us from behind. It was a very tense few minutes for we were all directly in the line of fire but at last the vehicle was free. I shouted my thanks as the soldiers disappeared but the officer remained in the driving seat. Tim raced over and climbed into the back while the officer manoeuvred the ambulance back onto the road. To my relief he offered to drive us into the city and I readily agreed: glad to put our lives in someone else's hands, for I was tired of the responsibility. As we headed toward the city he pushed my head beneath the dashboard and put his foot down. He was an excellent driver, fast and skilful and even though we'd reached the relative safety of the main street, he insisted on taking us right to the hospital and offered to wait and drive us back.

When I entered the hospital the doctors were surprised to see us. Tim went off to find August and Erna Cipra, a Jewish couple who had been trapped in the area since the siege began. August was very sick and his wife was desperate to get him treatment. Their grandson had been killed whilst playing in the school yard and his death had affected them both deeply. Erna had spent her own childhood in a Nazi concentration camp but she felt that was nothing compared to the pain of losing her beloved grandchild. They had packed a small bag, leaving almost everything they owned behind. There was also another Jewish woman who was married to a Muslim. She and her children would not leave without him and once again I found myself saying that I would try to return with the appropriate papers.

I was devastated to learn that Damir Greljo – the eldest of the little boys – had died within two hours of arriving at the hospital. Elmir, who was two and Lela, the baby, were waiting with their mother on the ward. She was still in shock and sat staring ahead, seemingly oblivious to everything around her.

When I returned to the ambulance I found Mirsad, Selma's father, had climbed into the back. He was refusing to budge, insisting that he leave with us. Tim explained how dangerous it would be for us to take him for he was a Muslim man of fighting age. He eventually got out but only after I promised to try and get him a visa.

We left Mostar as dusk was falling and once again I was in the passenger seat while the officer drove. Elmir lay on a stretcher in the back of the ambulance attended by Tim. With him were his mother and grandmother, who was holding the baby. August and Erna sat opposite. Thankfully, the ceasefire held and once we reached the last Bosnian checkpoint the officer got out. I gave him some chocolate and two cartons of cigarettes; which didn't seem much, considering he had just saved our lives.

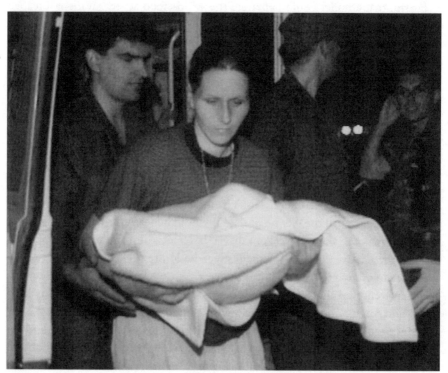

Ivan helps Elmir's mother.

After crossing the airfield, I became confused in the dark and missed our escort. To my horror, a group of HVO soldiers appeared and signalled for me to stop the vehicle. They were dirty and scruffy, their appearances suggesting they had returned from a long stint in the front line. I was immediately concerned for the safety of my passengers, some of whom were Muslim and I held my breath as they tried to peer inside. Sendzana, Elmir's mother, was too traumatised to know what was happening. She stared blankly at the fearsome faces of the men while her mother-in-law stroked her hand; August and Erna were relatively calm, even when the soldiers ordered everyone out of the vehicle. I was about to intervene when I spotted a familiar face among the crowd. It was one of the policemen sent to escort us and he ordered the soldiers to move away.

Lynne was waiting for us at the UN base in Medjugorje but when she asked the soldier on guard to open the gate, he refused. I looked around for someone to help us but there was only a dark empty road.

The Spanish Captain came to tell me that they were forbidden to assist us in any way. I asked if we could at least have some food and water for the evacuees and eventually a soldier brought some yoghurt and water. Jonathan Morris and Simon Dack, two journalists from the *Evening Argus* had been awaiting our arrival and Simon asked if it would be alright to photograph me with Elmir. Headlights came down the road and a Sky News van pulled up. To my surprise, Christopher Morris stepped out of the ambulance, followed by his film crew. I explained what was happening and one of the crew turned to the Captain. 'This is an ambulance,' she said slowly, 'an ambulance with sick children inside.'

'I don't understand,' said the Captain and then turned away.

When Elmir started to cry, my frustration turned to anger. I railed against the UN and all the major aid organisations whose policies were so rigid that they weren't able to respond in an emergency, even when wounded children were involved.

'They're funded by the taxpayers and charitable donations and I'm sure that people would prefer it to be spent on saving lives, rather than on bureaucracy!'

To the huge embarrassment of the United Nations, the scene was flashed around the world. To be caught on camera ignoring the cries of children in need was very bad PR. Inevitably, they denied all knowledge of the mission insisting that they hadn't been informed and they were therefore unprepared. Of course Lynne and I knew that this simply wasn't true.

Lynne made a call to Ivan and he and his colleagues arrived at the base. The doctors carefully transferred our patients into a fully equipped ambulance and they were driven to the main hospital in Split. The whole incident was filmed; Bosnian Croats helping Bosnian Muslims while the UN turned their backs.

When I returned to the Citluk hotel, Thierry took me to one side.

'Sally,' he whispered, 'You were not supposed to come back.' I was puzzled by his words.

'What do you mean?' He looked around to make sure no one was in earshot.

'The UN did not expect you to get out of there alive.' He refused to say anything more on the subject and when I pressed him he said that he daren't talk about it. 'Not now,' he said. 'But maybe one day.'

All the phone lines to reception were blocked as the media tried to get through. It had become a massive story – the human face of war – and we did our best to highlight the suffering on all sides of the conflict. I was going back to Britain to arrange for more aid to be sent out and on the way to the airport we visited the hospital in Split. Against all my expectations Elmir was sitting up and smiling. He had undergone major surgery to remove a damaged kidney, and although there was still shrapnel embedded in his eyes they had managed to save his sight. As I approached his bed he muttered something to me. The doctor seemed a little uncomfortable but I convinced him to translate.

'He says he wants you to move aside because you are blocking the view of his mother.'

The hospital staff gave me some flowers and a book about Croatia. As I stepped outside there were crowds of people pointing and waving. It was quite extraordinary. I had become a local celebrity even though the people I helped were from the opposite side.

I boarded the plane with Alan Little, a BBC reporter I had first met in the Gulf. He warned me that there would be trouble ahead owing to a statement that had been issued by the UN. There were so many journalists waiting at the airport that I had to be escorted through customs by the police and I soon understood why. The UN had accused me of spying.

At first I was amused for it seemed so ridiculous, especially as they implied that I was spying for them. The headline on the front page of the *Daily Mirror* wasn't that funny though: 'UN SIGNS SALLY'S DEATH WARRANT'. If this was taken seriously it could endanger me personally and threaten any future operations. Of course I hadn't learned any secrets because I had never been interested in political moves or military strategies, but the situation in Bosnia-Herzegovina was so tense that I could not allow the allegations to go unchallenged. I was invited to take part in a televised political debate with two politicians from the leading political parties in Britain. I was expecting a fight but within a few minutes it was clear they both supported my work.

Christopher Morris was interviewed on television and insisted that the accusations were rubbish. When he was asked why he thought the UN would make such an accusation, he said that it might be a case of sour grapes. I was given a chance to speak out on *Talkback*, a live phone-in broadcast on Sky. Calls came in from around the world and I found the questions interesting and challenging. Almost every caller began by congratulating me and expressing their support but one woman complained that I had not helped Serbian children. I explained that the children's ethnic background was not an issue; I was working on the basis of need, not creed. Another caller, speaking from Rome, suggested that we should leave the Balkans to its fate and he remained unmoved when I argued that innocent people would die if the aid agencies pulled out. The last question was from Laurie Mayer, the programme's presenter, who asked how I felt about being called a publicity seeker.

'Anyone who believes that I would risk my life for the sake of publicity has a serious problem. If publicity was my aim, I could have climbed the Post Office Tower naked. It would certainly have been a lot easier!'

The ICJW (International Council of Jewish Women) raised funds which would buy food for the Jewish community in Mostar and with the proceeds from an exclusive interview with the *Mirror*, I was able to buy blankets and shawls for the elderly. It would not be long before their problems were magnified a thousand fold by the bitter cold of a Balkan winter.

10 | THE EAST SIDE

WHEN I LANDED IN Croatia I was met by Roger, a South African filming for ABC news. Roger had been told that I was hoping to try and get a transit visa for Selma's father Mirsad so he could be reunited with his family in the States. This would not be an easy task because he was a Muslim adult male but I was hoping that the presence of a news crew might help.

Roger's fixer was a young Bosnian with the unlikely name of Elvis. They had rented an armoured vehicle but when I asked if Mirsad could travel in their vehicle, I was told no. Apparently it would be 'unethical' for them to assist the operation in any way.

I arrived at the Citluk hotel to find Lynne in a high state of anxiety: she had spent the last few days avoiding Eddo the Psycho. Before leaving, I had asked Ivan to keep an eye on him but unfortunately he had taken my request to the extreme. Eddo was arrested for being drunk and suspended from duty. Collette and the boys were away, so poor Lynne was subjected to his constant presence at the hotel and she had spent most of the time locked in her room.

Ivan was in Zagreb so he sent his friend Vava to help us with the paperwork. Vava could do a great impression of Ivan, whom he teased unmercifully, insisting he looked like Colonel Gaddafi. Throughout those few tense days, he remained at the Citluk hotel, keeping us amused and insisting that I remain optimistic when it seemed as though the mission might never come off.

Tim Clancy had heard about our plans and he called me from Zagreb and asked to be included. When I told Roger he was delighted, as this meant he would have a real American hero for his film. A British friend of his wished to come as well. He was also called Tim. He was working with a charity called War Child who operated a mobile bakery in Medjugorje. They were hoping the bakery could be moved to the East side and Tim had been asked to do a recce.

The conflict had escalated, with both sides pushing harder in a desperate attempt to gain territory. The Bosnian army had managed to take Hum, the mountain that dominates the valley and overlooked the whole of the city, so emotions were running high. Locals were directing their anger at foreigners – including myself and Lynne – and it was going to be difficult to secure the documents necessary for our forthcoming mission.

Although the Bosnian Croats had supported my rescue operations, the local people had very little access to the media and knew only that we helped the other side. They were unaware, for example, that I had also managed to highlight the problems in Nova Bila, and that as a result an evacuation had taken place.

When the transit visas finally arrived they caused some problems. Amongst them was one for Mirsad Handzar. Vinko, a young soldier, was hanging round reception as we were checking the papers and when he saw Mirsad's surname on one of the documents, he immediately launched into a torrent of abuse. When Lynne tried to talk to him about it he spat on the floor and muttered 'You help Muslims!'

'I'm sorry for his behaviour,' said Vava. He knew Lynne liked Vinko and considered him a friend. To his surprise, Lynne merely smiled wryly and shrugged. 'Life's a bitch and then you die!' she said. For a moment Vava looked quite shocked for he'd obviously never heard the saying before, but soon he started to laugh and kept repeating it to himself.

When Lynne and I were alone she admitted that in actual fact she was extremely upset. The situation was starting to really get her down and she didn't know how much more she could tolerate. Rather than make a decision she might regret, she agreed to wait until after the next mission before deciding what to do.

We still had no promise of a ceasefire and one day I was told that permission for the operation had been cancelled. I had just informed Roger, who could not hang around much longer, when to our surprise there was a phone call from the Minister of Health informing me that the mission could now take place after all. I was sceptical. It seemed a little odd to say the least.

Roger wanted to proceed immediately but I knew that the UN would not support us. This also meant that it was unlikely the Bosnian army would be forewarned of our arrival. Despite this, they were keen to go ahead. I insisted that we at least wait until the following day, giving me time to buy supplies for the hospital.

Tim had borrowed two flak jackets and helmets that he threw in the back of the ambulance. As we prepared to leave, Eddo suddenly appeared, having come to see us off. His suspension from the army was now over and he was off to the front to join his brigade. He was wearing his full kit and carried his weapons on his back and for some strange reason he presented me with a stack of personal photographs and his wedding ring, which he asked me to take care of until he returned. I handed them to Lynne for I didn't want to carry them through a war zone and I tried hard not to grimace as he gave me a hug. He wished me luck and told me that despite me being Jewish, he liked me very much. Saluting dramatically, and giving us a toothless smile, Eddo the Psycho proceeded to march off into the distance, never to be seen again.

We crossed the front line without any problems and proceeded towards the main street. Tim Clancy was attempting to give me directions but we took a wrong turning and ended up on a hill that overlooked the city. There was a loud burst of gunfire so I drove behind an apartment block for protection.

Within a few moments people started to venture onto the street and stood staring at our vehicle. We explained that we were lost and a man offered to show us the way to the hospital. As we headed back down the hill I could hear sporadic shooting and realised to my dismay that we were being targeted by a sniper. The blue light on top of the vehicle was shattered and I desperately looked around for somewhere we could shelter. Ahead of us was a tunnel, so I quickly drove inside. The ceiling was too low, scraping the roof of the ambulance with a grinding screech of metal. Unable to go forwards, I would have to reverse into the bullets.

Our lives depended upon what happened next and I was consumed with fear. Taking a deep breath, I put the vehicle into reverse and pressed the accelerator to the floor and as we came out of the tunnel I shunted the ambulance back and forth in an attempt to turn around on the narrow track. Bullets whistled past in quick succession and my heart was thumping so hard I could barely think straight. At last we were facing back the way we came and I quickly drove around the corner, where Roger and Elvis were waiting.

Our guide showed me the way to the hospital and when we pulled up outside I thanked him for his help and offered him some cigarettes and coffee. To my surprise he shook his head and grabbed hold of my arm.

'No need to thank me,' he said. 'You come to save our children.'

When we entered the hospital I was confronted by the director, Dr Dragan Malović. He accused me of being a traitor and at first I assumed he was referring to the UN allegations but Hafid took me to one side and explained. Croatian television had used each of my missions to create propaganda. The Croat doctors had been filmed helping my patients and Sendzana, Elmir's mother, had appeared on television thanking the Croats for helping her family.

The local commander of the Bosnian Army's 4th Corps, Arif Pasalić, was enraged by the film and insisted that the woman had been forced to say the words at gun point. Malović had received a dressing down for allowing the mission to take place and he was ordered to prevent any further medical evacuations.

I asked to speak to Malović again and spent a long time trying to persuade him that my actions were justified. Children, who otherwise might have died, were now safe and well. He was finally convinced but insisted that only the Bosnian army could authorise any further evacuations. Before setting off, I went to see the children and made a note of their details.

Elvis offered to accompany me to the Bosnian army headquarters and just as we were leaving, Selma's father arrived at the hospital. He had heard from the Red Cross that his family was safe in America and the relief was clearly visible on his care-worn face. He was desperate to join them, although he doubted whether the Bosnian army would agree to let him go. Nevertheless, he insisted that he would be leaving with me whether or not they gave him permission. He led us along the main street past three APCs manned by the unfortunate UNPROFOR soldiers who had been forced to remain behind. Once we reached the main junction, I saw a sign that read, 'Warning, sniper'. There was a nerve-racking wait while we prepared to dash across the exposed area, which was targeted by snipers from the upper storey of a bank that overlooked the square.

We arrived at the command headquarters of the 4th Army Corps only to find that the commander would not be available for at least another two hours. Not wanting to risk the snipers any more than necessary, we decided to wait. Sitting side by side on the front porch, we surveyed the damage caused by two years fighting. The Serbs had bombarded the city from the mountains in the east and since May their job had been taken over by the HVO attacks from the west. Few buildings had escaped entirely and many were blackened shells.

As evening drew near, Elvis became anxious. 'I'm not spending the night here, if we haven't sorted this out by 8.00pm we will have to go.'

'I don't want to leave without those I came in for,' I said,' I'll wait until tomorrow if necessary.'

After a while the Commander pulled up outside the building in a gleaming black Suzuki jeep. He was a good-looking man of 50 and after stopping to look at me for a moment, he strode past without a word.

A short time later, Elvis was summoned to see him but he was only gone five minutes before he returned looking annoyed. Mirsad was refused permission to leave unless he had a visa issued by the United States and the husband of the Jewish woman would need one from the government of Israel. As for the children, they were not his concern; I would have to get permission from the War Office.

To the people of this besieged section of the city, the man was a hero for holding off the enemy for such a long time and although frustrated by his attitude, I understood his antipathy towards me; the sight of a mother thanking her enemy for saving her child was damaging to morale. Nevertheless, I was surprised that he would be prepared to delay the children getting the medical help they so desperately needed.

Elvis thought we should leave but I was damned if I was going to abandon the children after we had risked our lives to get here.

Hafid had just removed a part of a young boy's brain by torchlight. The boy, called Amel Demić, had been blasted against a wall when a mortar exploded near his front door. His mother had been calling him to come inside and she was also wounded with pieces of shrapnel embedded in her stomach. Amel, whose skull had been shattered, was now in a coma and Hafid told me that it would be a miracle if he survived. His colleague had not wanted to waste the anesthetic which was in such short supply but Hafid pointed out that had it been his own child, he would want him to try.

There was no normal oxygen supply; instead they relied upon the industrial variety and amputations were performed where in other circumstances the limbs might have been saved. He told me that they were forced to play God, keeping back vital medicines for those who might have a chance.

Later that night Hafid showed me to a room upstairs where there were a few beds awaiting a new team of doctors who were travelling across the mountains from Sarajevo. The Tims chose to sleep in the ambulance parked in the hospital compound and Roger and Elvis slept in their jeep. I was kept awake by worry and the constant thump of explosions. By the morning I was desperate to be on my way.

Meanwhile, at the White Hill Hospital in West Mostar, Vava was having a few beers as he anxiously awaited my return. He was sitting in Ivan's office when a phone call was put through from my mother.

'Have you heard from Sally?' she inquired.

'She's fine, Mrs Becker, she should be here in the morning.' said Vava, crossing his fingers.

'Please send her my love when you see her.'

'Of course I will,' he replied, as he reached for another bottle.

I arrived at the War Office on the stroke of eight – I had one other card up my sleeve. I had a letter of introduction from Stipe Rozić to an old schoolfriend who worked there. Stipe had told me to ask him a question before handing over the letter. If the man answered correctly, then I would know he could be trusted. After all, the letter was in effect written by the enemy: a Croat.

I found Stipe's friend and promptly asked him the question, which was about a place where they had played as children. He gave the right answer and I handed him the letter; but the response was all too familiar.

'Firstly,' he said, 'it is impossible to help Mr Handzar without a visa from the US. He is of fighting age and although he has been wounded he must remain here.' The Jewish woman's husband is also liable for military service so as you were told, he will need a visa from Israel. Of course if his wife and children wish to leave, then that is fine.' I sighed with frustration.

'They won't leave without him.'

'Then they are foolish,' he replied, making it obvious that the conversation was at an end.

'But what about the others?' I persisted, handing him a list I had made. 'There are six children in need of medical treatment and a woman with a severe head wound whose son might lose his arm.' The man lowered his voice so as not to be heard outside the office.

'Maybe if you wait two, perhaps three days, we can make sure that the children have the necessary documents which would enable them to leave.'

'But there wasn't any need for documents last time,' I said, struggling to control my anger. 'I have permission from the Croats to bring them all out.'

'Either you can wait and try to help the children or you will have to leave without them.' He replied.

As he began to usher me from his office I asked whether there was anywhere that I could get some cigarettes as I had given all mine away. It was rumoured that there were vast amounts of hashish available in East Mostar but hardly any tobacco.

He took me to a small room and unlocked the door. Cigarette cartons filled the space from floor to ceiling. There had been an attempt to obscure the brand name but I could just about read it: 'Yugoslavia'. They had no filters and when I tried one it tasted very stale but I realised they would have to do – this wasn't the time to give up smoking.

Back at the hospital I broke the news to the others. Elvis wanted to leave but Roger preferred to wait a little longer. I left them and entered the reception area where the staff ate and slept. Behind a curtain were four beds, one of them Hafid's. A small team of doctors had arrived from Sarajevo and the dormitory upstairs was now full. Hafid insisted that I use the bed whenever he was busy, which was almost all of the time. He looked exhausted but I told him that his wife was in good health and being well looked after, which cheered him immensely.

The pillows were soft and I closed my eyes hoping to catch some sleep. There was a screaming whine followed by a loud explosion. A rocket propelled grenade had blasted the window just a few feet away from my bed and although we were in the basement, the windows were level with the pavement outside and dust and debris were hurled into the room covering every surface. My ears were ringing from the noise as I sat up, pulling slivers of glass from my hair. I pulled out a small mirror from my overnight bag and saw blood was trickling down my face, tracing fine red lines through the dust.

There was no one around so I tentatively stepped into the corridor where I found Dr Malović's three-year-old son sitting on the floor. I crouched down beside him just as another explosion rocked the building, causing me to flinch. He giggled with delight. He hadn't seen anyone react to bangs before; here they were just a part of everyday life.

A young woman was carried in on a stretcher and laid beside the injured from the previous night. I could hear her screams and cries echoing in the space between us. After a while the noise stopped and I asked if she had been given morphine for the pain.

'We don't have any morphine. Anyway she doesn't need it now because she's dead.'

11 | INCOMING

SIXTY-FIVE SHELLS HIT THE area in the first 24 hours and the stream of casualties seemed endless: men and women, boys and girls, babies. Many died while waiting for treatment. The HVO did not have direct line of sight to the hospital but their artillery was aimed in that direction and shells often exploded above or in front of the building. It was rumoured that the army kept their ammunition stores in the basement and that the doctors had been struggling to get them to move it.

Hafid ran from one operation to another like a man possessed, his hands bloody and his eyes frantic. Malović assessed each patient as they arrived, carried in on stretchers by two brave men. He looked at me and murmured, 'Your friends did this.' I knew that in a way he was right.

Roger had left to follow some soldiers but he returned a short while later unscathed. Elvis wasn't so lucky; he was wounded while anxiously waiting at the hospital entrance for his colleague to return. I watched the doctor extracting the jagged pieces of shrapnel from his back and realised that this young man represented the internecine mess that was Bosnia. His father's people were attacking his mother's people and he was one of the victims caught in between. He and Roger left the following morning during a lull in the fighting; the boys had arranged to leave with UNPROFOR when they changed shift later that day.

Dr Malović took me to the bedside of a young HVO soldier who had been captured and put to work on the front line. The soldier was wounded in the stomach and urgently needed a transfusion but he had a rare blood group so there was nothing they could do. I touched his burning forehead and he reached for my hand, staring at me with eyes bright with fever.

'Let's go, let's go,' he murmured, over and over again. Malović told me that he was one of four HVO soldiers caught in a grenade blast and they were all in the hospital. I suggested he send a message to the aid organisations based in Medjugorje.

'I have tried that before but whenever I talk to Médecins Sans Frontières or the Red Cross they say, "We would help you, but our actions are limited by the Croat HVO forces besieging the city." They always mention the HVO. They use them as an excuse for their own limitations.'

I suggested that he send a message to Bagarić giving him details of the soldier's blood type. He agreed that it could do no harm and we gave the letter to Tim.

To pass the time between visits to the war office I talked to the patients and when possible I gave blood. The conditions in the hospital were appalling. There were only three makeshift water tanks but no purification system, and the electricity supply was almost non-existent. There was a kerosene-powered generator that they tended to use for surgical procedures only. Most of the time the surgeons worked using headlamps. What equipment they had was sterilised in an old autoclave heated with wood.

The food consisted of dry bread for breakfast, a bowl of rice or beans cooked in salted water for lunch and the same in the evening. When I received my first ration of rice and 'gravy', I attempted to pick out the weevils but soon gave up. The woman in charge of the kitchen made 'coffee' from green beans and although it tasted nothing like the real thing, it was brown and hot. Better than cold water from the river, contaminated with decomposing bodies.

Malović asked me if I would like to speak on Mostar radio. I declined, not wanting to become further embroiled in the propaganda war. He thought that if they announced that I was staying at the hospital it might deter the Croats from shelling the building. Unable to convince him that it wouldn't make any difference, in the end I agreed.

Although determined to stay, I had never been so frightened and was unsure whether I would survive. Before leaving Britain I wrote a letter to my parents to be opened if by some chance I did not make it back; this was the first time I thought it might actually be read.

To my surprise a small contingent from UNPROFOR came to evacuate the Croat soldier. Their arrival was obviously the result of the message Malović had sent out with Tim but when he saw them he flew into a rage, shouting that he had included a list of the sick and wounded children but that had been ignored.

'Instead they come for a fighting man!' he cried and ordered them out of the building.

Following the announcement of my presence on Mostar radio, the shelling stopped for a while. I was convinced it was because of the four wounded soldiers but Malović thought otherwise, which meant that no one was in a rush to see me leave.

When someone left the building you could never be sure if they would make it back. Shortly after I arrived a man called Agim came to see me. He was President of the Albanian community and he asked me to tell his embassy that 200 Albanians were trapped in East Mostar and most of them wanted to leave. I promised to pass on the message when I reached the other side but he returned to the hospital several times each day to ensure that I wouldn't forget. Each time he came, he was risking his life unnecessarily, so I was exasperated when the cook mentioned him again.

'You don't understand,' she said. 'He's dead, killed by a sniper. His body has just been brought in.'

Amel Demić was still in a coma. The family kept a constant vigil beside his bed and Hafid told me that if by some miracle he managed to survive, he would be in

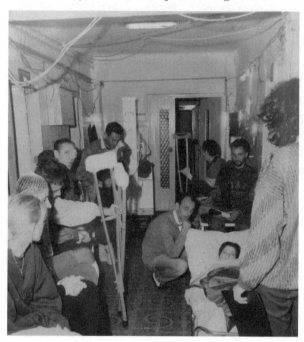

The wounded wait in the hospital corridor.

urgent need of specialist care. His brother Emir glanced at me.

'Please help him,' he said. Malović overheard him and took me aside, saying that he didn't think the boy would make it.

In Mostar, most activities took place at night as it was the safest time. People would use the cover of darkness to visit friends, bury their dead and collect water from the river or search for food. Most people were living in cellars or the lower floors of buildings, sleeping on blankets, mattresses or rugs, completely reliant on aid. There was no black market; all the roads into town were targeted by the HVO and the Serbs controlled the surrounding hills. The only food available came from a soup kitchen set up in a former department store where they served 3000 bowls of 'soup' each day.

Every evening Hafid set off to deliver half of his food ration to his sister who slept under the local pharmacy. On the way back he would stop to feed the wounded cat that lived in the ruins of his father's house. I insisted he take my share of the food, wishing there was more I could do to help.

Each day I went over to the war office hoping to secure the departure papers for the children. Sometimes I would pass a body left there from the previous night and the stench of rotting corpses mingled with the odour of excrement and garbage that littered the streets. If the shelling was heavy I would find it was closed, or they were busy and told me to come back later.

The main street ran parallel to the river and the side streets leading off it were targeted by snipers. I would wait anxiously at each intersection whilst trying to gather the nerve to race across. Occasionally a red pinprick of light would flash across my body from the laser beam on a sniper's rifle, which was truly terrifying.

The shelling soon recommenced and whenever the generator was working we watched the carnage on the news. The staff cheered when the presenter announced that the Muslim counter-offensive had gained ground. Then onto the screen came scenes of a massacre by Bosnian soldiers, including a young boy who had been butchered. 'They are all as bad as one another really,' said Hafid softly.

The woman doctor showed me the morgue which was actually just an ordinary room, for it had no refrigeration. Several bodies were piled inside, one upon the other, and she told me that hundreds of bodies had passed through since the siege began.

On the fifth day I was woken by a familiar French accent and to my delight I saw Danielle from UNICEF. She gave me a hug and then to my dismay announced that she was just about to leave. She had entered East Mostar with Jerry Hulme, head of the UNHCR in Bosnia-Herzegovina, so I quickly told her about the children and the difficulties I was having trying to arrange their evacuation. She suggested I come with her to meet him and we raced through the narrow streets to where he was parked with an escort of APCs. Jerry was a middle-aged man wearing a flak jacket and a blue UN helmet. He removed it for a moment to wipe the sweat trickling down from his bald head. His face was suntanned and he had twinkling blue eyes. After listening to what I had to say, he assured me that the UNHCR would be able to carry out the evacuation on my behalf.

Danielle tried to convince me to go with them and I hesitated for a moment, tempted to escape from all the death and destruction. Instead I gave them the list of names and urged them to hurry.

Watching them go left me feeling more alone than ever. I was becoming increasingly light-headed from the lack of food and water combined with the intense heat. After racing across 'sniper's alley' I wearily made my way back to the hospital past the blackened shells of burned out buildings, sharply delineated against the clear blue sky.

Following a night of constant shelling I awoke to find that the ambulance was damaged. I knew that no one would dare venture out long enough to try and fix it and I was unsure what to do next. My head was aching and I couldn't seem to think straight. When Hafid finished his shift that evening he found me sitting on the edge of his bed with my head in my hands.

'Sally, you are sick,' he said, feeling my forehead. 'You have a fever and I think perhaps it is time for you to leave.'

Knowing there was nothing I could do without transportation, I figured he was probably right. In any case I was confident that Jerry and Daniele would soon be back to carry out the evacuation. The UNPROFOR soldiers would be changing shift the following day and Hafid suggested I go with them.

That evening I went to see the woman with the head wound and found her young son still beside her, nursing his damaged arm. I visited the father of a sixteen-year-old girl with a spinal injury and explained the situation, assuring him I would do my best to help her. Following surgery most patients were taken upstairs where they were lined up on mattresses on the floor. Amongst the patients was a young girl who was obviously in a great deal of pain and I felt wretched knowing there was nothing I could do.

Early the next the morning I packed my bag and said goodbye to the staff. Tim had loaned the flak jackets to the stretcher bearers and I decided to leave them behind. They were made from Kevlar and cost £1000 each but I figured that no one needed them more than these two men who continuously risked death as they rushed to help the wounded. Hafid was in the middle of an operation so not wanting to disturb him, I left a short note on his bed. I thanked him for his generosity and kindness and I promised to make sure his wife received the things she needed for their baby. I handed the keys of the ambulance to Malović's wife and ran from the building.

On the main street I waited while a soldier faxed my details to the base in Medjugorje; they would need permission before I would be able to travel in their vehicle. I sat down on the dusty pavement and a scrawny young dog limped towards me. He was brown and white with a very large head and I saw a piece of shrapnel protruding from his paw. As I tried to remove it, he licked my face, perhaps sensing that I wanted to help. I was suddenly overwhelmed. Burying my face in his neck, which was thick with dust, I wept for this poor wounded animal and all the other wretched creatures of this once thriving city; for all the men, women and children who were living like rats in dungeons with death on their doorstep.

I left the city in a UN armoured vehicle and although it was small and very cramped it felt like heaven, for at last I felt safe. The vehicle broke down before we reached the airport and we had to be shunted along by another APC, so a journey that should have taken about 40 minutes actually took seven hours. As we passed through Citluk I asked to be let out but was surprised when they insisted on taking me to the UN base. As the hatch was opened and I finally climbed out, a crowd of people with cameras were waiting on the ground. A microphone was pushed under my nose as I staggered across the compound.

'How does it feel to be rescued by the UN?'

Back at the hotel I was greeted by Ivan, Lynne and Vava who were obviously relieved to see me. Vava told me that Ivan had hardly slept and had been to church each day, praying for my safe return. We were joined by the other doctors and they wanted to hear about my experiences in 'enemy' territory. To be fair they did not ask for any military information; they simply wanted to understand why the mission had failed.

I was exhausted and my cheeks were hollow, with dark shadows beneath my eyes. My clothes were dusty and spattered with blood. Collette pushed her way past the doctors insisting that I needed to rest. She took me to her room and put me to bed, as I was still running a temperature. As I lay between the clean fresh sheets she gave me some aspirin and camomile tea. There were no bursts of gunfire, no explosions and no screams of pain, only the comforting feel of Collette's cool hand upon my forehead as I drifted off to sleep.

12 | COLLETTE

AS SOON AS I was feeling better I went to see Ivan about blood supplies for the wounded Croat soldier. He suggested I ask Jerry Hulme to deliver it to the hospital so I drove to his office in Medjugorje. He gave me his assurance that the evacuation would be taking place within days. They were sorting out the paperwork and in the meantime he would be going in with a Medevac team to assess the patients. This seemed to me to be an unnecessary delay but he was adamant that it had to be done as part of the process. He seemed very genuine, if a little patronising in his manner, but at this stage I had no say in the matter: it was no longer my operation. Before I left he asked me for a favour. Would I use my influence with Ivan to get permission for him and Danielle to visit West Mostar? They wanted to inspect the orphanages and hospitals there.

It took me a couple of days to persuade Bagarić' to allow them to enter West Mostar on an unofficial basis. I pointed out that she had agreed to arrange an assessment of Nova Bila in return. Ivan agreed, on condition I accompanied them into the city, which was ironic. In spite of my somewhat fraught relationship with the UN, I was now to be cast in the role of chaperone.

A rather odd character had recently arrived at the Citluk hotel. He was known as Big Rod, a very broad man with dark hair swept back in a ponytail who had driven a customised vehicle from Britain in response to an appeal I made on Sky. I had been interviewed by Selina Scott immediately after the first evacuation and she asked if there was anything I needed. At the time I requested an armoured ambulance but had forgotten all about it. Rod heard the appeal and had been busy ever since, converting a vehicle using metal sheets which he'd welded on to the sides. He had a short temper and became very angry when told that the latest mission had been delayed. Jerry Hulme, who was wearing a UN cap, had come to collect me for the trip to West Mostar and caught the full force of his wrath.

'Unless those children are out within days,' Rod shouted in his face, 'I will make sure the media are informed of your incompetence!' He grew increasingly irrational and at one point I was afraid he might become violent but Jerry turned his back and returned to his Land Rover. As I climbed in beside him he muttered something about the strange company I kept. As we drove out of Citluk it occurred to me that I must seem quite mild mannered compared to someone like Rod.

While Jerry and Danielle were taken around the hospital I went to visit Damir and his family. Erna was still trying to get Damir to Britain but his permit would allow him no farther than Zagreb. He had relatives there who were desperately trying to sort out a visa but so far it had been refused on the grounds that he would need to be accompanied by his parents.

Damir's grandfather had at last returned home to his wife. The antibiotics had worked and he was beginning to walk again. Erna told me that the Rozic family had become very popular because they were friends with 'The Angel of Mostar'. I laughed, but Damir assured me that it was true and indeed when we passed through the checkpoint outside their apartment, the soldiers vied with each other to talk to me. It was the same in Citluk, where we were constantly turning down invitations to visit people's homes. Even the hotel receptionists, who had always seemed indifferent if not cold, now treated us with a grudging respect. It was either due to my stint on the 'other side' or because I was drawing attention to Mostar. Either way, I was pleased because it made Lynne feel much safer.

Three days later, Collette and Sean went with the boys into West Mostar to take some photographs of the damage. Before they left, Collette told me that she planned to join me on my next mission. She had decided she would rather use her nursing skills in East Mostar where she felt the people would benefit more from her help. Sean was against the idea but knowing how determined she was, he knew that he had little choice in the matter.

Collette was in a room at the top of an abandoned apartment block in an area known as The Rondo, where the boys were observing an area captured the day before. A grenade fired from an RPG-7 came through the window and exploded behind the couch where she was sitting. Collette was blown to the far side of the room, conscious but horribly wounded.

Sean was hurled backwards by the blast as he came through the doorway. Making his way through the smoke and the dust he saw that Collette was on the floor. The shrapnel had ripped through her abdomen and damaged vital organs. He shouted for help as Collette clutched her stomach in an effort to prevent her intestines spilling out.

The boys found an abandoned stretcher in the corridor and carried her down the seven flights of stairs. They immediately commandeered a vehicle and with the stretcher supported across the top of the seats, they drove her towards the hospital on the hill. All the while Sean held her hand and told her that he loved her.

As soon as they arrived at the hospital Collette was rushed into surgery. Sean waited outside the operating room while the doctors battled to save her and finally, after four hours, Vladlena appeared.

'Her injuries are very bad,' she said, looking exhausted. 'She is in a very serious condition. Go back to your hotel – there is nothing you can do here.'

Sean did not want to leave her but Vladlena insisted. 'You must get some rest and come back in the morning.'

That evening Sean appeared in the doorway of our room and told us what happened. When he finished he sat there in silence, his face pale and drawn. Thierry arrived a short while later and as he sat down he slowly shook his head.

'She won't make it,' he said softly. 'She's in a very bad way. Even if she survives the operation, she would be on tubes and machines for the rest of her life. Collette is too lively, too vital. She would not want to live like that.' We lapsed into silence once again, shocked by his words.

Sean decided to go and pack some of her things to take to the hospital. He had only been gone a few minutes when he reappeared at the door and announced that she was dead.

I could hardly begin to imagine his pain. In the few months since they got together they had rarely been apart and I recalled how he had gazed at her photograph on the bus and how we had teased him. I remembered the poems he wrote about her and the hundreds of photographs he had taken; Collette in her surgical greens, in his uniform, sitting by the lake at Ljubuški or with the boys. Those photographs were now all that remained of that vibrant, beautiful and caring young woman.

After a few minutes Sean announced that he was going to his room. When he left I wandered onto the landing, needing some time to think. I felt guilty, knowing how often I had tempted fate and feeling that it should have been me instead of her. When I eventually turned around to go back to my room, I saw one of the doctors who worked with Collette. Normally quite tough, with a confident jaunty manner; he looked drawn, punctured by grief.

'She was so pretty,' he said as tears streamed down his cheeks. Until then I was too numb to cry but seeing him in such torment I too wept openly. Tim and Thierry joined us and we talked long into the night about Collette, remembering how happy she was and the funny things she said.

That morning Sean returned to the hospital with Thierry, after spending the night in the bed he had shared with Collette. Later Thierry told us what had happened.

'It was terrible. The morgue was full so they had placed her body in another room. I begged Sean not to look at her, to remember her just as she was, young and beautiful. I have seen many corpses and in this heat, with the flies… I knew it would be bad but he would not listen. This is not Collette, I told him. This is just a body.'

We offered to call Collette's family as they still did not know what had happened but Sean insisted he would make the call himself. I asked him if he wanted a drink but he just sat staring into space. Thinking he would prefer to be alone, I started to leave but he suddenly reached out his hand. There was nothing I could say to ease his pain so I just held him close until his tears eventually subsided.

The Croat health authorities arranged for her body to be driven to Split and then flown to Zagreb for cremation. Sean and Tim accompanied the coffin and at the morgue in Split, 20 nurses stood in attendance, each holding a white rose in one hand and a candle in the other. A gold plaque was placed upon the wall at

Bijeli Brig hospital in remembrance of Collette, who had died in the very place where she had worked so hard to save the lives of others.

Another week passed with still no sign of the evacuation. Rod insisted that it would only happen if we carried out the mission ourselves but Ivan was adamant that he would not get permission for me to cross the line alone. He was not willing to let me risk my life again – but there was another factor. I had not yet managed to organise a similar mission to Nova Bila and Ivan's reputation was on the line. Why, his superiors wanted to know, had he allowed me to rescue fifteen Bosnian Muslims when I had not helped one single Croat? I knew that it was imperative that I try to reach Nova Bila.

Things went from bad to worse and Jerry told me that it would be at least two weeks before the evacuation of Mostar would take place. The whole operation had been passed on to the International Office of Migration, which meant that before the children could be brought out, they had to be allocated hospital beds in other countries. Only then would they be issued with visas. This did not make sense to me because I knew that Danielle had already arranged for beds to be available at the MASH hospital in Zagreb.

'Why can't the children be taken to Zagreb?' I asked, completely bewildered by the bureaucracy. 'Surely the visas can be allocated once they are safe.'

'The IOM doesn't work like that,' said Jerry patiently. 'They prefer to do all the paperwork first.'

'And what if somebody dies in the meantime?'

'That's the way the mandate works I'm afraid.' He said, seeming a little uncomfortable. 'It's their policy'.

'Then it's a load of crap! 'Children are dying because of these so called "policies". It's appalling! For goodness sake forget IOM. Instead of going in to assess them tomorrow, just bring them out.'

'Sally, we can't evacuate the children ourselves, not now that the mission has been given to IOM.' I couldn't believe what I was hearing.

'Why?' I asked him, softly this time. 'Why was the mission passed to them?'

He started shuffling some papers on his desk and he replied to my question without looking up.

'It was a political decision.' He said. 'The IOM want the kudos for themselves.'

Politics! It was always politics; politics and publicity, even if it meant risking the lives of the children. And I knew that behind the caring faces of aid workers like Danielle, behind all those brave UN soldiers on the ground, were the faceless puppeteers who pulled the strings for their own political ends. I was consumed with anger and frustration. When I returned to the hotel I broke the news to Rod, telling him what had been arranged.

'I'll do it myself!' he shouted,' If you've lost your bottle, I'll do it alone.'

This was the final straw. I had battled with the Croat authorities, with the Muslim authorities, I had battled with the UN. In between I had to sell everything

I owned and beg or borrow money to keep going while highly paid professionals turned their backs on wounded children. I had been shot at, shelled and branded a spy and I had just spent several days in hell. And here was this man implying that I'd somehow given up, 'lost my bottle'. I took a deep breath and rounded on him.

'The only reason I'm not prepared to go in by myself is because I don't have permission from the Croats. Without their permission I would have to bring the children across the front line without a ceasefire. And that's only if the Bosnian authorities allow them to leave without the transit visas. Do you understand? It's too dangerous! If you want to be the big hero, at least make sure it's safe, or as safe as it can be. I'm sure you wouldn't want a child's death on your conscience.'

Rod looked ashamed and said he was sorry, he was just frustrated; he'd come all this way and wanted to do something to help. I understood his frustration only too well.

'Tomorrow we'll buy supplies with the money given to me by the ICJW and deliver them to Mostar. It's Rosh Hashanah, the Jewish New Year, so we'll try to make it special for them. And after that, how do you feel about taking a young boy to Britain?'

The next day we drove to the Jewish warehouse, where Stipe and Zoran helped us to unload the aid. Rod had agreed to drive Damir to Zagreb and try to help him get a visa. If it wasn't possible, he planned to hide him in a section of the vehicle and once they reached the UK, Damir would declare himself to immigration. He had an aunt and uncle living in London who would take care of him until the war was over. Before we left, I handed the keys of the Renault to Stipe. 'You may as well have it,' I said, knowing that he would use it for the benefit of others.

The Croats had recently opened an embassy near Medjugorje where I was invited to meet the new Ambassador. We had lunch and talked a little about the situation but I felt uncomfortable when he proudly announced that the area under their control was now called Herceg-Bosna and Mostar would soon be the capital. Later Vava drove me to meet Mate Boban, the President of 'Herceg-Bosna', who congratulated me for what I had achieved in Mostar–and berated me for what I had failed to do in central Bosnia.

This was the opportunity I had been waiting for and I decided to take a chance. Would he, I asked, give me permission for a convoy to East Mostar, providing I did the same for Nova Bila?

'I don't care where else you go,' said the President 'You can take aid to all sides, evacuate the injured, so long as you include the area of Vitez, Novi Travnik, Bugojno or Nova Bila.'

At last I could realise my dream – I had his word. I also knew that I was looking at something on a much greater scale than anything I had tackled so far. I would need supplies, transport, volunteers and an enormous amount of money. And of course I didn't have much time, for the situation was growing ever more desperate as winter approached. I would have to go home.

Ivan and Vava drove Lynne and me to the airport and I asked them what they thought of Boban.

'He doesn't like me,' said Ivan, 'I was once in his office discussing the political situation and he asked me where I wished to be, so I pointed to his chair!'

We laughed, but in actual fact I too wished that Ivan had been sitting in the Presidential chair; the war might have ended by now.

'It isn't over,' I told Lynne as we walked through the airport. 'This is my chance to help the children of Nova Bila.'

'You know I won't be here to help you?' said Lynne.

'Do you mean that?' I asked, unable to imagine Bosnia without her.

She looked at me sadly. 'Everything changed when Collette died. And now the boys have gone …'

I suggested she might be exhausted. 'Perhaps you just need a good rest.' Lynne laughed.

'And what about you? Don't you need a rest?'

'Well I'll get one while I'm in Britain.'

'A rest?' she said, as they called our flight over the tannoy. 'You'll be lucky. You'll need volunteers and aid, funding and vehicles …'

'Sounds a bit like hard work to me,' I said, as we hurried towards the plane. 'I might have to reconsider!'

A few days later I received a letter from Hafid and I read it with tears streaming down my face.

> I am so sorry to have to inform you that despite their promise, the UN have not yet carried out the evacuation of the children. Medina, a child who was wounded by shrapnel, has died from septicaemia; there was nothing we could do. She was only eleven years old. This war is a travesty. It is destroying us and killing our children.

Naturally I blamed myself for what had happened. I shouldn't have relied on the UN. I should have been more insistent, I should have tried to go back in.

I wrote a strongly worded fax to the United Nations headquarters in Zagreb, demanding they carry out the evacuation immediately. A reply came back within an hour; the evacuation would proceed within days.

A short while later I was watching a television documentary about Mostar. Jeremy Bowen was speaking to Medina's mother.

'I thought that Sally Becker would help us,' she sobbed. 'But she didn't come and my little girl died.'

They are words I can never forget.

13 | OPERATION ANGEL

I SCRIBBLED THE SUMS on a piece of paper. We would need, I calculated, about £60,000 to get the convoy to Bosnia and I had arrived back in Britain with nothing. And yet on 10 December 1993, World Human Rights Day, Operation Angel assembled at Brighton Pier with over 200 volunteers and 56 trucks, ambulances and even a coach. It was the largest convoy to leave these shores; and it had all been done in three weeks. The story of how it came together is a remarkable testimony to the resourcefulness and generosity of the people of Britain.

It had begun extremely badly. In fact, before we were able to get underway I wasted five precious weeks trying to do things 'through the proper channels'. I had lunch with a man from the Overseas Development Administration, I sent faxes to John Major, the British Prime Minister telling him about the children and I tried every avenue I could think of but each was a dead end.

I also had fun for I was presented with awards from the Variety Club, the Celebrity Guild of Great Britain and the Ross McWhirter Foundation and I was invited to meet Princess Margaret at a luncheon for Women of the Year. When I received notification of the McWhirter award, I was invited to attend a dinner being held at the Inner Temple in London. I needed an escort for this event, so I asked Duncan Stewart to accompany me. It seemed appropriate. I had known him a long time and he was the first person to donate supplies for me to take to Bosnia. He was the perfect escort, tall, handsome and very charming.

Having lived in a war zone for some time, it felt strange to find myself sitting amidst members of the aristocracy, judges and other notables at a magnificent banquet. As they congratulated me, I wondered how I came to be there. We were joined by my parents and my brother Eddy, who brought my old friend Heather James, who was now a politician. As liqueurs were served, I asked Duncan if he would consider becoming the Medical Officer for Operation Angel; Dr Mark Porter from BBC *Good Morning* was supposed to come but he had peritonitis and was forced to cancel. Duncan shook his head and laughed. 'I'd love to but I'm afraid I'm far too busy.'

'Believe me Duncan' said my father, 'before the night is out she'll change your mind.' And he was right.

I was presented with the Unsung Heroes award by the actor Richard Wilson and when it was time to make a speech, I was astounded by all the famous faces

Duncan escorts Sally to the Inner Temple in London where she is presented with the McWhirter award for bravery.

Richard Wilson and Jeremy Beadle present Sally with an award. (Courtesy Sidney Harris)

in front of me. I could not quite bring myself to wear an evening gown and high heels (I had spent too long in jeans, T-shirt and trainers and thought I might look like a drag queen) so I settled for a pair of smart black trousers, white jacket and a black silk blouse. Various interviews were arranged through Mike Mendoza and I used the opportunity to highlight the mission. The *Sunday Mirror* had started an appeal but things were still moving very slowly.

I was asked to speak at an event organised by the JACS (Jewish Adult Cultural Society) that raised almost £2000. This enabled us to buy our first ambulance, a Bedford, similar to the one I used in Bosnia but this time fully equipped. From that point on things really began to happen as I was able to set up a headquarters with telephones and a fax machine; until then I'd been using my mother's kitchen. Then an old school friend called Stewart Weir offered to help me. He took charge of recruitment and immediately enlisted two women from the local business school to help me. Justine and Val were to prove indispensible, using their skills to type all the reams of necessary documents, letters and faxes, taking endless phone calls, interviewing prospective volunteers and keeping track of my appointments.

Duncan Stewart was President of the Halley Stewart Trust, set up by his grandfather to provide funds for worthy causes and they donated £1000.

Gloria Macari, who had a beautiful voice and a heart to match, wrote a song together with her colleagues Roger Ferris and Yolanda Beeny. It was called 'Hear the Children' and I found it so moving that I called Neil Morris, producer of BBC's morning television programme and played a recording of the song over the phone. He was very interested and the next day I was invited onto the show to talk about our mission. The BBC decided to get behind us and Anne Diamond and her co-presenter Nick Owen started an appeal.

Andrew Popkewiez, a friend of Duncan's, designed a leaflet that he printed by the thousand. The leaflet read: 'An angel rushes in where most of us fear to tread' and included a photograph of Elmir, taken by the award-winning photographer Simon Dack, just after we came out of Mostar.

> Surely you can see that innocent children must be rescued from their suffering. Through the intervention of Sally Becker and others like her, they have been, but there are many more Muslim, Croat and Serbian children who will perish this winter in the freezing conditions of Bosnia so now she's going back. But Sally and her team of volunteers need all the help they can get.

The leaflet was endorsed by Harold Pinter, Lady Antonia Fraser, Chris Eubank, Christopher Timothy, Andrew Bowden MP, Bob Marshall Andrews QC and Dr Mark Porter. At the bottom of the page were the details of UKJAID (Jewish Aid and International Development), a charity that had agreed to handle funds on our behalf – we didn't have time to apply for charitable status.

Briefing the volunteers. Left to right: John Morrison and Terri, Sally, Duncan and Lawrence.

Stewart Weir appointed half a dozen co-coordinators based around the country and they began to distribute the literature and start appeals within their own areas. John Morrison and his partner, a couple from Humberside, managed to get the police to lend us a mobile kitchen and as my cousin Ashley was studying to be a chef, he was put in charge of the catering. David, his older brother, had managed to convince the company he worked for to donate a truck filled with aid, which he would drive to Bosnia himself.

The response to the appeal was incredible. People right across the country began raising funds and collecting supplies. Elderly ladies knitted sweaters and children handed their pennies over in school.

Sadly, there wasn't time to release 'Hear the Children' so *Good Morning* chose another song already available on compact disc. The song was called 'Remembering Christmas' and was performed by the Bramdean Boys Choir. The BBC compiled a very moving video to accompany the song, which raised over £8000. The *Sunday Mirror* appeal raised a further £11,000 and Sally Line Ferries offered free passage to France; Nissan loaned me a brand new 4x4 and Trailblazers provided loudspeakers and Citizen Band radios for each of the vehicles.

An extraordinary man called Mansukh Patel, who ran an organisation dedicated to world peace, invited myself and Duncan to visit his multi-faith centre in Birmingham. He then marshalled all his followers to prepare hundreds of nutritious food parcels for the journey. A motto was printed on each of the parcels: 'Every little thing we do, no matter how small, can change the world.'

I received a message from Peter and Evelyn Rees offering us hand-knitted teddy bears, which we decided to include in the family boxes. The organisation, called Teddies for Tragedies, had started in 1985 and since then hundreds of thousands of teddies had been knitted, bringing smiles to the faces of children all over the world.

Having somehow managed to capture the country's imagination we were inundated with aid. Perhaps it was due to the fact that people were used to putting a few coins in a box never actually knowing where the money would go or how it would be used; whereas those who supported us knew where the aid was going and who we aimed to help – and they could even follow the whole mission on TV.

There were of course the occasional blunders. We appealed for family parcels destined for the refugee camps and a man who worked for the ambulance service had offered to help. He made an announcement on television that the parcels could be dropped into any ambulance station but unfortunately he forgot to inform his bosses. Consequently, ambulance stations right across the country were inundated with parcels and no one was available to receive them. The phone rang continuously for days until we finally managed to sort out the misunderstanding and arrange for the aid to be collected.

We appealed for volunteers, preferably ex servicemen or from the emergency services; we needed people who were used to discipline and not easily frightened. We tried to discourage those with young children by stressing that the areas we hoped to reach were very dangerous. Unfortunately, there wasn't time to vet each one personally but we did insist on good references and a clean bill of health. Each person was asked to raise sponsorship of £100 towards the costs. I contacted the AA and the RAC who kindly offered to provide breakdown teams for the convoy. They would remain alongside us throughout the mission, there to provide backup.

With donations of medical equipment from hospitals that were closing or refurbishing and medical supplies from various companies, we had over £1 million worth of medical aid; but we were still short of funds for the journey itself. The ship that would carry the convoy from Italy to Croatia would cost a further £30,000 and we hadn't yet reached our original target. It was then that Duncan kindly stepped in to offer the use of the building that housed his surgery as surety for a loan. By the time we were due to leave we had raised enough money and the loan was not needed after all but I was touched and honoured by his faith in me.

During this time I was busy trying to clarify the overall plan. It would be no use having the means if we had not sorted out the end. My aim was to help all sides in the conflict so I approached the respective embassies to request permission to cross their territories. The Croats and the Bosnians confirmed their agreement but the Serbs failed to respond to any of my requests. We would therefore head to East Mostar, where the Muslims were besieged by Croats and to Nova Bila, where the Croats were besieged by Muslims.

I contacted the UN in Zagreb to request protection for the convoy and to my surprise I received an immediate response. Karen Abuzayed was Chief of

Mission in Bosnia-Herzegovina and she sounded very enthusiastic about the mission, even asking whether I would consider including other enclaves such as Tuzla and Zenica. Her only stipulation was that the selection of the patients would be done by the UNHCR medevac team. I agreed and the UN issued a press release announcing a joint mission which they called 'Operation Angel.'

I soon found myself caught up in a bizarre Catch 22 situation. I kept receiving messages from the UNHCR informing me that Britain had refused to allocate beds. When I contacted the ODA, the government department responsible for such things, they told me that no beds had been requested. With the planned evacuation of several hundred sick and wounded children and their families, this allocation was essential so I wrote to them both and suggested they sort it out.

I was contacted by a representative of Veterans for Peace, an NGO based in the States who apparently had access to many hospital beds. They put me in touch with Bianca Jagger who was staying at the Savoy Hotel in London and Duncan and I went to meet her. She assured us that she would do her best to help but she would need details of the patients, so I sent a message to the UNHCR. The Veterans were already caring for some of the children I evacuated from East Mostar, including Maja Kazazić and to my great delight, they forwarded her letter.

My dearest Sally Becker

My name is Maja Kazazić, the 17-year-old girl that you helped to get out of Mostar in August 1993, having lost my left leg from below the knee. My right leg was broken in several places with deep infection and had I not got out of Mostar, by your dedicated effort, I doubt that I would be alive today. Words cannot express my respect and gratitude that I have for you.

We were brought to the Cumberland Memorial Hospital in Maryland USA where the good fortune that you bestowed on us by your dedication, was continued here for we were treated just like family by the Doctor, the nursing staff and the people of the area, who visited us and treated us as though we were related to them. We have repeatedly been taken to people's homes for dinner, for holidays, to football games and to the school where I hope to go. We have so much to be grateful for that it just boggles our minds. I have now a temporary artificial leg and am able to get around on a walker. I cannot put any weight on my right leg until it heals completely, which shouldn't be too long. We are now in a private home by ourselves; the house is furnished by the individuals of this support group. We are happy to be self sufficient, all due to your dedication, thanks ever so much.

I'll close now, with love and respect and yours truly forever grateful.

Maja Kazazić

If ever I found myself wavering through exhaustion or frustration, Maja's letter strengthened my resolve.

A few days before departure, my family was invited to accompany me to the Variety Club Ball. I found myself sitting at the top table beside Dame Vera Lynne. When we were introduced, I told her how honoured I was to meet her. She took my hand and said, 'You are a brave and courageous young woman and it is I who am honoured to meet *you*.' Hearing this from one of the best-loved and respected women in Britain, I can honestly say my heart nearly burst with pride.

Towards the last few days we were working day and night in order to meet the deadline but somehow we did it. On 9 December, 230 volunteers dressed in white sweatshirts and baseball caps with 'Operation Angel' emblazoned in blue, assembled at the Thistle and the Metropole Hotel in Brighton where they would be staying overnight, free of charge.

They were a wonderfully varied group of people, both in age and background. There were nurses of all ages, ambulance drivers, medics, firemen, policemen, two female doctors and a psychologist. There was also a team from Veterans for Peace who had flown in from the States, though unfortunately their offer of beds had not yet been confirmed.

As a result of the UN announcement, members of the press had arranged to meet us in Croatia but others, including a crew from the BBC and another from Meridian, would be travelling with us. Meridian was making a documentary about my work and they had been filming some of the lead-up to the actual mission.

We had arranged a final briefing prior to departure and when I stepped onto the platform in the conference hall the atmosphere was humming with energy. There was a heart warming ovation from 270 volunteers and when they eventually quietened down, I thanked them for coming. I then proceeded to explain as clearly as possible the current situation in Bosnia-Herzegovina. I made it clear how gruelling the journey across Europe would be and explained that the drivers would work in shifts, stopping only for fuel and the occasional meal. Using video footage from a hard hitting BBC documentary called 'Unfinished Business', I showed them the area where they would be going and stressed the dangers. I made it clear that they might become bitter and bad tempered from lack of sleep, that they would probably argue with one another but it was important to keep sight of our aim, to save lives.

Next on the podium was Lawrence Le Carré, an energetic man in his fifties with a mop of bright red hair and a booming voice. Lawrence had run convoys to Bosnia before and he explained the driving rules and emergency procedures. When he had finished, Duncan stood up and briefed the volunteers on the medical aspects of our mission.

The briefing lasted from ten until three in the afternoon when the volunteers were then free to spend the evening as they pleased. The mood amongst them was

The volunteers gather in Brighton at the start of Operation Angel. (Courtesy Stewart Weir)

a mixture of exhilaration and trepidation. Many had said goodbye to their families, not sure whether they would make it home for Christmas and perhaps even wondering whether they would return at all.

Later that night a fax arrived from the UNHCR. It was a document I should have received much earlier containing a detailed list of the evacuees. There were more than 80 in Mostar alone, including Amel Demić who was still in a coma. The list also included names from Zenica, Tuzla and Sarajevo, all predominantly Muslim enclaves. It was then that I saw there was only one patient coming from Nova Bila and my heart sank. According to Ivan there were still many seriously injured children at the monastery who were in desperate need of specialised medical treatment. The fax stated that heavy snow had blocked the roads into central Bosnia and it would therefore be impossible to take the convoy in with us. Instead they had arranged to fly me and Duncan to Sarajevo and bring the evacuees out by air.

I was filled with dismay, knowing that the Croats would be enraged. Not only would it now be impossible to take aid into Nova Bila, only one person would actually be brought out. I was sure that the Croats would feel that I had reneged on the agreement but there was nothing we could do so soon before departure. Nevertheless, I was determined to get the list amended as soon as we arrived.

Early the next morning when all the supplies had been loaded onto the vehicles the press began to film the convoy leaving the hotel. As we prepared to pull out onto the main road, a traffic warden appeared and began working her way along the line issuing parking tickets; seemingly oblivious to the whirring of cameras and gales of laughter.

A crowd of well wishers had gathered at the pier to see us off. Among them were Gloria, Roger and Yolanda together with around 30 children from the Torah Academy and St Christopher's primary schools.

The convoy was comprised of 56 ambulances and trucks and one by one they began to line up along the promenade. Most of the vehicles were white and emblazoned with the Operation Angel logo and stickers from Sally Line Ferries.

'Don't worry, I'll take good care of her,' said Duncan, hoping to reassure my father.

'More likely she'll take care of you!' he replied, to the amusement of those within earshot.

I started my engine, a signal to the rest of the convoy that we were leaving, and as we pulled away from the kerb my mother was crying. Issuing from loudspeakers at the entrance to the pier, Gloria Macari's voice filled the air.

'Can you hear them? Do you care? Listen to the children, crying out there. All their pain and suffering, they never asked to play our games.'

Sally gives her mother a hug before leaving.

The Nissan Patrol.

The convoy departs from Brighton seafront. (Courtesy Simon Dack)

This was followed by the chorus which was sung by the children.

> We are the children,
> Listen to our voices,
> We are the future but all our dreams are dying.
> We have the gift of life;
> We have the right to survive.
> Oh mankind, please don't take away our world.

One by one each of the vehicles pulled up behind me, the blue lights of the ambulances flashing in unison. Glancing in the rear view mirror my heart swelled; Operation Angel was at last underway.

14 | JINXED

THE CONVOY SEEMED JINXED from the start. The canteen trailer loaned by Humberside police had jack-knifed on the road leaving Brighton. No one was hurt but we had lost our mobile kitchen and Ashley and Nick who were in charge of the catering would now have to travel in the bus.

We made it to the ferry port just in time and found the coach waiting for us. The driver had removed most of the seats and spread mattresses on the floor, much as we had done on previous convoys to enable people to take a proper rest. Somehow Stewart had enlisted too many volunteers but I hadn't the heart to force anyone to leave. Instead I borrowed a minibus from Sally Line Ferries to accommodate the extras.

Once we had boarded the ferry, I went to call our representative in France. He was trying to trace the documents that would enable us to pass through the motorway tolls without paying. This was standard for all humanitarian aid convoys but there was a lot of paperwork involved. When I returned from the office I over-heard a man making an announcement in a broad Scottish accent.

'We shouldn't follow their route,' he was saying, slurring slightly from an excess of alcohol. 'I know a better way. Anyway it's all being done wrong and I don't think we should continue with this woman.'

I tugged at his sleeve, for he obviously hadn't noticed me come in. '*This woman* would prefer you didn't continue at all,' I said, to the sound of cheering. 'First of all you're drunk- and drinking is strictly forbidden whilst driving in convoy. Secondly, I made it very clear that anyone attempting to stir up trouble would be asked to leave. We are travelling to a war zone for goodness sake.'

There was silence as everyone waited for his reaction. I knew that this incident could make or break my authority with the volunteers. The man lurched towards me and started to shout in my face.

'Well, I have to tell you,' he slurred, 'that firstly I'm not drunk and that secondly I plan to bring out a couple of soldiers who are stuck in central Bosnia, so I really have to go there.'

I could hardly believe what I was hearing. If this man was being serious, he was actually prepared to jeopardise the whole mission by attempting to smuggle soldiers through a war zone.

'You are no longer part of this convoy,' I said coldly. 'Please remove the logo from your vehicle and travel separately. I'm sorry but I will not risk you being connected with us. This is an official evacuation and we are working within UN regulations. I have signed a paper that states I will not make any unauthorised evacuations and as leader of this convoy I am responsible for the actions of the volunteers.'

On arrival at Dunkirk I still had to sort out the authorisation for the tolls, so while the volunteers were left to catch some sleep, I remained in the office while a persistent Frenchwoman endeavoured to clear our path. It took until dawn but at last we set off and Duncan took the wheel of the Nissan Patrol so I could get some rest. When we stopped to fuel up, John Morrison suggested that we go on ahead to the next toll in order to make sure the convoy would not be delayed. It seemed a sensible idea at the time but I was to regret it bitterly later.

The BBC crew had followed us to the next toll and to my surprise I saw Stewart was with them. He was supposed to be our personnel officer, in charge of the volunteers, so I was disappointed to learn that he was being paid as the BBC's driver instead.

Everything was now in place for the convoy to pass through the tolls and we waited for them to catch up. Hours went by but still no one came so we drove to the nearest service station to find out where they were, mobile phones not yet being ubiquitous. After a night of frantic phone calls to Meridian TV, we finally had an answer. The convoy had stopped to unload some excess weight from some of the vehicles. The Red Cross later picked up the discarded boxes, which contained clothes and blankets and were sent on to Bosnia. Unfortunately, the scene had already been filmed by Meridian who gave the impression that the aid had just been dumped. This would do our reputation immense harm before we were able to set the record straight.

The Morrisons had arranged a meeting to sort things out, sidelining Lawrence and appointing the firemen as convoy leaders instead. They had sensibly split the vehicles up into separate groups, easier to manage and able to make quicker progress but they had failed to inform Lawrence. The vital medical supplies and equipment had been transferred to the three largest trucks, which left more space in the ambulances for the drivers.

As each group arrived, Duncan and I spent hours sorting out their grievances and giving encouragement to those who had begun to lose heart. I was disappointed that even at this early stage, some of them already seemed to have lost sight of our aim. One man was complaining that he had not had a hot meal in hours and I reminded him that there were poor souls in Mostar who hadn't had a hot meal in months.

Duncan obsereved that we had included a few volunteers with a package holiday mentality. It was our own fault, in the sense that we hadn't had the time to interview each person in order to weed out those who had neither the stomach nor the stamina for such an exercise.

Ashley and Nick had rigged up the primus stoves and while the volunteers ate a hot meal in the car park, I received a phone call that was patched through the BBC crew saying that the Italian police wanted a word with me. Feeling exhausted I set off with Duncan, Lawrence and Mick Fegan, a former policeman who had been driving one of the large trucks. To my dismay, I saw that the man at the border post was the loud-mouthed drunk I had dismissed from the convoy. He was held up at the border and I noticed that he had not removed the Operation Angel logo from his Land Rover. It soon became apparent that he was demanding free access through the tolls under our name.

Lawrence became angry, his outrage fuelled all the more because a volunteer had reported that the Scotsman had been boasting about smuggling weapons into Bosnia. A scuffle broke out and Lawrence landed a punch on the man's nose. As I watched him run off, I shook my head in disbelief. My dream was rapidly turning into a nightmare and we hadn't even reached our destination.

My next concern was an elderly man being cared for by one of the paramedics. His vehicle had broken down and he had slept in the open waiting for a lift. The paramedic told me that he was suffering from a mild form of hypothermia and was not fit to continue the arduous journey, so we arranged to fly him back to the UK.

We drove on ahead once again to sort out the tolls and arrived in Ancona ahead of the others. Planning to have a well earned rest for a few hours while we waited for the groups to arrive, we checked into the Hotel Jolly. The hotel could not have had a more inappropriate name. As soon as I entered my room, I received a call from Mike Mendoza; the news was filled with reports that our coach had crashed and there were apparently several casualties.

I knocked on Duncan's door and told him what had happened and we frantically tried to call the hospital where the injured had been taken. The coach had been struck in the rear by a speeding truck but fortunately the reports of serious injuries were unfounded; the coach driver had whiplash and some of the passengers were bruised. A few of them were traumatised by the accident and felt unable to face the ordeal ahead so we authorised the funds to fly them home and Mike arranged for them to be picked up at Gatwick airport. We then spent the rest of the night making sure their families had been informed.

The remaining coach passengers insisted they wanted to continue the journey and they joined us on the quayside a few hours later. Amongst them were Ashley and Nick who had been sitting on the rear seats of the coach until ten minutes before the crash when they happened to transfer to David's truck. Had they not done so they would have been seriously injured, perhaps even killed.

There were showers and hot food on board the ship and cabins were allocated to those most in need. I was invited to dine with the ship's captain to discuss the forthcoming mission and he asked me which route I preferred to take and what time I would like to dock in Croatia; having never been 'in charge' of a ship before I found it quite exhilarating. As we crossed the swelling waves of the Adriatic, however, I began to feel seasick and was relieved when we finally sailed into port.

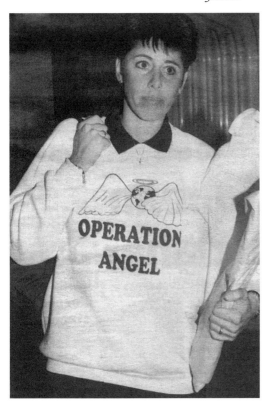

On a mission.

As we docked in the pouring rain, we were met by UN personnel who appeared very friendly and polite. They explained that Duncan and I would be taken to Sarajevo while the convoy was escorted to the hotel in Makarska to wait for our return. We had booked the hotel so that while we were in Sarajevo, the volunteers would be able to rest from their journey.

Following a series of interviews with the press who were hanging around the port, I overheard a briefing being given to the volunteers by one of the very same officers. He was informing them that they would be travelling to Mostar the following day. I marched through the crowd and climbed some scaffolding so that all the volunteers would hear me.

'Please ignore what you have just been told.' I said, 'You will *not* be going to Mostar tomorrow at all. I have given my word to the Croatian authorities that the mission will not take place until we have carried out the evacuation of Nova Bila. They have made it very clear that this is the way it will happen and I am not prepared to jeopardise that. We cannot pass through territory held by the Croats without their permission; it would be foolish as well as dangerous and the operation could fail.' Some of the volunteers nodded while others just stood there looking confused.

'As soon as we return from Sarajevo, then and *only* then will we have permission to enter Mostar. In the meantime you will be staying in a comfortable hotel where you can eat and drink whatever you wish and take a well earned rest.'

'Suppose something happens to you and you don't make it back?' called one of the doctors bluntly.

'Then the situation would be out of my hands.' I replied. '

The UN Official apologised, saying there had been a misunderstanding. I accepted his apology but remained a little sceptical as we said our goodbyes. The volunteers gathered around to wish us good luck and afterwards I took Lawrence aside. 'Regardless of what happened en route, you are still in charge of the vehicles and the aid.'

At the UN headquarters in Split we were joined by Mark Dowdney, the foreign correspondent for the *Daily Mirror* and Rob his photographer. Also following us was a freelance cameraman from Meridian. Each of us was issued with a UNHCR identification card that would enable us to use UN transport and placed us under their official protection. Beneath my photograph was the word 'Consultant', which caused me to chuckle. I had been given a flak jacket but it lacked the vital Kevlar plates that were supposed to be inside. Duncan had a bulletproof vest loaned to him by one of our volunteers but he was told by an officer to leave it behind; he would be issued with a better one in Sarajevo.

As we crossed the tarmac to the plane, he was suddenly prevented from boarding.

'You are not allowed to travel without a flak jacket,' shouted the soldier. 'It's forbidden under UN rules.'

'He has to come,' I replied, raising my voice in order to be heard over the roar of the engines. 'As our Medical Officer he will be needed to assess the patients not yet included on the list.' The soldier shrugged. 'Well he ain't going nowhere without a flak jacket so I suggest you either travel without him or stay behind yourself.'

He seemed unnecessarily aggressive so I stepped in front of him so that we were virtually nose to nose.

'Firstly there is no need to be so rude! And secondly, your boss has caused this problem by insisting that he leave his flak jacket behind. Something smells a little odd around here and I'm telling you now that I will not be going anywhere without him.' At that moment a BBC cameraman came over. He had forgotten to bring his passport, thinking that the UN pass would be sufficient and now he too was unable to travel. He offered his flak jacket to Duncan and at last we were able to board. After stowing our boxes of food and medical supplies destined for Nova Bila, we sat down beside the Medevac representative, a Frenchwoman called Genevieve Begkoyian who was in charge of this part of the mission.

The flight was very short and once we landed in Sarajevo we raced to unload the boxes from the hold. The surrounding area was controlled by the Serbs so the airfield was exposed to snipers and there was the continuous sound of shelling and gun fire. The sounds, so familiar to me, were completely new to Duncan but he seemed quite calm as he struggled back and forth beneath the heavy loads.

Beneath the tarmac was a tunnel that bypassed both UN controls and the siege lines. Protected from Serb shelling and sniper fire, thousands of people, tons of food, arms, and other supplies were smuggled through the tunnel each day; 800 metres long, it had taken six months to build. The UN denied its existence but it provided a lifeline for the city throughout the siege.

We took shelter within a darkened room while we waited for transport to our hotel. Mark Dowdney resembled a bank manager, with his grey hair and glasses, incongruous in the stark surroundings. He was chatting to Duncan, who despite his exhaustion was smiling; his fair hair curled by the drizzling rain and his eyes a cornflower blue. He caught my gaze and I felt my pulse quicken as he smiled.

Seemingly unconcerned by the darkness and the danger, his courage gave me an unfamiliar sense of security. For the first time in months I didn't feel afraid and at that moment he seemed like a knight from a fairy tale, wearing a flak jacket instead of shining armour.

A UN soldier appeared and informed us that our transport had been delayed; the vehicle had been detained inside Serb lines and would not now make it before curfew. We were eventually taken into the city in an APC to the Holiday Inn Hotel. The surrounding buildings were pockmarked with shrapnel and bullet holes and blackened by fire. The city had been under siege for over a year and very few people dared venture out onto the streets. Those who did were desperately trying to avoid the snipers as they raced from one side of the road to the other.

Built to house the athletes during the 1984 winter Olympic Games, the Holiday Inn was now the only functioning hotel in Sarajevo, a battered yellow building that had become a familiar backdrop to news reports around the world. Several floors were missing, struck by a shell earlier in the conflict.

The power only ran long enough for the chefs to prepare a meal. The darkened atrium was strung with fairy lights. We followed Genevieve through the reception area to an alcove in which a woman sat behind a glass partition. She noted down our details by the light of a candle and we paid for the rooms by credit card, increasing the feeling that we were in the midst of some strange dream. Genevieve announced that she would see us in the morning leaving us to climb several flights of stairs to our rooms. The bathroom had no running water but to my delight the power suddenly came on. There was a tap on the door and a maid came in to turn down my bed. Duncan handed her a large bar of hazelnut chocolate in lieu of a tip and she gave him a beaming smile.

'She can probably sell it on the black market and buy some food,' I told him.

'She can probably buy a house with it!' he replied, making me laugh.

'We should have got a discount for the rooms.' I pointed out wryly, '$80 per night seems a trifle expensive for a view of the Serbian guns.'

He turned on the television and a western came on. After watching for a moment he turned down the sound.

'Why did you turn off the sound?' I asked curiously.

'Because we've got the real thing outside,' he replied.

The room was very cold. It was snowing outside and there was no heating. I was tired and wanted to climb into bed but first we needed to eat. Duncan said he would scout around for food and left me alone in the room. After about ten minutes had passed, the lights went out and I realised he hadn't taken the torch. I sat there worrying as I pictured him wandering around in the dark but after what seemed like ages, I heard a noise in the corridor. He had managed to find his way back by feeling for the numbers on the doors.

'Madam,' he said, offering his arm, 'would you care to join me for dinner?'

I took his arm and we carefully made our way down the stairs by the light of the torch. As we entered the dining room I gasped at the extraordinary scene before us. Tables were laid with white linen cloths and cutlery gleamed beneath subdued lighting. Waiters dressed in peach coloured jackets with starched white shirts and black bow ties bustled between the tables carrying trays laden with food. There was a low buzz of conversation and nearly all of the tables were full. Fortunately, Mark had saved us a place and as we sat down, I felt as though we'd been transported from war-torn Sarajevo to a high class restaurant in Mayfair.

The meal however, was a stark reminder that we were far away from London. The rolls were freshly baked but the meat had a strange flavour and I almost choked when Duncan suggested it might be horse flesh. A bottle of house wine cost $40 and the coffee was $10 per cup; we were dining in a city where people were known to strip bark from the trees to fill their empty bellies. Most of our fellow diners were journalists and UN personnel and Mark informed us that the management paid protection money to the Serbs in order to stay in business.

When the meal was over, we returned to my room to discuss arrangements for the morning. It was still very cold in spite of the fact that we were wearing our coats and we huddled together for warmth. We chatted about mundane things and for the first time in days I began to relax.

The following morning we were driven to Kisiljak, a former ski resort with panoramic views. We were taken into the UN compound and given our itinerary for the day, which included visits to a hospital and an orphanage from where children would be evacuated as part of the mission. Nova Bila had now been removed from the list; according to Genevieve the only patient to pass the medevac assessment did not now wish to leave. I insisted that we go there anyway, if only to deliver the medical aid and to see the situation for ourselves.

The church of the Holy Ghost in Nova Bila was still being used as a hospital for the sick and the wounded and we were greeted at the entrance by Fra Franjo Grebenar, a Franciscan Monk who said that he had been expecting me for a very long time. All the beds were full so many of the patients were lying on wooden pews in the chapel.

There was a sudden commotion and a man with a bullet lodged in his head was rushed into a room where operations were performed. A television crew appeared and as the doctors prepared to try and help the wounded man, cameras began to whirr. No

The church at Nova Bila.

one attempted to stop them filming, much to our surprise. In fact one of the doctors, with blood still dripping from his hands, twisted the poor man's face towards the camera to emphasise the horror of their situation.

We were taken around the makeshift hospital and listened to the patients histories; soldiers wounded in the fighting, missing limbs or eyes and sometimes both; women, young and old, maimed by shrapnel, and children, one with no legs and another with no arms; a child who was seriously ill and another horribly burned. Someone placed a baby in my arms. He was eight months old and almost blind but no one knew why. They did not have the facilities to run any tests and as I held his small limp body his mother broke down and cried.

'My husband has been killed and I am alone with my children. Please help us. Take us out of here so that my son can get treatment,' she pleaded.

Rage welled up inside me. 'Why were these children not included on the list?' I demanded to know. Genevieve began shouting angrily.
'You promised beds. But your government knows nothing about it. In any case this child isn't dying – there are others more in need.'

'He's going blind,' I said calmly. 'Doesn't that count as serious? Surely we ought to try and help him?'

'We don't have enough beds available Your government insists that you didn't request any and those we have are needed for more serious cases.'

I was outraged, thinking of all the meetings and phone calls with the ODA, the letters I had written to John Major, the IOM and the Home Office. I had tried every tactic I could think of to get this sorted and so had the various people I had approached. Yet the answer had always been the same; the beds must be requested by Medevac and approved by the UNHCR and the International Office of Migration.

On impulse I spun around to face the cameras with the child still lying in my arms.

'Please don't leave the children here to die. John Major I am begging you to help them. Let us have the beds so that they can be saved.'

We were taken to the staff room where I explained that we desperately wanted to help their children but were being prevented from doing so. The doctors told me that Genevieve had not been near the hospital in weeks and that the only patient to be included on the list was a man who decided he would rather a child left in his place. We told them that we would continue to push for the evacuation and if it didn't happen, I would find a way to do it myself.

To our surprise we heard that a convoy was due to arrive later that day. Dr Slobodan Lang, a Jewish Croat from Zagreb, had negotiated with the Bosnian Muslims and each side was bringing a convoy of humanitarian aid to the area. One was destined for the area of Nova Bila and the other for Zenica; so much for the roads being impassable.

Duncan and I were invited to the maternity ward and watched enchanted as a jolly midwife placed a new-born in the arms of its young mother. There was only one obstetrics bed for the hundreds of women living in the area and this was the 110th child to be born there. We felt immensely cheered by the mother's joy and the midwife's obvious pride in her work. Despite the horrors of the war raging beyond the doors, despite all the confusion and fear, there was still new life to be cherished.

As we prepared to leave however, the frustrations soon resurfaced. I found Genevieve in the midst of a television interview lambasting me for misleading the UN. I felt suddenly weary at the thought of defending myself yet again so I just turned away. Fra Grebenar requested an Operation Angel sweatshirt and gave us gifts in return; a black and white print inscribed with the words 'with thanks to the Angel of Nova Bila' and a watercolour for Duncan. We were touched yet saddened for in spite of our efforts, we had been unable to help them.

When we left Nova Bila, our vehicle was caught in cross-fire and as the bullets ricocheted off the armour plating, we were grateful for the skill of the British soldier who was driving. We stopped in Vitez and were greeted by an officer from the Cold Stream Guards who briefed us on the local situation. All sides were encouraged to pass on information knowing that it would remain confidential, with the result that not a soldier or a weapon moved without UNPROFOR knowing about it. Major Tohler was informative and amusing and despite the setbacks of the day, we found ourselves still able to laugh. He told us about an arms factory, coveted by all sides, which was situated beside a marmalade manufacturers and Duncan pointed out that if the factory was blown up; it could create a very 'sticky' situation. (It wasn't Oscar Wilde but it made us laugh.)

That evening we ate in the officers' quarters and spent a pleasant couple of hours watching them rehearse their Christmas show. Duncan and Mark were then led away to the barracks together with the other journalists while I was told I would be spending the night at the home of the commander of the British Battalion, Colonel Peter Williams.

The gallant Colonel led the way, stamping a path through the thick, slimy mud – the bane of every soldier's life – so that I could literally follow in his footsteps. As we made our way across the base, I told him about the children who had been excluded from the evacuation list and he assured me that if I came back for them his men would be ready to assist with the evacuation.

Despite all the conflicting information whirling around in my brain, I slept very well that night and awoke feeling refreshed. I had a hot shower, a change of clothes and was served with coffee by a young soldier who insisted on calling me 'Ma'am.' I was filled with admiration for these soldiers. For some it was their first deployment and their job was made even more difficult by the increasing desperation of the local people. So bad had it become that some of the adults encouraged their children to run in front of the aid trucks, forcing them to stop. Other youngsters would then board the vehicle and throw down as many packages as they could. The soldiers lived beneath the constant threat of the heavy guns in the surrounding hills.

Genevieve rejoined us as we waited for transport and we clashed almost immediately. I suggested that she was wrong for criticising me to the press but she called me a liar, almost spitting the words out, her mouth twisted with fury. She then accused me of 'exploiting a child' and I was incensed.

'I held the baby in front of the camera to convince the Prime Minister to change his mind,' I said angrily.

On the way back, we heard that Britain had offered sixteen beds as a result of my plea. We cheered and Duncan squeezed my hand but unfortunately Genevieve was riding in another vehicle so I couldn't see her face. Silvana Foa was later quoted as saying, 'Sally Becker turns up in Bosnia with a TV crew, and sixteen sick children get promises of admission to the UK in three days, including visas for relatives. It usually takes at least three weeks, and usually the Health Secretary doesn't get involved personally.'

Upon our arrival at the UN base in Kiseljak, we were informed that we could not return to Croatia as there were no more flights that day; the rest of the mission would therefore have to proceed without us. I was shocked and at the same time concerned, for the permission that would enable our convoy to cross the front line into East Mostar rested with me.

'How will my volunteers pass through the checkpoints?' I inquired.

The officer replied that they wouldn't be going. Instead, the evacuation would be carried out by the UN. I knew this made sense on one level – the patients would be safer inside the armoured vehicles – but I didn't see how they would carry 80 patients unless they had suddenly acquired a huge amount of transport. I voiced my concerns to Duncan and he reminded me that the new arrangements also meant that our aid would not be delivered to the hospital.

The more I thought about it, the less I believed in the likelihood of the evacuation taking place. East Mostar was the quid pro quo for Nova Bila and nothing had happened there yet. The officer was called to the phone and returned a few minutes later looking worried.

'The Croats have called off the mission,' he said despondently. I urged him to help us.

'If you can get us back to Croatia I will try to sort things out.'

He was obviously not convinced that I could overturn a decision by the Croatian Ministry of Defence; but then neither was I.

15 | 'YOU HAVE PUT PEOPLE'S LIVES AT RISK!'

IT WAS NO REAL surprise when the officer informed us that he might be able to arrange a flight after all and 20 minutes later we were on our way to the airport. Inside the small terminal a makeshift sign read ; 'Maybe Airlines', a satirical reference to the number of planes that never left the ground and listed amongst the choice of destinations was Heaven.

It was a great relief when the plane eventually left the tarmac for we were desperate to get back and continue with the mission. Lawrence and Mick were waiting to meet us when we landed in Split. They both looked worn out and with very good reason; the UN had taken command of the convoy and ordered the volunteers to transport the aid to a warehouse in Metković. I was so furious I could hardly speak as we headed along the coast to Makarska.

The hotel was impressive, nestled among some pine trees within a few yards of the sea. We were greeted by Major Need, the liaison officer acting on behalf of the UN and I immediately demanded to know why the trucks had been emptied.

'The aid is in a compound at Metković,' he replied. 'Some of the volunteers are there too.'

'Why? What are they doing there? They were all supposed to wait here until we got back.' I followed him through a door on which a sign read 'Operation Angel' and sitting inside was John Morrison and his partner Terri Kelly.

'We thought that you weren't coming back,' said John. 'So we decided to proceed without you.'

'Why wasn't I contacted? And who authorised the aid to be removed from our trucks?' Morrison sighed and continued in a patronising tone.

'I don't know why you're so perturbed. The bulk of the aid is safely inside the UN warehouse and the volunteers have been distributing the family boxes to local refugee camps. Oh and yesterday the UN took a couple of the firemen into Mostar to deliver some of the medical supplies.' I stared at the Major in disbelief.

'When Mate Boban agreed that I could carry out these missions, it was on the understanding that Nova Bila would be first. The evacuation of Mostar is now in serious jeopardy.'

I marched out of the office with the Major following behind. He was attempting to explain but I was beyond listening. When I reached the reception area I turned to face him.

'Hopefully I'll be able to arrange a meeting with Dr Bagarić but I just hope to God that you guys haven't screwed up the whole operation.' He told me that he would ensure the volunteers returned before nightfall.

'And by the way,' he said as I began to walk away, 'don't say, *you* guys. I am a Royal Marine who has been appointed to liaise between you and the United Nations and that is all. I do not make the decisions.' I knew that he was in a difficult position, caught in the uncomfortable position of go-between and in spite of my anger I liked him.

A short while later the other drivers returned. One of them, older with a grey beard, stood right in front of me and started shouting into my face.

'You must never organise anything like this ever again. You have put people's lives at risk!' My cousin David prepared to move between us, obviously concerned that he might become violent.

'We believed in you,' he continued, 'and we followed you, but you've let us all down. I have been saying this behind your back so I feel that it's only fair to say it to your face. People could have died in that coach crash!' As I looked around, I noticed that the ever-present cameras were filming his outburst.

'You're not just saying it to me, you're saying it to the whole of Britain,' I said, pointing to the cameras. Mick moved towards the television crew.

'No!' I cried, 'Leave it, he has had his say and now I'll have mine.'

'The crash was an act of God, I could hardly have prevented an Italian lorry from hitting the back of our coach. When I started out on this mission, I made my aims clear and invited others to join me. I know that the journey was hard and there were setbacks but we made it clear from the start that it wouldn't be easy.'

I was worried. Nothing was as it seemed and it looked as though the mission might fail. In addition to this I was losing the support of my own volunteers. I was feeling despondent and very weary.

A short while later Major Need informed me that a briefing was underway in the conference room. I entered the room to find John Morrison and his partner sitting side by side in front of the volunteers. When he saw me he grinned and somewhat facetiously made an announcement; 'Ladies and Gentlemen, your leader has returned.'

The volunteers responded with a slow hand clap and I could feel the hurt rising inside me. I clutched the edge of the table to prevent my hands from trembling as I started to speak.

'I'm sorry that we haven't been around but Duncan and I have been in central Bosnia trying to arrange the first part our mission.' One of the drivers stood up.

'The journey from Britain was exhausting and we were assured that we'd get to rest when we arrived. Instead, we were taken to Metković and told to wait in our trucks! We've spent two days sleeping in a UN compound.'

'I'm really sorry,' I said earnestly. 'I know you must have been exhausted when you arrived but that's exactly why we'd arranged for you all to spend a couple of days here in this hotel. Any alternative instructions you've been given were certainly not mine.' I glanced meaningfully at the Morrisons before continuing.

'As I told you during the briefing back in Brighton, people in East Mostar are dying for want of the most basic medical supplies. The area has been under siege for several months so they only get one meal a day. They live in basements and cellars like rats because it's too dangerous to go outside.' I paused for a moment, looking into the sea of faces, some of them openly hostile.

'This mission was my dream, and the day we left Brighton, the day it all finally came together, well that was one of the happiest days of my life. We came here to help the innocent victims of a war not of their making and beyond their understanding – so let's focus on that and do whatever we can now to help make a difference.' As I prepared to leave the room, some of the nurses came over.

'Sally, we joined this mission because we believe in what you are doing,' said one. 'Be assured that you have our undivided loyalty, no matter what.' I thanked her and then turned away, not wanting them to see my tears.

When I finally got through to Ivan's office I was told that he was unavailable. They put me through to his secretary who informed me that the UN had requested the mission be delayed until Tuesday. 'But that's impossible!' I said, urging her to let me speak to Ivan. The volunteers were supposed to be leaving on Sunday and our budget would not stretch to the costs of further accommodation and food for 200 people. Apart from the costs, those who worked for the emergency services would be expected back at work, especially over the Christmas period. I asked her to explain all this to Ivan and she promised to call me back. After pacing the floor for a while I finally got a call to say that Ivan would discuss the situation with his colleagues and get back to me later. I repeated the conversation to Major Need but he insisted that it was the Croats who requested the delay, *not* the UN. The situation was becoming more confusing by the minute. We went upstairs to wait for Ivan's call to be put through and when the phone rang it was Vava on the line.

'Vava, I don't understand what's going on,' I said, relieved to hear his voice. 'According to the UN, the Croats have requested a delay.'

Vava assured me that this wasn't the case. He said that he would try to persuade Ivan to come to the hotel. I repeated the conversation to Duncan and suggested that we were being misled. Duncan looked a little embarrassed and nodded towards the Major who was standing in the doorway.

'How dare you insinuate that we have been lying!' His face was red. 'I've had enough of this whole business,' he said and before I could reply he turned on his heel and left the room. Now it was Duncan's turn to lose his temper; cool, calm Duncan from whom I'd hardly heard a word uttered in anger.

'For goodness sake Sally, you've blown the whole operation now. Why on earth can't you be more diplomatic?' I was surprised and disappointed by his outburst for he was the one person I thought would understand.

'Diplomatic? *Diplomatic*? It wasn't diplomacy that enabled me to cross the front line, or diplomacy that stopped me getting killed by the snipers! In fact the last time I depended on the *diplomacy* of the United Nations, a little girl died!' He ignored me.

'You should apologise immediately, I'm going to try and prevent him from leaving,' he said, heading for the door. 'I just hope that it's not too late.'

'He won't be going anywhere Duncan.' He ignored me and strode off down the corridor, leaving me dismayed that he had so little faith.

'They've been using me,' I called after him. 'Don't you see?' He was on his way to the elevator and I followed him. 'This is all about publicity, it must be. Why do you think they were so keen to include the press on this mission?' He seemed to hesitate.

'Think about it Duncan, they have commandeered our aid and convinced the volunteers that we wouldn't be coming back.'

The doors of the elevator closed quietly behind him and I returned to my room feeling emotionally drained. It was all so stressful and twisted and nothing was as it appeared to be. There was obviously something going on behind the scenes but I did not know what. Alone in the room I decided to take a shower to cool down. Ivan would be here soon and I felt I should at least make an effort to look present-able; the success of our mission now rested on him.

A short while later Duncan reappeared and told me that the Major was still around. 'You were right' he said grudgingly 'he isn't leaving after all, but he said that he came very close. Apparently he's never lost his temper before.'

I decided that Duncan was probably right; perhaps it was time for some diplomacy after all. The Major was sitting at the bar, though he was only drinking coffee. 'May I join you?' I asked and he immediately gestured to a chair. 'I just wanted to say that I'm sorry. I know that you aren't to blame for all this.' After ordering another coffee he told me that the UN had arranged to carry out the evacuation of East Mostar without me.

'They would have collected the patients in their APCs and transferred them into your ambulances at Metković. But now that the Croats have cancelled the mission what happens next is anyone's guess.'

That evening Ivan arrived with Vava and when he entered the room I could see the bitter disappointment in his eyes. We spent over an hour trying to clarify the position and he remained adamant that the UN had requested the delay. I pointed out that it was irrelevant now and asked him to arrange for us to proceed with the evacuation as soon as possible; preferably the following day. He shook his head emphatically. 'It would be impossible to get a ceasefire agreed at such short notice, and besides', he reminded me, 'you have still not helped the children who are trapped in Nova Bila.'

Dr Lang was planning to create a route through Bosnia-Herzegovina that would provide safe access to all the hospitals, enabling aid and medical staff to be taken in and patients to be brought out. This was the White Roads project that

Ivan had started several months earlier in which I had played a very small part. Dr Lang's convoy would enable the project finally to be fulfilled, but Ivan explained that the vehicles were currently being held up by the Bosnian army; one man had already been killed and the drivers were being held hostage.

'If you wish to go ahead with your mission, you must try to get the other convoy released,' he said, causing my head to spin. It was all becoming more and more confused. I wondered how on earth I would mange to salvage anything out of this mess. Leaning forward I looked into Ivan's eyes,

'If you allow me to carry out the evacuation of Mostar, I give you my word that I'll travel to Nova Bila the very next day and remain there until the convoy is released.'

I could see him giving serious thought to my proposal. Ivan knew that the press were following me and this would put pressure on those who were preventing Lang's convoy from reaching its destination. He stood up, gathering his papers together and putting them into his briefcase.

'I cannot promise anything,' he said. 'But I am Ivan Bagarić and I too want to save lives. Therefore I will do whatever is in my power to help Sally Becker, Angel of Mostar and Nova Bila.'

16 | 'THEY COULD HAVE DONE THIS WITHOUT YOU'

LATER THAT NIGHT WE were invited to attend another briefing in the hotel basement. Major Need explained that the UN had decided to proceed with the mission into East Mostar without official permission.

'Surely you don't intend to defy the Croats; that would put the patients' lives at risk. In any case you'd be stopped at the very first checkpoint.'

'That is where you come in. You'll travel at the head of the convoy and as usual the press will follow you. If the Croats hold us up, you'll use the media to embarrass them into letting us pass.' I stood up and looked him straight in the eyes..

'Well I'm telling you now that you can forget it!' I will endeavour to carry out this mission without resorting to blackmail.'

The next day the convoy was invited to the airport at Split to see the first 50 patients arrive under the auspices of Operation Angel. I was escorted across the tarmac to where the Sea King helicopters had landed with their precious cargo and my anger and frustration disappeared. The patients came from Tuzla, Zenica and Sarajevo. Amongst them was an eleven-year-old boy called Senad Zukić. He had been playing in the garden with his friend when a grenade exploded, causing serious injuries to his stomach and legs. On his head he wore a baseball cap bearing our logo and as he was carried across the tarmac there was a broad smile on his face. I wasn't the only one profoundly moved by the moment. The volunteers were watching from the terrace above and many of them were crying.

Upon our return to the hotel I was given a message from Ivan. He stated that I would need to send a fax to Mate Boban's office confirming my intention. I knew this was a sign that it could all be ok and within a few hours we were told to prepare for the mission.

At the final briefing we were informed that Duncan and I would be entering Mostar with the three British doctors and the Veterans for Peace. When I asked about the supplies I had brought for the hospital, they said it would be impossible to take them as we would be travelling in an APC.

'And what about all the paediatric medicines and the antibiotics? These are things they really need.' The officer thought about it for a few moments and then made a suggestion.

'The only way you can take those in would be in your own vehicle,' he said, rubbing his chin thoughtfully. 'Though of course that would be dangerous, and might be considered reckless.'

'We went to a great deal of trouble to get those supplies and we've brought them all the way from Britain. I certainly don't plan to leave them in a UN warehouse.' He sighed irritably.

'Ok. We will sandwich your vehicle between the APCs to give you some protection.' Duncan offered to travel with me but as much as I wanted him beside me, there seemed no point in both of us taking a risk.

That night we went to bed early as we would be leaving in a few hours. Most of the volunteers would be waiting in Metković which was just a couple of kilometres from the front line, so it was important they remained alert. As I prepared to get undressed, Mick knocked on my door. 'Sally, please take care of yourself,' he said, giving me a hug.

I couldn't sleep, my mind reeling with the forthcoming mission. I was truly terrified at the thought of crossing the front line once again, even with protection. Having made the journey three times under fire, I could not help feeling that my luck might be running out.

We left Makarska at 3.30am and arrived in Metković two hours later. I was finally issued with plates for my flak jacket and headed towards the rendezvous point on the outskirts of Mostar. As we reached the last HVO checkpoint, we could see the UN convoy parked up ahead. There were several armoured vehicles driven by the Spanish UNPROFOR and Jerry Hulme's bulletproof Land Rover. He seemed slightly bemused as he came over to my vehicle to collect Duncan. As we waited for permission to continue, I tried to hide my fear, gripping the steering wheel to prevent my hands from shaking. Duncan wished me luck and I watched him walk away, a tall slim figure silhouetted against the light of dawn.

The officer from the briefing appeared at my window and demanded that I hand back the identity pass issued by the UNHCR; I would no longer be under UN protection.

'You have chosen to travel in an un-armoured vehicle, therefore we are no longer responsible for your safety and you will have to travel at the rear of the convoy.'

That isn't what he'd told me at the briefing but there wasn't time to argue; the convoy was already moving. The back of the Nissan was loaded with boxes of antibiotics, liquid paracetamol for children, dressings, antiseptics and a sterilisation unit. I also carried some personal things for Hafid, such as a powerful torch he could use for operations and a whole load of surgical equipment. There were also plenty of cans, dried food and coffee.

As we approached the now familiar front line, I remembered the faces of all the children, those I had managed to help and those I had been forced to leave behind. When I reached the main street a Bosnian soldier stood in the middle of the road and refused to let me pass. Instead he directed me to the war office where I was ordered to park the vehicle and get out. He led me up the stairs to the first floor landing where a man was waiting to speak to me.

The fifteenth-century bridge targeted by the HVO.

'I want to thank you,' he said, smiling warmly. 'You saved my daughter. She had a serious injury to her spine and because of your persistence the UN finally came to get her out. She has had an operation and thanks to you she is now safe and well. We will always be in your debt.'

Before I could respond I was taken into an office where I was told to sit down and wait. Mark Dowdney was already there with another reporter, both of them looking confused. Decorating the wall was a mural of Stari Most, the beautiful old bridge that gave the city its name. Having survived 500 years of war, earthquakes and other disasters, after heavy shelling by the HVO, it had finally been destroyed on 9 November. A symbol of civic pride and tradition, its loss had been a terrible blow to Mostar's citizens, regardless of their ethnic background. EC Monitoring Mission Observer Brendan O'Shea noted the significance of this 'senseless vandalism' in his book *Bosnia's Forgotten Battlefield: Bihac*:

> While it made if obvious to everyone that the values of the past were now well and truly gone, it also triggered a reaction from the politicians who were at least theoretically supposed to be in control of their military … Mate Boban fired his top General Slobodan Praljak, replacing him with the more moderate Ante Roso … Five days later in Geneva all three sides signed a declaration … purporting to guarantee the free passage and security of all humanitarian convoys operating in Bosnia.

How would that translate into practice on the ground?

Two men entered the office. One of them, a soldier, was pale and his eyes were red.

'You do not have permission to enter the city,' he said, interpreting for the larger older man dressed in civilian clothes. He looked feverish and was trembling as he spoke. 'None of you were included on the UNPROFOR list. We have new rules which state that UNPROFOR must provide a list of all names to be included on a convoy and the list must be submitted 24 hours in advance of any operation.'

'Surely my name must be on there somewhere; I organised the mission.' The interpreter repeated my words to the official who looked puzzled.

'He wants you to explain what you mean,' said the young man, looking as though he was about to pass out. 'This is Operation Angel. An official UN mission.'

'She is Operation Angel' said Mark, 'this whole thing was her idea.'

The two men withdrew and we waited for almost an hour. I thought of the supplies in the Nissan and wondered how to ensure they reached the hospital. As we sat there discussing what had happened, it slowly dawned on me what might be going on. Perhaps the UN had deliberately withheld our names from the list in order to prevent us from reaching the hospital; that way they could still take the credit for the evacuation. I was becoming used to the way in which they worked but if only they had told me. It wouldn't have mattered to me *who* got the credit so long as the children got out.

After a while the journalists were told they could leave but I was ordered to remain behind in the office. As I stood alone, looking out of the window, I spotted Duncan standing on the pavement below. I called to him and he looked up in surprise.

'I'm being held here against my will' I shouted, hoping he could hear me. A short while later a man came to take me downstairs.

'There has been a misunderstanding,' he said apologetically. 'We know who you are and if you still wish to visit the hospital then you may.' As I came out onto the street, I found Duncan talking to Jerry Hulme.

'This whole thing is utterly pathetic,' I told Jerry, who stood there in silence while I continued to rage. 'You allowed me to drive in without protection on the understanding that this was the only way I could bring in the supplies. You failed to protect my vehicle and then made damn sure I was prevented from reaching the hospital. It's appalling and you ought to be ashamed of yourselves.' An ITN cameraman began filming the row and Jerry addressed me as though trying to calm a petulant child.

'Now, now Sally,' he said, 'if you want to reach the hospital so badly, I'll take you myself. Unfortunately a man has just been shot by a sniper but of course if you'd rather they welcomed you instead of helping him, we'll go now.' I felt sick to my stomach.

'Of course I wouldn't expect to go to the hospital while they're recovering the wounded.'

'Then you'll leave with us now,' said Jerry. 'The patients are already in the vehicles, 44 in all.'

'There were supposed to be 84' I said miserably.

'Unfortunately some of those on your list did not reach the hospital this morning.' He replied.

'Well can't we go and find them?' I asked, aghast at the news.

'No' he said emphatically. 'There was shelling last night and they are scattered all over the place.' Seeing my despair Duncan pulled me close.

'We have to go now,' said Jerry, striding towards his vehicle. Duncan offered to drive the Nissan but I was past caring about the snipers and oblivious to the danger. As I climbed into the vehicle I was thinking of the other names on the list, so near yet so far. My thoughts were interrupted as I heard a familiar voice and looking up I saw a mop of red gold hair. It was Tim Clancy, the American volunteer who I hadn't seen for weeks. I jumped out and gave him a hug. 'What are you doing in Mostar?' I asked.

'We've got permission to bring a mobile hospital unit across the front line. It should be here any day now.' I realised that this meant Tim would be staying.

'Please, take these things to the hospital,' I said, opening the rear of the vehicle. He helped me to unload the heavy boxes onto the pavement and then I reached in to get the packages for Hafid. I pulled out the last of the boxes which contained all manner of clothing, food, chocolates, vitamins, coffee, beer and cheese. There was even a small Christmas cake. Tim called to his friends to come and help while I scribbled a quick note to Hafid.

'I'd better go now,' I said, seeing the convoy approaching. 'Take care.' My flak jacket still lay beside me on the passenger seat and I handed it to Tim. As I drove along the muddy track that wound its way along the side of the hill, the vehicle started to slide and I panicked. I couldn't remember how to use the four-wheel-drive and fearing that the vehicle was about to go over the edge, I squeezed my eyes shut. To my surprise, somehow the wheels began to grip and I managed to regain control. Looking back I saw that I had just missed a series of stick mines protruding from the ground.

Once we were out of the war zone, I passed through the Croat checkpoint and stopped to wait, in case the HVO soldiers tried to hold up the convoy. I was carrying my original documents signed by General Praljak and the Minister of Health and I hoped these might prove useful if a problem arose. Jerry was waiting up ahead and when he saw me he put his vehicle into reverse. Both he and Duncan got out of the Land Rover and strode towards to my vehicle.

'Come on,' said Duncan sharply, 'move over, I'll drive.' He thought that I was having some kind of breakdown but I explained that I was fine.

'I'm waiting for our patients,' I said. 'But you're welcome to join me.' He shrugged and slid into the passenger seat as Jerry wrenched open my door.

'You can't stay here,' he said abruptly, 'We're going on to Metković.'

'You go. We'll follow on behind with the others.' He hesitated for a moment and then looked at me.

'Stay if you must, but I wish you'd stop being paranoid. Operation Angel was a UN thing. Oh, you helped us of course because without your ambulances we wouldn't be able to carry the patients to Split, but the rest of it had nothing to do with you.'

When all the armoured vehicles had passed safely through the checkpoint, we followed on behind; 40 minutes later we pulled into the UN compound at Metković and were greeted by a wondrous sight. Our ambulances were arranged in a large circle like a wagon train camp in a western. Beside each of the vehicles were our medical teams, waiting to escort those who could walk while others were borne in on stretchers. Having spotted Major Need, I went over to say goodbye and to my surprise he put his arms around me and gave me a hug. 'Well done,' he said smiling.

As I returned to my vehicle, I saw one of our paramedics from West Sussex talking to the Meridian presenter. 'Yes,' she was saying in reply to a question, 'seeing this today has made it all seem worthwhile.'

'Would you do it again?' asked the presenter.

'Yes,' she replied with tears streaming down her face. 'But without Sally Becker. The woman was never around.'

I didn't care what she said, for at that moment a stretcher went past me carrying Amel. It looked as though Hafid would have his miracle after all.

As the convoy headed back along the panoramic coast, the sun was setting and the sky was a myriad colours. In the mirror I caught a glimpse of the flashing blue lights of the ambulances following behind us and I caught my breath: for inside each of those vehicles were the children – safe at last.

Once we reached the airport in Split, we drove onto the tarmac and watched as the patients were transferred to the waiting aircraft. Someone came with a message from Ivan. Dr Lang's convoy had reached Nova Bila, so I wouldn't need to go there after all. Duncan and I were invited to escort the patients to Italy so we said goodbye to our volunteers who were preparing to catch the ferry.

When we arrived in Ancona there was only one more job to do; transfer some of the patients and their families onto a medevac flight to Britain. The plane had been chartered by a team of paediatric specialists from the trauma centre at the Staffordshire Hospital in Stoke on Trent. Veterans of Operation Irma, they would be involved in the ongoing care of our patients.

As we flew home, I talked to Suad, Senad's older brother, who told me that he hoped their mother would be able to join them one day. Those patients who were well enough to eat were given a hot meal and some of them were taken to visit the flight deck.

We landed at Birmingham airport to a media scrum and at the press conference a journalist called out; 'Sally, the United Nations say they could have done this without you.'

'Then why the bloody hell didn't they?' I replied.

17 | NOVA BILA

THE PRESS WAS CRUEL; 'Angel Has Wings Clipped,' read one of the headlines. 'A Tarnished Halo' read another. One minute I was hailed as a heroine and the next I was a 'loose cannon' a 'maverick' or a 'self aggrandising publicity seeker'. The old saying about 'sticks and stones' that I sang as a child no longer applied. I was terribly hurt by the things that were said for despite all the setbacks, the quarrels and confusion, we had come through; 98 people were safe at last and for them at least, the war was over.

I was planning one more operation, this time by air, taking supplies into central Bosnia and bringing out the wounded. I called the UN headquarters in Zagreb and wrote to the Chief of Missions with a request for assistance with the evacuation of Nova Bila. At the end of January I received a reply: the UN had no plans to evacuate the children and they were certainly not willing to assist me.

When I approached other avenues, Paddy Ashdown MP, leader of the Liberal Democrats was the only politician who bothered to reply. He wrote to the Secretary of Defence Malcolm Rifkin and General Sir Michael Rose, the newly appointed chief of the UN in Bosnia asking them to support my next mission. He could not be involved any further than that but I was immensely encouraged by his support.

I also made contact with Dr Lang who was planning another convoy but this time with the extraordinary combination of Muslim and Croat drivers. He was aiming to reach Zenica, Sarajevo and Nova Bila and I immediately offered to help.

I had heard nothing from Bagarić since my return, despite sending a stream of faxes and making endless calls. It was obvious that he hadn't yet forgiven me for letting him down.

Dr Lang invited me to join the convoy and within five days I was ready to go. Before I left, Duncan took me away for our first weekend together. We spent two days in a quaint hotel deep in the Sussex countryside. We savoured every moment of our short time together, aware that very soon I would be back in the war zone. On Sunday evening, 4 February, we drove to Heathrow Airport and as I prepared to go through passport control, Duncan took me in his arms.

'I love you Miss Becker.'

'I love you too Doc.'

Tears pricked my eyes as I waved him goodbye. Leaving wasn't so easy now that I had fallen in love; especially as I was going to a war zone where a bullet might have my name upon it.

The Rt Hon Paddy Ashdown MP

HOUSE OF COMMONS
LONDON SW1A 0AA

Lt Gen Sir Michael Rose
Commander Of UN Forces
In Bosnia

Our ref :- DAC/FA/Bosnia
Date :- 25 January 1994

Dear General Rose

I have been approached by Sally Becker, who organised the 'Operation Angel' airlift of children from Bosnia to Britain in December last. I enclose a copy of her letter to me regarding this matter.

Sally tells me that she has requested that the UN supply her with air transport from Split to central Bosnia and back in March, in order for her to bring out the mothers of the children now in Britain, plus some ten other sick youngsters. I understand that Sally has received assistance in this way from the UN on a previous occasion.

As you know, I have visited Bosnia five times, and believe that anything that can be done to alleviate the suffering of the Bosnian citizens, without jeopardising the UN mission, or other lives, is worthwhile.

Like all of us in Britain, I saw the coverage of Ms Becker's last mission. I recognise that there are always reservations about freelance operations and some criticisms were expressed, but I also realise that sometimes achievements in humanitarian missions depend on having a relaxed attitude to red tape.

I do not know all the details of Ms Becker's proposed mission so I cannot make a judgement on its operational merits and relation to UN activities. However, the evidence suggests Ms Becker is sincere in her purpose and she tells me she has the co-operation of the British commander in Vitez, in providing escorts from Kiseljak.

I do know that Ms Becker's activities do serve to keep Bosnia in the public mind, and remind people of the everyday suffering. For a fortunate few this also results in deliverance from the war.

If there are no over-riding objections to Ms Becker's request, I would urge you to grant it. If there are strong objections, I would be grateful if you would inform me of these.

Yours sincerely

Paddy Ashdown MP

Paddy Ashdown pleads Sally's case to Lieutenant-General Sir Michael Rose, 25 January 1994.

The tension in the conflict zone was heightened by the threat of air strikes against the Serbs. They had been given one more chance to lift the siege of Sarajevo and the countdown was about to begin. The flight was almost full. British soldiers, UN personnel and aid workers filled the seats and when we landed, the airport was teeming.

I took a taxi to the Hotel Split in the centre of town where I would have to wait while arrangements were made. The hotel had few guests apart from some EC monitors but it was packed with refugees. I spent the first couple of days in my room trying to make contact with the Bosnian-Croat Ministry of Defence and waiting to hear from Dr Lang. To while away the time I watched the news on CNN.

Being quite restless, I found the waiting almost intolerable. I had already wasted several weeks and was impatient to get on with the job. I was also increasingly concerned about the impending airstrikes and their affects upon the people of Bosnia-Herzegovina. Having lived through the Gulf War, I knew just how imprecise so-called surgical airstrikes could be.

Eventually I received the long-awaited call from Dr Lang. He told me that the convoy was delayed due to the atrocious weather in central Bosnia, where thick snow had again made the roads impassable. He told me that the only way to get there would be to fly and he suggested that I travel with him to a conference the following day. There would be important people there who might be able to help me. I had already tried the aid organisations but either they had halted operations due to the threat of air-strikes or they were grounded because of the snow. There was one organisation that might try going in but they were unwilling to take an outsider with them.

Dr Lang arrived at the hotel accompanied by Dr Kraus, President of Zagreb's Jewish Community and as I joined them in the chauffer-driven car, I saw that we had a police escort. Lang had become a heroic figure since the success of his White Roads mission in December and upon hearing of my own experiences, he urged me to press my case with the Croat authorities. I knew however that the first person I had to convince was my first and best ally.

I saw him as soon as we arrived; Brigadier Doctor Ivan Bagarić, a head taller those at his side. He gave me a bear-like hug but I still sensed some distance between us. After a few moments he excused himself and I was left alone to watch the proceedings.

The conference was vital – chosen by Mate Boban to announce his resignation as President – but it was all in Croatian and I could hardly understand a word. It was freezing cold in the auditorium and I could not stop shivering despite my fleece-lined jacket. I eventually managed to corner Ivan during the lunch and tried hard to convince him of my sincerity.

I was here, I said, to keep my promise to the people of Nova Bila but I would need a helicopter to reach the area. His first reaction was to laugh until he realised I was serious. I pressed him throughout the day and towards the end of the conference he finally agreed to make some inquiries.

I had to wait a further ten days for his decision and my only solace was Vava, who kept in touch with me by phone. At last the news came; a helicopter was standing by in Posušje to take me to Nova Bila; we would take off as soon as the weather permitted. I immediately packed my bags and drove down to Čitluk where I had been told to await final instructions.

As soon as I set foot in the Čitluk Hotel the memories came flooding back. I received a very warm welcome from the staff and was given a key to one of the rooms. It was similar to the one I had shared with Lynne for so many weeks and I could almost hear her voice and those of Thierry, Domi, Paul, Paddy, Sean … and of course, Collette.

The weather was the only thing that had changed. Instead of the oppressive heat of the previous summer, snow now lay several inches deep and the temperature was well below freezing. I called Stipe and Erna as the phone lines were working and they came over with a couple of their friends; a police inspector and his Muslim wife. They arrived in the Renault Four and we drove to a restaurant that had been their favourite before the war robbed them of an income. I saw that Erna had put on a little weight at last and she looked lovely. They both missed Damir but he wrote often and occasionally they managed to call him on the phone. He was staying with Erna's sister in London and with support from the ICJW he was able to continue his studies. We ordered a platter of seafood, Erna's favourite, and we shared a bottle of wine. Over dinner we talked politics and I caught up on the news.

Ivan had arranged for Zoran to deliver mail and parcels to the people living in East Mostar. Those who'd been separated from their friends and families during the war could now keep in touch. Hafid's wife had given birth to a healthy baby girl and was now living abroad. Erna told me excitedly that Bella, her little dog, had a litter of puppies. 'The father,' she said, with a serious expression on her face, 'has been killed, so she is now a war widow.' As they prepared to drive back to Mostar they all wished me luck with the forthcoming mission.

'We have constant electricity now,' said Stipe 'So we'll be able to follow your work on television.'

Ivan's driver came to collect me a couple of days later and we drove to Siroki Brijeg to pick up Vava. I had been feeling nervous about the forthcoming mission but his warmth and humour immediately lifted my spirits. I had bought him a bottle of Jack Daniels, which he opened on the way to the Ministry of Defence in Posušje.

'Do you think the NATO ultimatum will affect what I'm trying to do?' I asked as we drove across the snow-covered landscape. He laughed out loud.

'Are you crazy? It's just talk, as usual. We lost our faith in them a long time ago. Their threats are empty.'

I spent the night with some friends of his in Posušje. Dr Jurić and his family made me very welcome but it was even colder than Čitluk. I found it impossible to sleep because my teeth would not stop chattering. In the morning I was taken to an office where I was able to make some phone calls. I rang the helicopter pilots; I rang my mother, who was torn between wanting me to succeed yet wanting me out of danger; and finally I called Duncan. This would be the last time we would talk for a while and I wondered whether I would ever hear his voice again.

I called Karen Abuzayed at the UN headquarters in Zagreb and asked whether there were any plans to evacuate the children from Nova Bila. She was adamant that there was nothing on record and when I requested permission to enter the No-Fly zone in central Bosnia; she assured me that Croatian military helicopters used the route often so permission wasn't necessary.

The days dragged by and I thought I would go crazy. Each time I prepared to set off, a message would come through; fog has come down, we can't fly. I passed the time sending messages to Nova Bila and the Bosnian army and fretting over the weather reports. I had never before taken such a keen interest in meteorology.

On 20 February 1994 the fog finally lifted and a pilot agreed to take me in. Five surgeons were travelling with me who would remain in Nova Bila for one month. Vava was also coming, which was immensely reassuring. He had been trapped in Sarajevo for several months during the siege and after hiding in the airport for several days in fear of his life, he had managed to escape. He always swore he would never go back and when I asked him what had changed his mind, he shrugged.

'We'll fly in, wait for the children to be carried on board and we'll fly back out. I won't even have to get off.'

'If that's the case, why don't they carry out the evacuation themselves?' I asked. 'Why would they need me?'

'In wartime there are things that take priority over wounded civilians – even children. Don't ask me why. I'm not a soldier or a politician. Also it is considered too dangerous to evacuate civilians as the helicopter could be shot at. You're presence here and the fact that you have informed the Bosnian army has enabled Ivan to convince the military authorities to make an exception. They have allocated one slot.'

The helicopter was a Russian MTV-8, which was missing some essential equipment. Peter Churdo, the pilot, had never flown that type of helicopter before but he had volunteered because he wanted to help the children. He managed to convince his commander to let him go and he found a co-pilot and a flight technician willing to join him. The helicopter was loaded to the roof with medical supplies and we had to sit astride the boxes. Vava winked at me from his position behind a huge pack of dressings as the propellers whirred into action.

We flew without lights, unseen but not of course unheard and I tensed as I pictured the big anti-aircraft guns below and the damage they could do. The flight took around 30 minutes and after circling the area three or four times, we finally landed in a quarry thick with snow. Quickly the supplies were off-loaded and the patients were then lifted in on stretchers. I saw they were all wounded soldiers – where were the children? I searched around for Vava but couldn't see him.

The helicopter blades were already turning, faster and faster as the heavy machine prepared to lift off from the ground. However much these people needed help, I had not waited so long and travelled so far to abandon the children, but what could I do? I knew I only had a few seconds to make my decision.

I cursed under my breath as I picked up my bag and jumped to the ground, the powerful blades whipping the snow into a blizzard. I was wearing a soft white scarf which I wrapped around my face but icy particles blew into my eyes half blinding me. It was much too dark to see anything in any case and I had no idea in what direction the hospital lay.

Suddenly a figure appeared in front of me and to my relief I saw it was Vava. 'Hi man,' he said, as the helicopter rose into the air. He grasped my hand and helped me to my feet. 'I saw you leave so I jumped out.'

'Why didn't you go with them?' I asked, surprised he hadn't left while he had the chance. He glanced at me as we trudged along side by side, knee deep in snow.

'How could I leave you alone here? Firstly you don't speak the language and secondly … Ivan would never forgive me!'

18 | THE PROMISE KEPT

WE SCRAMBLED UP THE side of the quarry and found an ambulance parked at the top. It was the vehicle that had been used to transport the soldiers and was just preparing to leave. Vava asked the driver to take us to the hospital, assuming that our messages had not got through. We were met in the entrance by Fra Grebano who pulled down the neck of his robe to show me that he was wearing his Operation Angel sweatshirt. 'You came back,' he said and led us to a warm room and an even warmer welcome from the staff. To my astonishment, their phones were working so Vava started to make some calls while I was taken to the ward.

'The children were told that you were on your way back,' said a woman doctor. 'It will give them great pleasure to see you have arrived.'

I was surprised to see that Robin White, a reporter for ITN was there. Having been accused of being a publicity seeker by the UN, we deliberately had not informed the press about this mission. Without the media it would have been impossible to highlight the plight of victims of war, and without them we would never have managed to raise funds and aid for Operation Angel. However, I was funding this mission myself and I was working alone, so there was no need for the press to be involved.

Ironically, Robin had heard about the mission during a briefing by the UN. The army based in Vitez had been told to refuse entry should I turn up with the children. 'It would be a shame for Becker to grab the limelight!' read the UN staff order. That was not part of my plan but I was disappointed to think that British soldiers would have been forced to turn away injured children. In fact I'm sure that Colonel Williams would not have approved.

The room was filled with young patients and their relatives and I visited each child in turn, explaining that I had come to take them to safety. A fourteen-year-old girl called Marija had lost both her legs in an explosion which killed her father. 'Thank you for coming,' she said quetly, 'I have been on a waiting list for months.' One of the doctors handed me a sheet of paper with 55 names on it and when Vava had finished making his calls I asked him if we would be able to fit them all in. 'We'll just have to try,' he said.

Vava was told there would be no more flights that night but they would send the helicopter back the following evening, 'providing there isn't any fog.' I resigned myself to another long wait and was offered a bed in the staff room. It was three in the morning and I was pretty worn out.

The next day I spotted Elvis, the fixer from ABC news I had last seen in Mostar. He was now working for another news crew and he told me that his shrapnel wounds had healed well. A few hours later a British soldier arrived from the battalion at Vitez and informed the doctors that an evacuation would take place the very next day. One of the doctors confronted him.

'We have been asking you to evacuate our wounded for several months, so why would you decide to do it now? Could it have something to do with Miss Becker's arrival?' The soldier looked extremely embarrassed. He was obviously only following orders.

'I have my own thoughts on that,' he replied, 'but I am not allowed to express them.' He turned to me.

'Please can I see the names of the children you plan to take out? I think three of them might be on our own list and we don't want a mix up.' Fra Grebenar stepped between us and insisted that I was not to give him the list.

'We would prefer you to take them out yourself,' he said, 'The UN have let us down too many times and we are not willing to trust them again.'

That evening the children and their relatives were gathered together at the entrance to the church. A small boy was clinging to a nurse and crying. He had an ugly leg wound which was pinned together by an external fixator. The nurse explained that he had been orphaned by the war and she and the other nurses had become his family. His cries broke my heart but she assured me that he had an aunt in Croatia who was waiting to take care of him.

We planned to fly all the children and their mothers to Split because many of them had relatives in the city. The hospital had the facilities to treat all the patients and of course they could speak the same language. One by one the patients were carried into the ambulances that waited outside.

When they were ready to leave, I climbed inside and sat opposite a woman with a baby on her knee. He had a dummy clamped firmly in his mouth and was staring at me with wide-eyed curiosity. Beside me was Marija who was lying on a stretcher. She was shivering from the cold so I took off my scarf and placed it around her neck. We soon began the treacherous descent down the side of the quarry and she screamed as each jolt of the vehicle sent an agonising pain through her mutilated body.

The vehicles finally stopped outside a hut built into the hillside and completely covered in snow. First the stretchers were carried inside followed by the walking wounded and the relatives. The cold bit into my face and hands and I could feel my toes going numb inside my boots.

With the patients safely huddled inside around a warm stove, I stood outside with Vava and scanned the night sky, straining to see any sign of the helicopter. It was inky dark but we could just make out the silhouettes of trees surrounding the quarry. A group of soldiers were standing guard a few feet away, their cigarettes glowing like fireflies. The cold wind whipped against me, slowly freezing each part of my body.

Israeli children wearing gas masks during an air raid in the First Gulf War.

Sean and Collette. (Courtesy Sean Vatcher)

Mama and Baba in the refugee camp at Posusje.

Brigadier Doctor Ivan Bagaric.

Sean enlists as a war photographer. (Courtesy Sean Vatcher)

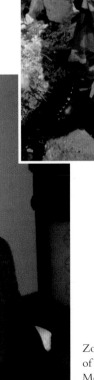

Zoran Mandlebaum, President of the Jewish Community in Mostar.

View from
Zoran's office.

War damage.

The front
line. (© Nigel
Chandler/
Sygma/Corbis)

A body lies on the Bulevar close to Mostar's front line. (Courtesy Sean Vatcher)

Mostar. (Courtesy Sean Vatcher)

A patient with shrapnel wounds is brought to Higijenski, the makeshift hospital in east Mostar. (© Patrick Chauvel/Sygma/Corbis)

The exterior of Higijenski hospital in Mostar.

A UN soldier helps Maja. (Courtesy Simon Dack)

The UN refuse to open the gates.

Sally tries to persuade the UN officer to help the children.

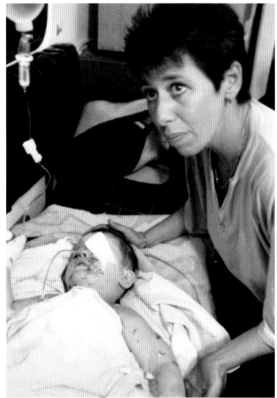

Inside the ambulance with Elmir. (© Syndication International)

The Croat
doctors transfer
Elmir to the
hospital in Split.

Neurosurgeon Hafid Konjihoddzic.

Vava (left).

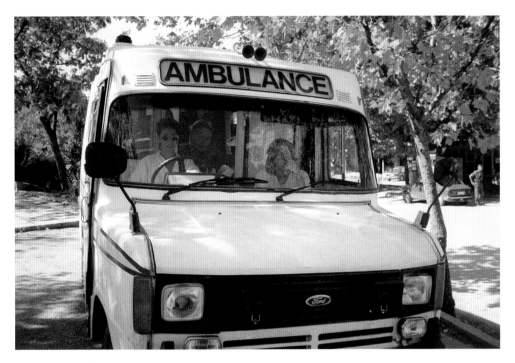

The trusty ambulance.

Mostar during an offensive. (© Nigel Chandler/Sygma/Corbis)

Operation Angel is underway. (Courtesy Simon Dack)

Preparing to leave Brighton seafront.

Team Drenica. (Courtesy Ted Vandegrift)

Rob Penny with some of the children. (Courtesy Ted Vandegrift)

Locals form a chain to unload the aid. (Courtesy Ted Vandegrift)

The children
wave goodbye.
(Courtesy Ted
Vandegrift)

En route to
northern Albania.

The Accursed
Mountains.

UNHCR, ECMM and OSCE wait at the border.

Sally arriving at Stansted Airport following her release. (© Michael Crabtree/Reuters/Corbis)

Distributing aid in Tropoje.

Lake Koman.

Crossing the new
'Old Bridge'.

Maja and Sally,
Florida, 2009.

With Elmir and Lela, Mostar 2012.
(Courtesy Darren Fletcher)

With Billie, beneath the arch of Stari
Most. (Courtesy Darren Fletcher)

'Will they come?' I whispered anxiously. Vava shrugged and bent over to light a cigarette, shielding the flame with his hand.

'They said so,' he replied, though his voice betrayed his uncertainty. In the distance I heard the crack of rifle fire and I hoped to God that the doctors were right when they said that the quarry was hidden from view.

All of a sudden from out of the darkness, a young couple appeared with two small children. I could see one of the doctors ushering them away so we went over to see what was happening. One of the children, a five-year-old boy, was in urgent need of an operation and he had been on an evacuation list for over six months. Hearing of our arrival, his father had decided to try and get him out and they had walked for miles through the snow. The doctor was adamant that we could not take them; they had not been included on our list and there was no space.

The man told me that he didn't care about himself but he begged us to take his wife and children. The doctor became angry and started shouting, insisting that they go back. My heart ached as I watched them turn to leave, the young man's shoulders slumped in defeat. I pleaded with the doctor and offered to give up my place but he ignored me. Vava offered to do the same and finally he looked at us both and sighed. They were trudging back up the hill huddled together for warmth when we caught up with them and explained that they might get to leave after all. 'Thank you,' said the man, tugging the boys' woolly hats down over their ears.

Suddenly one of the soldiers looked up and pointed and we could hear the murmur of anticipation amongst them. Straining our eyes we peered into the sky and saw a small dark shape passing in front of a cloud. I held my breath as the shape grew larger until at last I could see the outline of a helicopter. There were no lights on the ground but the soldiers darted forward with torches and helped to guide it into the quarry. When it was almost overhead, the pilots switched on the landing lights and the helicopter settled clumsily on to the snow like a giant bluebottle.

The women came rushing outside, overjoyed at the sight of the machine and as the blades whipped up the snow, I quickly removed my coat to cover the two little boys. Snowflakes melted into icy rivulets and ran inside my sweater but I barely noticed in the joy of the moment.

We had to wait for an hour while they unloaded the supplies, stamping our feet and rubbing our arms in an effort to keep warm. Finally the stretchers were carried on board while those who could walk followed behind them. The doctor ticked off each of their names. At last they were all inside but there seemed to be no space left at all. The doctor looked at me helplessly. 'I'm sorry,' he said. I turned to Vava, desperation on my face.

'We have to get them out. Please, try and convince him!'

'I really don't think there's any more room,' he said despondently.

The doctor suddenly pushed us towards the doors but I gestured to the family waiting patiently at my side.

'Please, let them go instead of us.'

He looked at me for a moment and then shrugged. 'Ok' he said and told them to climb on board. While the woman was saying goodbye to her husband I felt a small, icy hand slip into mine. It was the youngest boy and I choked back the tears as I lifted him gently inside. I turned to Vava. 'Sorry,' I said, feeling wretched that he was stuck there because of me. He shrugged.

'Life's a bitch!'

As they prepared to close the doors the doctor suddenly insisted that we get inside. I did not see how we could possibly fit but before I could say anything Vava grabbed my arm. We carefully edged our way through the crush of bodies. It was dark and absurdly cramped; arms, legs, feet and elbows dug into my back as I squeezed in behind the cockpit. Sitting with my knees against my chest, I tried hard not to crush the medical records given to me by the doctors. The soldiers heaved and pushed against the mass of bodies as they struggled to close the door.

During those first few tense moments nobody made a sound, and then suddenly all the faces were bathed in a glow of light as Marija's mother lit a candle in prayer. As she spoke, her face pale in the flickering light, Vava translated her words.

'Thanks be to God and all good people; for we are saved.'

Her careworn face was transfused with a look of utter peace, such as I had never seen.

The pilots soon strapped themselves in and the rotors started turning overhead. Vava gripped my hand and I hoped with all my heart that Marija's mother was right. The great machine lifted from the ground, swaying from side to side as it rose into the air. I could just make out the faces of those around me; some were anxious, others were filled with anticipation. Only the babies were oblivious to the danger.

The helicopter climbed higher and time seemed to stand still as we flew over Bosnia where the war still raged below. I kept up a silent treaty, 'Please let us make it, please, please …'

And then the lights of Split appeared below us, like a carpet of jewels in the night. Vava passed the news around and suddenly everyone was laughing and cheering, trying to hug one another in that cramped space. Tears streamed down my face as we came in to land and I made no attempt to wipe them away. I had kept my promise.

I returned to a media storm. Lyndell Sachs, spokesperson for the UN was quoted as saying that my mission had caused 'the entire aid operation in the area to grind to a halt'. Ray Wilkinson, spokesman for the UNHCR issued a statement to the press announcing that I had hijacked a UN operation and had put the patients in danger by using a helicopter in a no-fly zone. They also stated that we had been shot at, which of course was not true.

Wilkinson was busy making the rounds of all the national television and radio stations and although I was invited onto the programmes, I declined. Mike convinced me that I ought to defend myself against the allegations and in the end I agreed to do an interview by telephone. When I was asked to respond to the accusation that I had hijacked a UN mission, I pointed out that Karen Abuzayed had assured me that there were no plans to evacuate Nova Bila. I tried to say that some of the children had been on a list for months but Wilkinson kept interrupting and my words were lost. When I asked him to account for what happened to our aid, the question was ignored.

Duncan registered our charity under the title 'Operation Angel' and whilst the ceasefire in Mostar seemed to be holding, Nick Jacobs, an ophthalmic surgeon, offered to carry out some surgery. Although the snipers were still occasionally taking pot-shots across the front line, the shelling had ceased. The fortifications and checkpoints that divided the city had been dismantled and in West Mostar, for the first time in two years, the sidewalk cafes were full. Even on the east side of the city, people were beginning to venture out from their underground shelters, taking advantage of the uneasy peace. Based in the mobile hospital that Tim had helped bring into the city, Nick performed 35 successful operations.

When I returned to Mostar, Duncan came with me. We were staying with Erna who told me about a project that she thought might interest me. Edina Kajtaz and a vibrant redhead called Azra Hasanbegović had set up a centre for Muslim and Croat women called Žena BiH. The association, which started with 32 women, enabled them to work and earn an income. Apart from providing support for one another, the women made clothes and toys for local refugees and as more women began to attend they needed more space and materials. We applied for a grant from the Sir Halley Stewart Trust and Zoran, who had known Azra for some time, set about finding more appropriate accommodation. With the money from the trust we were able to pay for a lease and supply them with sewing machines and the materials they needed and within three months the membership increased by several hundred.

Damir was keen to return home and now that the ceasefire seemed to be holding, his parents relented. The European Union had sent a police force to Mostar to help keep the peace so Damir applied for a job and was soon working as an interpreter for them, earning more in one month than Stipe received in a year.

During my next visit, Erna and I went to meet Damir at the Hotel Ero during his break. Since the ceasefire, the restaurant had become popular with staff from the international organisations and I saw Jerry Hulme sitting in the bar. His skin looked jaundiced and he had lost a great deal of weight. He invited me to join him and to my surprise he apologised for what happened during the Operation Angel mission in December 1993.

'It seems that I was grossly misled.'

I was about to ask him what had changed his mind but someone came over with an urgent message. 'We'll meet again and have a talk.' He said, as he hurried away. Sadly that wasn't to be, for he died a short while later. He was a remarkably brave man who helped a great many people. As can be seen from the following letter from Herceg-Bosna President Prlić, he shouldered a heavy burden and his problems had been our problems, but multiplied and complicated by official responsibility.

No. 01 – I – 567/93
Mostar, 24 September 1993

UNHCR
To: Mr Jerry HULME personally

<u>MEDJUGORJE</u>

1.   In a number of official talks with the Croatian Republic of Herceg-Bosna/HR HB/ officials in relation to the organisation, transit and distribution of humanitarian aid on the territory of central Bosnia, we have demonstrated our readiness to facilitate unimpeded transit and distribution of aid, but at the same time we advised you of the need to distribute aid equally to all who need it, irrespective of which people, ethnic or religious group they belong to. We rightfully believe that you have been assured of the HR HB authorities' readiness and cooperativeness, which has been proven in practice when a number of humanitarian aid convoys organised by the UNHCR and other humanitarian organisations were transported across the territory under the control of our armed and civilian authorities. Believing that this was the way to provide the needed aid to the Croatian people as well, we facilitated unimpeded passage through our territories even at the time when Muslim units were engaged in a strong offensive in the central Bosnia area.

However, the information that we have been receiving (attached) shows that recently aid in fuel, clothes, etc., has been going to the areas, towns and places under the control of Muslim authorities, and not even one convoy was sent to Busovača, Novi Travnik or Vitez in the last 25 days. This has created a dramatic situation in the above enclaves and may create an atmosphere that will prompt the citizens to self-organise and stop humanitarian aid convoys for their own needs or prevent them from going to other areas until they receive such aid. There have been such cases before, of which, we believe, you are aware. In order to avoid this kind of situation we request that the UNHCR organises, prepares and dispatches convoys of the needed aid for the Busovača, Novi Travnik and Vitez enclaves, including all aspects of humanitarian aid, particularly fuel, so that there is no break in the work of aggregates in hospitals and bakeries or the transport of the wounded.

2.   We were informed today that Muslim authorities in Konjic have been expelling the local Croats so that there are about 800 civilian refugees (women, children, the elderly) who are seeking urgent evacuation to the free regions of Herzegovina. As you are aware of numerous examples of serious casualties in such circumstances, we would appreciate it if you undertook urgent measures with regard to evacuation, accommodation, and temporary care of refugees from Konjic.

HR HB HVO PRESIDENT
Jadranko PRLIĆ
[signed and stamped]

I visited Senad in Birmingham where he lived with Suad and his mother. He had undergone countless operations at Heartlands Hospital and although he could only move around on crutches, the prognosis was good. Although he had got taller he hadn't really changed much and still had the same beaming smile. He was doing very well at school and spoke English with a broad Brummie accent.

Zena BiH continued to grow and very soon there were 2000 members; most of them refugees. Amongst the women were 250 former prisoners of war, many of whom were severely traumatised. I was taken to meet one of these women who lived alone in a darkened basement, barely eating and afraid to go out. During my visit, she sat with her arms wrapped around her body and trembled as she told me her story.

Mira was driven from her home in North West Bosnia and had taken shelter in the UN compound at Potocari when it fell to the Serbs. Srebrenica was a UN-mandated and NATO-protected 'safe haven' but when Ratko Mladić, the Serbian commander, ordered his forces to surround the area, the UN

Reunited with Senad.

were unable to protect the refugees. While his bodyguards handed out chocolates to the children, Mladić, who was responsible for the siege of Sarajevo in which 10,000 people died, assured their mothers they would not be harmed.

The men were separated from the women and taken to collection centres around Srebrenica. Everyone was terrified and Mira remembered two girls being dragged outside and returning later with their clothes in shreds. Following negotiations between the UN and the Serbs, the women and children were eventually herded onto buses to be deported but as she prepared to leave with her young son, he was taken from her arms and she never saw him again. She was obviously severely traumatised and in need of counselling but as she did not feel able to go to the centre, we arranged for a psychologist to visit her at home. Azra and her colleagues took statements from these women and prepared a series of reports, which were later submitted to the United Nations Human Rights Commission.

In August 1995, following the Srebrenica massacre in which 8000 Bosnian Muslims were killed, NATO ordered airstrikes against the Bosnian Serb Army, code-named Operation *Deliberate Force*. Two months later the Dayton Peace Accords were signed, bringing an end to a conflict that had claimed at least 100,000 lives and driven around two million people from their homes.

PART TWO

19 | KOSOVO AND THE QUEEN

WHEN THE DAYTON PEACE Accords were signed, there was little attention paid to Kosovo, which continued to remain under Serbian control, nor any mention of the fact that 300,000 Serbs were still living as refugees, having been ethnically cleansed from the Krajina. As author Brendan O'Shea so presciently pointed out in his book *Bosnia's Forgotten Battlefield: Bihac*, before the tragedy of Kosovo had begun truly to unfold, 'Milosovic may well live to regret that no provision was made for this region when the Dayton deal was cobbled together.'

Since 1989, when Milosevic revoked their autonomous status, the ethnic Albanians who made up 90 per cent of the population of Kosovo had suffered oppression under the Serbs. Ibrahim Rugova, who became President of Kosovo in 1992, led a civil resistance movement, insisting on a path of nonviolence. Despite years of peaceful demonstrations and appeals to the international community, the situation continued to worsen and those who were not of Serbian origin were subjected to random assaults and mass arrests. 185,000 people were dismissed from their jobs in the State-controlled economy and forced to travel abroad for work in order to support their families.

Hashim Thaci, a young Albanian known as 'The Serpent', went underground to join the hitherto unknown UCK (*Ushtria, Clirimatre e Kosoves*) the Kosovo Liberation Army and Rugova's pacifist tactics were abandoned in favour of the KLA's campaign of armed struggle. They began attacking Serb Forces, wearing masks to prevent identification and subsequent action against their families. The Serbs called them terrorists but the members of the KLA saw themselves as freedom fighters, determined to release their people from the tyranny of the Serb regime and they were all prepared to die for the cause.

In December 1997, I began a campaign on behalf of the people of Kosovo. Having experienced the horrors of the war in Bosnia, I wanted to try and prevent it from happening again. The majority of the International organisations based in Kosovo came under the authority of the Yugoslav Red Cross. As a result they had problems trying to retain their impartiality and the ethnic Albanians suffered from lack of aid, especially in outlying areas.

We began to raise funds for aid and medical supplies whilst appealing for vehicles and volunteers to drive them. Mitsubishi Motors loaned me a white Shogun with a long wheel base which was customised with our logo. Most of our volunteers were from the emergency services or veterans of the mission to Bosnia in 1993.

Sean Vatcher offered to be convoy master. He had formed a close relationship with a young British woman and although he was obviously still grieving for Collette, his new girlfriend accepted the fact and was very supportive.

On the eve of departure, 29 March, which happened to be my birthday, Mike Mendoza had arranged a fundraising event at the Metropole Hotel in Brighton. He invited a number of celebrities including two famous drag queens David Raven (a very good friend of mine known as Maisie Trollette) and Colin Devereaux (Dockyard Doris) who provided the entertainment. June Brown and Michelle Collins, two of the stars of Britain's most popular soap turned up and although Paul O'Grady was not able to attend in person, he sent a video of himself making an appeal on our behalf. Katie Price also came and the event raised a few thousand pounds.

The next morning we left Brighton seafront with a convoy of 30 vehicles carrying several tonnes of aid. We were escorted to the motorway by Betty Walshe, the Mayor, who had given her full support to the mission. Brian Johnston, a young man who was suffering from ME and confined to a wheelchair, was a computer whizz and he had designed and built a website for the charity. Computers were completely new to me but under his guidance I learned how to upload digital photographs and text for the internet. Thanks to him, those who had computers were able to follow the progress of our journey through France, Italy and Montenegro.

Upon our arrival in Kosovo wer were taken to the Mother Theresa Charity, the only organisation still openly assisting the ethnic Albanians. By 1998 the organisation had over 7000 volunteers and 1700 doctors, with 92 clinics around the province. The society also operated a maternity clinic in Pristina, provided special services to the disabled and elderly and distributed food and clothing to over 30,000 needy families a year.

During a briefing Jak Mita, the director, told us that the Kosovo Albanian population constantly risked being harassed or arrested

Brighton Mayor Betty Walshe ready to lead the convoy out of Brighton.

Waiting for permission to continue. (courtesy Ted Vandegrift)

The volunteers pose for a photograph with a representative of the Yugoslav Red Cross. (Courtesy Ted Vandergrift)

The volunteers attend a meeting with Jak Mita and Marta from the Mother Theresa Charity.

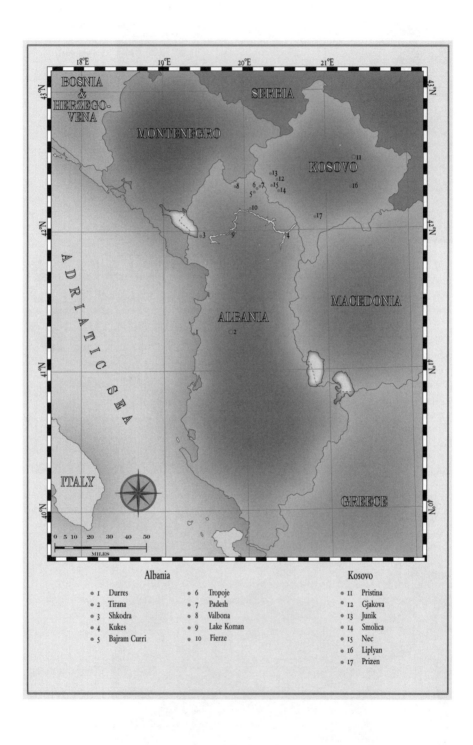

Albania

- 1 Durres
- 2 Tirana
- 3 Shkodra
- 4 Kukes
- 5 Bajram Curri
- 6 Tropoje
- 7 Padesh
- 8 Valbona
- 9 Lake Koman
- 10 Fierze

Kosovo

- 11 Pristina
- 12 Gjakova
- 13 Junik
- 14 Smolica
- 15 Nec
- 16 Liplyan
- 17 Prizen

at one of the numerous police checkpoints. This risk was all the greater since many ethnic Albanians did not have the requisite papers.

We were taken to a school in Pristina that was in serious need of help. Since taking control of the region, the Serbs insisted upon Cyrillic being used in educational establishments and Albanian textbooks were banned from the classroom. The Albanians rebelled and chose to fund their children's education from their own pockets but as the majority were now unemployed, this wasn't easy.

Unable to tolerate this rebellion, the headmaster ordered a wall to be built through the centre of the school, dividing the children by their ethnic origins. On one side of the wall there were 2500 Albanian students sharing two toilets. Broken glass littered the playground and the children studied cross legged on the stone floor. The walls were bare and the books were old and tattered. On the Serbian side, where 500 students gathered to study, the classrooms were well stocked with books and educational materials and the furniture was new.

The state hospital in the capital, Pristina, provided free treatment for Serbs but the unemployed Albanians, unable to afford insurance, were forced to pay. They were also forbidden to speak in their own language, which caused difficulties when trying to explain a medical problem to a Serbian doctor, creating an environment of fear and mistrust. As a result, Marta, a vibrant woman in her forties had set up a number of clinics which were funded by the Mother Theresa charity. Most Albanians preferred to use the clinics rather than the state-run hospital but there was a lack of equipment, so the staff could only provide the minimum of care.

Although we had brought supplies for both the State hospital and the clinics, upon our arrival, we were told that it wouldn't be possible to give any of the medical aid to the Albanians as they were classed as separatists. We were also refused permission to take food and other supplies to Drenica, one of the areas most in need.

Following a meeting with the Mayor of Pristina, it still wasn't clear whether we would be allowed to make the delivery. I raised the subject again during a meeting with the Yugoslav Red Cross and signalled to one of our volunteers, who was carrying a camera. The presence of the camera seemed to sway the decision and with obvious reluctance, permission was duly granted.

With help from Jak Mita and Marta, we negotiated our way through Serb paramilitary check points and apart from some worrying moments when the male volunteers were ordered out of their vehicles; we were able to reach our destination. As we arrived in one of the small villages, we were greeted by women and children who were poorly dressed and looked mal-nourished. Heavy grey clouds hung over the landscape and I caught a glimpse of some men watching from the hills. They were armed with Kalashnikovs, their faces hidden behind masks and I guessed they must be the soldiers of the Kosovo Liberation Army. A gust of wind whipped across the hillside causing me to reach for my jacket and by the time I looked up they were gone.

Delivering medical aid and equipment to the Serb-run hospital in Pristina.

Children greet the convoy at a small village in Drenica. (Courtesy Ted Vandegrift)

Talking to the children. (Courtesy Ted Vandegrift)

Upon our return to the UK, I received an invitation from The Queen and Prince Philip to attend a 'Reception for the Arts' at Windsor Castle. On approaching Windsor Great Park I was caught up in traffic and began to worry that I would be late. Fortunately the Shogun still sported the Operation Angel logo so I was seen by a policeman on horseback. He immediately stopped all the traffic and escorted me into the Long Walk that leads to the castle.

Smoothing down my skirt and trying not to trip in my high heeled shoes, I followed the other guests through St George's Hall. The walls were lined with paintings by artists such as Rubens and Van Dyke and we passed fine tapestries and suits of armour. I had been gazing up at the incredible gilded ceiling when I found myself standing beside the actress Joanna Lumley. We chatted about my forthcoming convoy. I told her that we were aiming to recruit female volunteers this time in the hope that we would appear less threatening to the Serbs. She said that if she hadn't currently been under contract to the BBC she would have willingly joined us.

There was a sudden hush as the Queen entered the room, looking far smaller and more beautiful than I had imagined. She was escorted by Prince Philip the Duke of Edinburgh and Prince Edward, her youngest son. As she stopped to speak to some of the guests her equerry informed me that I too could be introduced to Her Majesty if I wished. Feeling understandably nervous and wondering whether I'd be expected to curtsy, I was shocked when a man she was talking to started to shout in her face. The Queen seemed completely unperturbed by his outburst and addressed him calmly but firmly before moving on.

'Her Majesty will see you now,' the equerry informed me. I inclined my head and placed one foot behind the other in what I hoped was a curtsy but probably looked more like a bowling alley lunge. The Queen shook my hand and I was surprised to see that she was not wearing gloves.

'I know about the wonderful work you have done in Bosnia. What a tragedy that was. Do you believe the same thing is going to happen in Kosovo?'

When I told her that it was already happening there was genuine sadness in her eyes.

'Those poor people,' she said, 'it must be so awful for them.'

The room was filled with famous faces and I wandered around feeling completely out of place. Each of us was given a booklet that listed the names of each guest and I was surprised to find myself described as a 'war artist'.

I was invited to meet the Duchess of Gloucester, wife of Prince Richard, the Queen's first cousin. She seemed genuinely interested in my work and after we sat and talked for a while, she introduced me to Anne Wood CBE, creator of some of the world's best known children's television programmes. Anne told me that her Ragdoll Foundation was considering becoming a sponsor of our charity and within two or three weeks, a large truck arrived at our warehouse with a delivery of aid.

During an interview with Lorraine Kelly on Talk Radio, I was invited me to make an appeal for volunteers. When the phone lines lit up with women keen to apply, I made it clear that the trip would be dangerous so we would prefer to enlist those with relevant experience. Having learned a harsh lesson, we were planning to interview all prospective volunteers in advance but this was not always possible as some of them lived too far away.

On 29 May, a Serb policeman was killed and another wounded in the Decani region. This was followed by a Serb offensive that left over 60 Albanians dead, some of whom were children. As a result the fighting intensified and one week before we were due to depart, the Yugoslav embassy informed us that our visas had been refused. I met with Isa Zymberi, head of the Kosovo Information Centre in London and asked him what he thought we should do. 15,000 refugees had just crossed the border into Albania and knowing they would be in desperate need of help, Isa suggested we take the aid there. He offered to speak to some people he knew who would help to facilitate the mission.

By the end of June, we had enlisted 26 volunteers ranging in age from 30 to 65. I bought an old camper that would serve as a mobile office as well as somewhere to sleep and we managed to rent six large vans. We were also taking the ambulance and a coach and I still had the use of the Shogun. All the vehicles would be loaded at our warehouse in Brighton and the day before we were due to depart, Karen and I waited to greet them.

Mary Banks, a bus driver from Yorkshire, had offered to pick up the coach, which would carry some aid as well as providing a place for the drivers to rest en route. Karen and I were waiting on the pavement when the vehicle pulled up alongside us. The doors opened to reveal a short woman with a round pale face and bleached blonde hair. Although close to 70, she posed on the step with her hands on her hips and announced in a broad Yorkshire accent, 'My real name is Mary but my friends call me Doris Day!'

'More like Dockyard Doris!' muttered Karen.

Mary was accompanied by Maud, a retired bus driver who had agreed to co-drive the coach. She was a tall, slim woman with wavy blond hair and a broad Irish accent. Although quite outspoken she was funny and very kind. Pat, a local woman in her sixties with short grey hair and piercing blue eyes had spent many years in South Africa where she led a high-profile campaign against apartheid. Pat and Marie, another local woman, came along to the warehouse every day to help sort out the aid.

Liz Dack, a nurse who worked in the intensive care unit at Southlands hospital, had volunteered as our medical officer. She had short brown hair with a fringe that flopped across one eye and a great sense of humour. Brian wanted us to take his girlfriend, Jenny Wheatley, but I wasn't sure if it was such a good idea. She had no relevant experience and no driving licence but he pointed out how helpful she had been in the warehouse, so in spite of my reservations, I agreed.

Joycey, a paediatric nurse, was now retired after many years working as a missionary in isolated parts of the world. She was the oldest volunteer but very fit and capable and I knew that we could depend upon her if any difficulties arose. There were also a few former soldiers who had flown over from Guernsey. Each volunteer had managed to raise sponsorship money to contribute to the costs of the journey (except Mary Banks). Susan, a hospital matron, took charge of the funds and a former police inspector called Brenda was appointed Convoy Master.

20 | TO BAJRAM CURRI

THE CONVOY SET OFF at the end of June and two days later we reached Bari where we boarded the ferry to Durres. Just as the ship was preparing to dock, I was told that Mary Banks was suffering an asthma attack. Weeks before, like all the other volunteers, she had signed a form confirming that she had no health problems, so I was surprised and concerned to find her wheezing in her cabin. I suggested we fly her back to Britain but she was adamant that she would be fine and insisted on remaining with the convoy.

While the vehicles were being checked by customs we were approached by a young Kosovan called Riki. He was in his early thirties with thick black hair and a warm friendly face. Riki had been living in Switzerland but was hoping to visit his family. He had been chatting to one of our volunteers, an attractive blond nurse called Paula, who was also from Switzerland. She told me that Riki had offered to be our guide and interpreter and as none of us spoke Albanian, I readily agreed.

When all the vehicles were finally through we were met by Ismet Shamolli, a Kosovan who had been sent by the Albanian government to assist with our mission. Ismet was a member of the LDK – the Kosovo Democratic Party – headed by President Rugova. He had been sending truck-loads of aid into Kosovo since the conflict began.

Infrastructure limitations are a normal way of life for the people living in the mountainous region of northern Albania. Roads are few and far between and those that do exist are in a serious state of disrepair. Ismet had arranged for us to travel on the Koman-Fierze ferry but we were so long getting through customs it was now too late. He explained that by the time the convoy reached Koman, the ferry would be gone and there wouldn't be another for at least three days. We had no choice but to make the journey by road, so Ismet suggested that he take us to his warehouse where we could set up camp for the night.

We set off early the next morning and drove through Tirana, a bustling city that still bears the grey patina of communism. The road was clogged with small trucks and ancient buses belching clouds of black smoke. Weaving dangerously between the traffic were primitive carts pulled by horses and mules. Mercedes Benz limos with darkened windows played dodgems with rusty old bangers and the air was thick with dust and diesel.

Operation Angel volunteers (front row from left), Mary Banks, Maudy, Diane, Jenny Wheatly, Pat and Marie.

Mary McDermott (left) and Karen Turner.

Ismet had arranged an armed police escort for the convoy; the area through which we would travel was a haven for bandits. As we left the town and headed north we passed the rusted carcasses of automobiles and mountains of discarded rubber tyres. The dry, barren landscape was dotted with grey concrete domes that resembled giant mushrooms. The bunkers, installed by Enver Hoxha, Albania's communist leader until 1985, were built with slits in the walls for snipers, ostensibly to protect Albanian citizens from foreign invasion.

Although the escort changed at various points throughout the journey, one police officer remained with us constantly. He was a big fellow with black hair and a thick moustache who chose to travel with Janey, a buxom blond with a sharp wit. In between staving off his advances, she kept us amused with her impressions and often we would hear Mary Bank's raucous tones echoing from the CB radios fitted to each of our vehicles, only to find that it was in fact Janey.

As we headed into the mountains the road began to twist and turn and we were forced to negotiate a particularly narrow pass where the coach got into difficulties. I was in the lead vehicle when the call came through and above the sound of screaming, I could hear Mary Banks shouting and swearing. Once I made sure it wasn't Janey doing one of her impressions, I ordered the convoy to stop and went back to see what was happening. Hurrying past the long line of vehicles, I was shocked to find that the back end of the coach was jutting over the edge of a ravine.

Mary and Maud were in the midst of a blazing row while six of our volunteers and two armed guards looked on. Jenny Wheatly explained that Mary had insisted on driving while Maud was told to navigate. Somehow they had taken a bend at the wrong angle and Maud was now being blamed.

I asked the police to help move the coach and under their direction, Mary gamely inched it back and forth until the entire vehicle was back on solid ground. Jenny was telling me how frightened they all were so I suggested that they travel in the Shogun.

'We won't leave the coach without Mary,' declared Jenny. 'If she stays, we stay! I offered to swap places with Mary but her face darkened in anger.

'Nobody drives this coach but me!' she said emphatically and I saw Maud raise her eyes.

We reached our destination about 10.00pm and as we drove down the main street we had to avoid stray dogs that were roaming around in packs. Bajram Curri is a small town in the isolated region of Tropoje, not far from the Kosovo border. The local population, already stricken with unemployment and poverty, had increased by thousands over the past few weeks as refugees fled from the fighting. The police led us to a secure compound where we left the vehicles under guard. We were taken up the road to a hotel and as we reached the entrance I was surprised to see someone I knew.

Bob Edge was a tall, lean man who was rarely seen without his baseball cap. He had been part of Operation Angel in 1993 and was now working for Children's

The main street in Bajram Curri. (Courtesy Martha Grenon)

Drinks on the terrace at Hotel Ermal.

Aid Direct. He introduced me to the Hotel director Halil Gjongecaj, a short, slightly built man with shifty eyes. He did not speak English but he reminded me of Mr Rigsby from the TV show 'Rising Damp'.

The hotel Ermal, a mustard-coloured four storey building, was originally a government guest house. When members of the OSCE (Organisation for Security and Co-operation in Europe) arrived to take up residence, the building was abandoned, having been vandalised by the locals. The rooms had no windows but they offered one month's rent in advance and within a day, four of the rooms were habitable. Each room cost $50 per night and electricity and water were not always available.

Halil demanded a cash payment in advance for the ten days accommodation we required. There were only half a dozen rooms available but fortunately some of them were quite large. I bunked in with Liz Dack and Christine, another nurse. The toilet, situated just down the hall, was a hole in the ground which also doubled as a shower. It stank and we were disappointed to learn that there was currently no water. We had just unpacked our belongings when the lights went out too because the electricity had been shut off owing unpaid bills.

Bob appeared with his torch and invited me to his room, which was stacked high with tins. He explained that he was currently in charge of the distribution of canned meat on behalf of ECHO (European Community Humanitarian Organisation); the people of Bajram Curri were deemed to be undernourished and the cans were from a consignment left over from the 'European meat mountain'. This had earned him the nickname Bobby 'Mish'; the Albanian word for meat. He poured me some Raki and I began to relax after the long, stressful journey.

Bob was a mine of information and advised me on the best way to distribute our aid, suggesting that we deliver the medical equipment and supplies directly to the local hospital. We were also carrying large quantities of rice, pasta and canned food, as well as blankets and cooking materials for the refugees in Tropoje. None of us got much sleep that night because a dog started barking, which set off all the others; a common chorus throughout our stay.

Although an idyllic setting, nestled at the foot of snow-capped mountains, the town has witnessed a great deal of violence. After the fall of communism in 1991, Albanian inexperience with capitalism led to the proliferation of pyramid schemes left unchecked by a corrupt government. The schemes eventually collapsed, resulting in anarchy and following a nationwide raid on Albania's armouries, law and order became virtually non existent.

We spent the first day exploring the area whilst trying to avoid being knocked down. Mercedes Benz cars with foreign plates cruised down the main street honking their horns as they passed. Bob told me the vehicles were stolen but the local police could do nothing about it. After years of lawlessness, no one in the region was without his own gun, usually an AK-47 or a pistol jammed in a belt and the sound of sporadic gunfire put all our nerves on edge.

Presiding over the town square was a statue of Bajram Curri, the Kosovo-Albanian leader after whom the town was named. With his rifle in hand, Bajram Curri is the picture of the rebel outlaw. Originally from Kosovo, he was hailed a hero in 1912 when he fought against the Turks and a few years later he became one of the leaders of the Committee for the National Defence of Kosovo. He served as Minister for War in the Albanian government but fell out with Ahmed Zogu (the future King Zog). Pursued into the mountains of the Valbona valley, Bajram Curri is believed to have shot himself to avoid capture by Zog's troops.

We were invited to a meeting with the local representatives of the UNHCR, where an English field officer called Mark Cutts requested our assistance for refugee families unable to reach the town. The next day our teams set off with boxes of food and medical supplies, which they delivered to the addresses provided by the UN. The nurses were able to use their paediatric skills to help sick children in these outlying areas while the rest of us stayed in the vehicle compound, sorting out aid for further deliveries. It was gruelling in the heat and I was filled with admiration for the older volunteers who kept going regardless.

Escorted by the OSCE and the local police, we took the bulk of the aid to the UN warehouse in Tropoje, not far from the Kosovo border. We also delivered individual boxes to families housing refugees and therefore desperate for extra food and clothing. Claiming to feel unwell, Mary Banks spent most of the time in her room together with five of the women from the coach.

Riki knew of a place on the outskirts of town so we all decided to go there for a break. Taking only the Shogun and the coach, we drove across the ancient Ottoman bridge to a perfect spot where locals were gathered on the shore of the turquoise river. Rays of sunlight danced on the surface of the crystal-clear water and after the long journey across Europe followed by several days working in the intense heat, it seemed like paradise.

Mary McDermott served lunch from her camper van that served as our mobile kitchen. A resourceful and energetic woman, Mary's resumé included missions on behalf of various British charities and she had recently been awarded the MBE. In her late fifties she was still very attractive, with blond hair piled on her head in a bun. She reminded me very much of the stereotypical Englishwoman abroad; the sort of character one would see in old films, well spoken, practical and rarely seen without lipstick. (One you might find in India during the British Raj, or in Japanese POW camps in the Second World War.) Mary had befriended a local girl called Elizabeth who was keen to practise her English so she and her sister joined us on the picnic.

Maud, an excellent swimmer, dived into the river and swam to the other side while we splashed and swam around closer to the shore. Suddenly the tranquility of the scene was shattered by a loud explosion and I called to the women to get behind the coach. A small group of teenagers were laughing and jeering and Elizabeth explained that the explosion was caused by a grenade thrown into the lake to stun the fish. It seemed that the method was quite common locally.

Dawn, Alison and Jenny seemed particularly disturbed by the incident so we decided to leave. Liz and I set off in the Shogun while the others boarded the coach and as we drove onto the bridge, two boys climbed onto the roof and asked for a lift into town. As Maud prepared to follow us, another boy jumped onto the steps of the coach. Not realising that he was just hoping for a lift, she pressed the button to close the doors and started to pull away. The boy clung on and started waving a gun in the air but instead of being afraid, Maud lost her temper. She shouted at him and though I'm sure he couldn't understand a word, he soon got the message and jumped down.

That evening the boy came to reception and offered his apologies to the women on the coach, but Dawn, Alison and Jenny had decided to go home. Mark Cutts was going to Tirana the very next day so he offered to give them a lift. I wasn't aware of their decision until the next morning when Jenny came and told me they were leaving; 'I suppose you think I'm a coward!' She said, somewhat defensively.

'Not in the slightest,' I assured her,' Our aim was to get the aid here safely, which you have helped us to do. We're just waiting for Ismet to collect some things for Kosovo and then the convoy will go home. Please don't feel bad. You've done a brilliant job!' I found Dawn and Alison waiting in the car, but they chose to ignore me.

Mary went to a local shop and bought fresh bread for breakfast each day and when eggs were available she made omelettes. In the evenings when there was electricity we usually ate in the hotel. The food comprised of tough pieces of meat described in the menu as steak and kebab or there was pasta with cheese. The meat was served with chips and a little salad and was just about edible but most of us supplemented the food with Imodium, a treatment for diarrhoea. Alcohol was cheap and some of the volunteers, relaxing after a hard day's work, helped to boost the bar takings.

One evening we were all having dinner on the terrace when a man strode over to our table. He had wavy copper coloured hair and a moustache and was wearing a metal hook in place of his left hand.

'Major Bill Foxton, OSCE,' he said, 'It's an honour to meet you Miss Becker!'

Throughout the mission Bill afforded us every assistance, from briefing the volunteers daily about the local situation to arranging armed escorts for the convoy.

Some of the volunteers complained that their bras and cameras had been stolen so Bill spoke to the two Albanian women who did the cleaning for the hotel. He'd nicknamed them 'Wagon and Trailer' because they went everywhere together. The bras eventually reappeared but the cameras were never returned. Each week, Bob Edge wrote a satirical news sheet based on local gossip which he copied and distributed to all the aid workers. We provided the perfect material and much to our amusement we saw that he called his latest article *Hell's Angels*. We delivered some toys and food to the orphanage and later the women challenged the local schoolchildren to a football match. The children won by twelve goals to three but nobody minded.

Bill introduced us to Phil Figgins, the OSCE field station co-ordinator who had just arrived in Bajram Curri and Liz and I were invited to join them for dinner. Bill led us to a small 'restaurant' in the back streets of town where we were seated at the only table. There was no menu but our order was taken by an elderly woman who was both the waitress and chef; I think we were in her front room. We had four bowls of a rich beef stew called *ferges* and while the three of us shared a bottle of the local red wine, Bill called for a large beer.

This was Phil's first visit to Bajram Curri and over dinner he recalled the events of the day.

'We decided to come via the Lake Koman ferry in order to avoid the dodgy road route through the aptly named villages of Puké and Rrape before potentially getting robbed at Qafe Malit, a popular place to be stripped of everything. When we arrived at the entrance to the tunnel that leads through the mountain to the ferry terminal there were vehicles trying to force their way in both directions through what can best be described as a collapsed cave with room for the width of a couple of donkeys. How we got through was baffling. 40 minutes and 400 yards later, we reached the far end. I was beginning to think we should have travelled the road route after all.' he said, as Bill called for another large beer.

'Boarding the ferry ahead of us was a camper van with so much weaponry and ammunition aboard it had to be eased onto the ferry by ten men trying to take weight off the inverted springs. I was leaning against one of the upper deck rails eating a burek when a gun went off about 10 feet away. Some crazed diaspora Albanian (probably from California) was blatting away into the hillside. The captain of the ferry appeared at the top of the ladder and rushed over to the young gun and I was expecting him to have a go at the idiot. Instead, he grabbed the pistol and started firing into the same patch of ground 50-odd yards from a bunch of scuttling villagers. Welcome to north east Albania I thought, as me and Bill withdrew to a safer hangout!'

A few days later Ismet arrived with a truck destined for Kosovo and amongst the medical equipment we gave him was a mobile x-ray machine. Although he hoped the vehicle would get through, nothing was certain. The situation across the border was becoming desperate; no aid had reached the area for some time and since the aid organisations had pulled out, supplies had to be taken in across the mountains on the backs of mules.

Knowing that there were sick and wounded children in need of help, I had brought a large bag of paediatric medicines that I planned to deliver to Kosovo myself. Thousands of refugees had crossed the border in recent weeks so I figured it should not be too difficult.

One afternoon I was asked to come to the office of the UNHCR to speak to Daniel Enders, the young Frenchman in charge. He told me that there were many children in need of medical treatment unavailable in the region and he asked whether I would be able to organise some hospital beds in Britain.

'If you can do this,' he said in his charming French accent, 'I can guarantee that the International Red Cross will assist with the evacuation and we will provide our full support.'

I told him that I would send a message to Duncan who would in turn speak to his medical colleagues. A few days later, Daniel Enders was replaced as Head of Office by an Italian woman called Alessandra Morelli. Having heard of my intentions, she wanted to know how I planned to enter Kosovo now that the borders were closed.

I shrugged. 'To be honest I have no idea, but it's vital these medicines reach the children.' I was expecting her to tell me that it was a bad idea but instead she said that she had received a report that over 100 refugees were supposedly trapped in the forest just across the border and she suggested I try and locate them.

'As you know, the UNHCR have been pulled out of the region so there's nothing we can do. If you happen to find them perhaps you can try to bring them out.'

Later that same evening I was summoned to the OSCE office by John Mattson, an American who worked with Bill Foxton. Bill was waiting to speak to me and once I sat down, John left the room.

'I know about your plans,' said Bill, 'and although I don't doubt there is a shortage of medicines, it is just as important that you use the mission to highlight what's happening. You can focus on the kids who've been wounded and those who'll be at risk if nothing's done to protect them. You managed to bring a spotlight to Mostar so I'm sure you can do the same in Kosovo; with your reputation people will take notice.' He popped his head around the door as if to ensure that no one was listening.

'We've had reports that Junik is virtually surrounded and will soon be taken by the Serbs, so you'll need to get in and out fairly quickly. Of course the only way to get there at the moment is across the mountains but the Serbs have tightened their security to prevent smuggling of arms by the KLA. I suggest that you would be best to cross the border at night to avoid Serb patrols. Artan, my interpreter, will take you to Tropoje and someone will meet you there and arrange an escort for you. I'll give you a long range walkie-talkie so that we can keep in touch and if you come across the refugees let me know and we'll arrange to meet you at the border.'

I was very surprised to be offered this kind of support from what was in effect a government agency and I said so.

'You must not mention this to anyone and if you get captured do not, under any circumstances, reveal who gave you the radio. It would cause an international incident.'

On the eve of the convoy's departure, we were warned that bandits were operating in the area and that they might target the vehicles. Bill suggested the volunteers leave after dark; they would then drive straight to Fierze to await the early ferry.

Gathering in the gloom of the reception area we said our goodbyes. Marie, an Irishwoman who lived not far from me in Brighton, admitted that before leaving Britain she had begun to have doubts. 'But actually I'm delighted that I came,' she said, giving me a warm hug. 'It's been an amazing experience and I wouldn't have missed it for the world!' Karen was in tears, worried about leaving me behind and concerned for my safety.

'I'll be fine. I'll deliver the medicines and then come straight home.'

21 | DANGEROUS CROSSING

THE MUFFLED SOUND OF explosions echoed from the rugged mountain range that loomed before me. These 'Accursed Mountains' run the entire length of the Kosovo border from Montenegro to Macedonia. Spectacular and virtually impenetrable, a few high passes link the small number of farmsteads to the valleys below. The landscape is savage and journeys are measured in days rather than hours. As I reached the tent above Padesh, the distant explosions reminded me of Bosnia and I hesitated, almost overwhelmed with the familiar sense of trepidation and doubt.

I entered the tent dragging a bag filled with antibiotics, dressings and liquid paracetamol destined for the besieged hospital across the border. Originally set up by Médecins Sans Frontières as a rest station for the sick and exhausted refugees fleeing from the conflict, the tent was now serving as a refuge for the Kosovo Liberation Army. Around two dozen soldiers were sprawled across the floor while an older man in army fatigues was heating some coffee on a camping stove.

'Angel of Mostar!' he declared with a smile.

I was surprised that they were expecting me. This was an isolated region in a country with a poor communications system. It turned out that Avdyl was the father of Artan, Bill's interpreter. He usually worked in the Ujeze Highland close to Padesh but since Médecins Sans Frontières pulled out he also took care of the rest station. A few of the soldiers gathered around us and I noticed they wore sneakers instead of boots and their uniforms were mismatched. The badges on their upper sleeves bore a twin black-headed eagle against a red background with the letters UCK (*Ushtria Climintare e Kosovos*) embroidered in yellow; this was the official badge of the Kosovo Liberation Army. Kalashnikov rifles, grenades and ammunition belts were littered across the floor.

'It is an honour to meet you,' said one of the soldiers, speaking in French. 'You have saved many lives.'

I thanked him and gratefully accepted a cup of sweet Turkish coffee. Having no idea when or with whom I would be continuing my journey, I asked Avdyl to enlighten me but he simply shrugged.

Stepping outside to find the toilet, I soon realised it was non existent and headed towards some foliage on the brow of the hill. In the distance I could hear the sound of shelling and occasional gunfire, but apart from the soft murmur of voices

Padesh.

coming from the tent, the immediate area was quiet. Dusk was approaching and by the time I returned, an oil lamp had been lit, casting shadows across the canvas.

My rucksack had been placed on Avdyl's camp bed where he insisted I should sleep. I was debating whether to remove my outer clothing when another group of soldiers arrived. Their commander was in his late twenties with a thin tanned face and heavy lidded eyes. He had shoulder-length brown hair and carried a Guryanov machine gun. A large hunting knife hung from his belt. Unlike his colleagues, he wore green camouflage uniform and strong army boots. With bandoleers of ammunition across his chest, he reminded me of a character played by Sylvester Stallone.

'Rambo,' I declared smiling, and to my surprise he nodded and held out his hand. Soldiers of the KLA used pseudonyms in order to protect their families and this was the name he had chosen for himself. We shook hands and following a short discussion with the caretaker, Rambo asked me some questions. Speaking in German, he wanted to know how and where I intended crossing into Kosovo. I explained that I was was supposed to be travelling with an escort to Junik. After briefing his men, whose eyes were red from strain and fatigue, Rambo announced we were leaving.

As we made our way along the mountain ridge, two of the soldiers carried the heavy bag of medicines between them on a stick. I found it hard going but Rambo reached out to help me whenever the track became too steep. The light was beginning to fade and it was becoming difficult to see. We stepped around a dead mule with a bullet wound in its flank and fresh blood stained the stony ground on which it lay, indicating that it had died quite recently. After a while we stopped to rest and Rambo offered me a cigarette but feeling somewhat breathless, I declined. As he inhaled the smoke, he cupped the lighted end within his hand to shield the glow from snipers.

When we set off again, I caught a glimpse of the soldiers struggling along with my bag. We kept going for a while and when we finally stopped to take a rest, Rambo went on alone to scout the area. I had no idea how, where or when we would cross the border and I realised that I had put my faith in a complete stranger.

I could hear the drone of a HIP 8 helicopter, used by the Serbs for reconnaissance of the border. The tension rose. Rambo reappeared and in hushed tones he explained that the appearance of the helicopter made the crossing far too dangerous. He ordered his men to turn around and I found myself following him back down the track. I was disappointed and frustrated, impatient to proceed with my mission. When we arrived back at the tent I asked him when he thought it might be safe to try again but he just shrugged.

While the soldiers climbed into sleeping bags or covered themselves with rough army blankets, I lay on the camp bed wondering how to get a message home. I wanted to let Duncan and my family know that I hadn't yet crossed the border. I had the radio Bill had given me but I was loath to use it in case the men became suspicious. They trusted very few people and often refused requests from journalists wanting to interview or accompany them, on the grounds that information could be passed to the enemy. I decided to try and sleep for I was exhausted.

I awoke the next morning to find Avdyl heating a small pot of coffee while Rambo paced up and down. The tent was virtually empty now and I went outside and found a tap where I brushed my teeth and splashed my face with the icy water.

'You have friends close by in the valley,' said Rambo appearing alongside me. I looked at him blankly.

'Italian journalists who say they know you.'

I recalled three Italians who had turned up at the office of the OSCE in Bajram Curri. They came to interview Bill Foxton and when they asked him whether anything interesting was happening in the area, he suggested they talk to me. They were apparently hoping to follow some KLA soldiers into Kosovo but as this was the intention of most journalists in northern Albania, I hadn't taken much notice.

'I remember meeting them,' I said,' but they're not part of my mission.'

'We are going to join them in the valley,' he said, dunking his head in the icy cold water. I collected my rucksack and thanked Avdyl for his hospitality. It was mid-July and the sun shone brightly as we strode across the Alpine landscape.

We made our way into the valley where a few soldiers were sitting around. A number of small fires had been lit and the smell of wood smoke scented the air. The journalists were sitting slightly apart from the soldiers, beneath some pine trees on the edge of the forest. Rafaelli Cirielo, a slightly built man with dark hair, invited me to join them. Before sitting down, I removed the heavy blue waistcoat in which I carried the walkie-talkie, my passport, a penknife and two disposable cameras. Around my neck were the dog tags bearing my name and blood group. He asked me when I intended crossing the border.

'We are really hoping they'll take us with you,' said Rafaelli. 'We've wasted a lot of time getting here and now we're being told that we just have to wait.'

Gian Micalessin and his colleague Fausto Bilaslavo worked for an Italian television station. They both had glasses and were wearing light grey waistcoats with bulging pockets and baseball caps turned back to front.

Rafaelli produced a tin of tuna and some bread and using water that had been heated over a fire, I made some instant coffee from sachets I carried in my backpack. It was obvious that we would have a long wait, as there would be no chance of crossing during daylight. A low hanging mist enveloped the valley so I pulled on my jacket and using my rucksack as a pillow, I lay down to sleep. When I awoke a few hours later I found Rambo huddled in conversation with a group of young soldiers.

'We'll be leaving shortly,' he said and suggested I gather my belongings. 'The medicines you brought will be taken ahead of us on the back of a mule.'

The journalists asked if they could follow me and Rambo agreed, on condition that they keep their cameras hidden. The soldiers would not want to be filmed for fear of Serb reprisals against their families.

Kosovans who had been working abroad were now returning to fight and northern Albania had become a launch pad for some of these units. Training camps had been set up in Kukes, Bajram Curri and Tropoje. They included disused or appropriated commercial properties including a factory and a hotel. Rambo, whose real name was Abedin Sadrija, had been living and working in Germany until the recent escalation in fighting had brought him home.

Following a rag tag band of new recruits, we made our way along a shepherd's trail towards the high mountain meadows. The jagged crags and snow-capped peaks of the mountains rose above us, in some places 6000 feet high. According to local folklore, the area was created by the devil himself, unleashed from hell for a single day of mischief. It was late afternoon by the time we reached the mountain ridge that separated Albania from Kosovo and beyond the ridge was a forested valley framed by steep limestone cliffs.

We took cover in the elephant grass where we would wait until nightfall before moving on. Rambo went ahead to scout the area and by the time he returned it was so dark I could barely see. He signalled for us to follow and keeping our heads and shoulders low to avoid being spotted we ran as fast as possible through the long grass.

As we reached the open meadow there was little cover and I tried not to stumble as we scuttled along in single file. All of a sudden I found myself lying flat on the ground with Rambo's hand across my mouth.

'Serb patrol,' he hissed in my ear.

Small pinpricks of light were moving up ahead and I held my breath, wondering what would happen if we were caught. A couple of young Americans had recently been discovered in Pristina without visas and were subsequently arrested. They were released again after a few days – but they were not travelling with members of the KLA. I had been advised to wear dark clothing and had replaced my white T-shirt with a blue one. I knew that in the dark I could easily be mistaken for a soldier and I was terrified, knowing the Serbs might shoot first and ask questions later.

When it was safe to move on, I looked around for Rambo but he had disappeared. Rafaelli, Gian and Fausto were still with me but we had no idea which way to go. Bill had been adamant that the area was not mined but I couldn't help thinking of Paddy in Bosnia who had lost both his legs. The others were thinking of turning back but I wasn't sure what to do. I really didn't want to give up but travelling without a guide would be too dangerous.

Suddenly there was a noise, something between a bird call and a whistle and Rambo appeared. He had come back to find us and as he stood in silhouette against the night sky, I was reminded once again of his namesake. He took hold of my arm and with the others following behind, we crossed the border into Kosovo.

Rambo was much fitter and faster than I and it would have been hard to keep up with him if he hadn't kept a tight grip on my hand. Brambles and branches tore my face and hands as I followed him blindly through the forest. As he pulled me down a slope, I caught my foot on a tree root and hit the ground with a thump, twisting my ankle. Before I had time to complain I was hauled unceremoniously to my feet. Rambo wrapped his bandoleer around my wrist and the bullets dug into my flesh but this left him free to carry his gun in both hands.

I felt as though I were in a painful waking dream, stumbling on and on through the darkness but seemingly getting nowhere. I tried to ignore the throbbing pain in my ankle as I was pulled along the banks of unseen rivers and streams, over slippery rocks and through the icy water.

We continued this way for an hour before the column stopped and signalled for us to rest. I immediately sank to the ground, not even bothering to remove my rucksack and I cursed myself for wearing the wrong kind of shoes. They were made of canvas, more suited for the beach, but my boots had been stolen in Bajram Curri.

It was nearly midnight and I was dismayed to learn there was still another four or five hours travelling before we reached our destination. The years of smoking and lack of proper exercise were taking their toll. I was exhausted and wanted to rest awhile but when the signal came to leave, Rambo put my rucksack across his shoulders and pulled me along behind him.

As we penetrated deeper into the forest, he used a special torch with a diffused light and although this improved matters a great deal, even he was beginning to tire. The journalists were still with us, somehow managing to carry their camera equipment as well as their personal kit.

We had left the valley at seven in the evening and it was 4.30am when we finally arrived. By this time I was unable to bear any weight on my foot so I was helped by Rambo and the officer, who half carried me along a dirt track to a farmhouse.

The soldiers went off down the road, leaving us at the door. It was dark inside as there was no electricity and Rambo explained that Serb forces had cut the local power supplies. He led us upstairs where there were two bedrooms. The journalists went into one of the rooms and I took the other but to my surprise Rambo followed me inside.

I pointed to the fact that there was only one bed but he just shrugged and took off his jacket. Having left my shoes at the front door as is the local custom, I removed my heavy waistcoat and stretched out on the bed. The yielding comfort of the soft mattress felt like heaven beneath my aching limbs, and I was already drifting off to sleep when Rambo climbed in beside me.

22 | 'WELCOME TO KOSOVO'

WHEN I AWOKE I went downstairs and found that my shoes had been washed and were drying in the sun; an old Albanian custom, typical of the warm hospitality shown to guests. Rambo was sitting outside in the garden talking to an old man beneath the shade of a tree. The man was wearing the traditional white domed cap of an ethnic Albanian and Rambo explained that he and his wife were refugees who were staying at the farmhouse.

I sat down beside them and in a faltering voice the old man told me how Serb paramilitary police had driven him and his wife from their home. The tanks had surrounded their village while soldiers set light to his house and then burned his cattle. They had walked for miles with what little they could carry, eventually reaching this farm on the outskirts of Junik where they were given refuge. He told me of his relief that his children and grandchildren were living in Switzerland. He had angina and the medication he needed was no longer available so his health was suffering. His face was brown and wrinkled and he gazed at me with watery blue eyes.

'I don't expect to live much longer,' he said, 'Kosovo is dying so I may as well die too. I only wish that I could have kissed our grandchildren, just once.'

'There will soon be intervention,' I said, trying to instill some hope. 'The British Prime Minister said they will not allow another Bosnia to happen.'

The old man patted my hand. '*In Sh'Alla*,' he said, 'Let it be God's will.'

We were called in to breakfast and sat on cushions around a low wooden table. The farmer's wife served flat bread, sheep's yoghurt and a plate of fried green peppers, which we ate with our hands.

'What happens next?' asked Rafaelli, licking the salt crystals from his fingers.

'You will be taken to Junik,' said Rambo. 'What you do then is up to you.'

As the farmer's wife handed me a glass of sweet black tea I asked Rambo whether he would be coming with us.

'Of course,' he replied, seeming surprised by my question. 'My orders are to help you accomplish your mission. I will be with you the whole time.'

'We would like to film Sally in Junik if possible,' said Gian.

Rambo shrugged. 'You aren't my responsibility. I'll take you to meet the commander and he will decide.'

A car pulled up the track alongside the house and we thanked our hosts for their hospitality. I climbed into the front of the rusty old vehicle, which had a bullet hole through the windscreen and Rambo and the journalists squeezed into the back. The driver informed us that there were snipers up ahead and that we would have to travel at top speed. I couldn't help wondering what top speed might be for such an old banger and inadvertently slid further down into my seat. The car backfired as we pulled away causing me to duck, and we were careening down the bumpy track towards the town.

Once again I was reminded of Mostar, experiencing the same cold tingling on the back of my neck as I wondered whether a sniper was about to pull the trigger. I was greatly relieved when we finally reached the town and the driver slowed down to light a cigarette.

Junik is a small town in south-west Kosovo, situated between the districts of Decani and Gjakove. Being so close to Albania, the town was a major staging post for the KLA and the Serbs had recently begun a major offensive into the area. By the time we arrived they had virtually succeeded in surrounding the remote mountain stronghold and the only way in or out was across the mountains.

We pulled up outside a large concrete building set back from the road, which seemed to be the command headquarters. The walls were pockmarked with shrapnel and there were bullet holes in the glass. Young men in combat fatigues were hanging around the parking area and in the hallway, watching us closely. After about ten minutes we were taken upstairs to an office on the first floor where a man came forward to greet us. Gani Shehu, a former officer in the JNA, (Yugoslav Army) was about 30, clean-shaven with a rounded face and thick dark hair and unlike the other soldiers, he was dressed in a grey flying suit.

With Rambo interpreting, the journalists requested permission to visit the local hospital and talk to the doctors and if possible they also wanted to interview some officers from the KLA. We were offered glasses of warm Coke while Gani explained that the only hospital inside the town was a small health centre just along the road. As for meeting with KLA officials, he said that would have to be discussed.

'We will find you somewhere to stay,' said Rambo. 'In the meantime, he wants to talk to Miss Becker.'

When the journalists had gone, we were served with Turkish coffee and Gani addressed me directly in English. He was actually an Albanian American from Manhattan, a former lawyer fluent in English, German and French. He had returned to Kosovo as Chairman of the LDK, the Democratic Party led by Rugova and was now commander of the battalion based in Junik. He looked at me and ran a hand through his shock of black hair.

'I know of your work Miss Becker and we are glad that you have chosen to help us. There is a shortage of everything so we are very grateful for the medical supplies that came in last night. If we can assist with your mission in any way, please do not hesitate to let me know. In the meantime you are invited to our military canteen for lunch.' He stood up and escorted me to the door.

'Welcome to Kosovo.' he said.

As we walked along the street, I noticed that many of the buildings bore the battle scars of war. Some of the roofs were completely destroyed and one house had a hole blown through the side.

The mess hall was lined with long wooden tables and benches and as soon as I sat down I received a bowl of thick soup and large hunk of bread. A soldier dressed in the green camouflage and black beret of the KLA, came and joined us. He had short black hair, a neatly-trimmed beard and glasses.

'Miss Becker, it is a pleasure to meet you,' he said, shaking my hand. 'My name is Lum Haxhiu.' Formerly a political prisoner, Lum, a writer and poet, had spent several years living in Denmark and was now the KLA's 'Morale Officer'.

A couple of weeks earlier, he and Gani Shehu had hosted a meeting in Junik with Richard Holbrooke, the United States envoy who had come to Kosovo to negotiate a peace agreement between the Serbs and the ethnic Albanians. Upon his departure, Holbrooke admitted that the meeting was unsuccessful. Lum spoke fluent English, which was a relief to me after struggling with Rambo in German.

'How do you hope to help us?' he asked, leaning a worn Kalashnikov against the table.

'I don't know exactly,' I replied. 'I wanted to bring you the medical supplies but I am also here to highlight what is happening. When atrocities take place, the media flock here and you have the ear of the world, but as soon as the journalists disappear, people forget that the innocent are still suffering.'

'But how do we change that?' He tore off a piece of bread and dipped it in the soup. 'We have requested help from the international community for a very long time but no one cares. As a result we have been forced to take up arms in order to fight for our freedom.' I nodded, for I knew only too well how hard it was to make people listen.

'But you can't expect to beat the Serb army with a handful of guns and grenades,' I said. 'I know that your soldiers are prepared to lay down their lives for Kosovo but that won't save your people. In Bosnia it was the media that eventually made people sit up and take notice. In order to get help, you need to highlight the effects of the war on the women and children.' He looked thoughtful.

'That wouldn't be easy,' he said finally. 'Most of the children are living in cellars and basements on the outskirts of town.'

'What about those in need of medical treatment?' I asked.

We can't get them to the hospital because snipers watch the roads so it is extremely dangerous.' said Lum.

'That's exactly the kind of thing I want to highlight.'

'But you would need to travel through Serb territory in order to reach them.' I told him that I was willing to take the risk.

'And suppose you get hurt, or even killed?' he asked, looking straight into my eyes. I shrugged.

'Well that would certainly get their attention.' He nodded slowly and stood up. Lifting the rifle onto his shoulder he shook my hand and told me we would meet again. When he had gone, Rambo took my hand.

'I'm honoured to have been chosen to accompany you, Sally.' He said. 'I understood some of what was said and I will do my best to protect you.' I smiled and thanked him as we walked out onto the street.

Around the corner we came to a house built in the style of a Swiss chalet. It was two storeys high and backed onto a large garden where chickens were roaming. A cow pulled lazily at the grass and in a shaded corner of the garden five old people sat around a large wooden table while a cooking pot rattled on a wood burning stove.

Alberta, a tall slim woman about my age, explained that she was looking after the place for her neighbours, who had gone abroad. She lived next door with her husband and sister but her daughter was living in Britain and she had been unable to make contact for several months. All the phone lines were down and the post no longer operated. I suggested she give me her daughter's address so I could pass on a message.

She showed us into the house which was bright and airy with modern furnishings and I smiled with delight when I saw the shower room. Then they told me there was no water supply to the building. Instead she fetched me a bucket of hot water heated on the stove. Apart from clean clothes and underwear, I was carrying a toothbrush, toothpaste and shower gel. Stripping off my clothes, I rinsed the dust from my body and washed my hair. I dressed in a clean pair of jeans and a white T-shirt but decided not to wear shoes as my ankle was swollen. Alberta looked horrified when she saw I was barefoot and she rushed to fetch me a pair of slippers, kept on the doorstep for guests.

Sitting in the sunshine beneath an azure sky, it was hard to believe that the town was the target of an offensive. They told me that the shelling usually went on day and night and this was the first peaceful day in weeks. She invited us to join them for some chicken soup and I guiltily eyed the hens pecking in the grass, wondering if they were related to the contents of my bowl.

When we finished eating, Rambo took me to meet his family, with whom the Italian journalists were staying. I was shown over the house by three giggling teenage girls and was served with the inevitable sweet Turkish coffee. I noticed that Rambo turned his small cup upside down on the saucer when he had finished and when I asked him about it, he told me that his uncle could read the coffee grains left in the cup. He suggested I turn my own cup over so his uncle could read mine too. After a few minutes an old man joined us and Rambo spoke to him in Albanian. The old man nodded and began peering into my cup though it seemed a long time before he finally spoke.

'You have a long and arduous journey before you and there will be children involved. 'He said, 'Success will be the eventual outcome, but in months to come you will suffer and the suffering will take its toll.' When he looked into Rambo's cup he spoke in Albanian so I couldn't understand.

Later that day we were driven to a hospital situated on the outskirts of Junik. The journalists did not accompany us and Rambo explained that they were not trusted. In one of the wards there were about twelve men, some of whom had lost a limb and others with stomach or chest wounds. Bekim, who was 20, had a bullet wound that had paralysed part of his neck and shoulder. The doctor in charge informed me of the grave lack of medication. He showed me the store cupboard in which there were just a few packets of antibiotics and a small number of dressings.

'We have no anaesthetics at all and the only medicines we have are what was brought in last night.' His eyes were ringed with dark circles from lack of sleep. 'Serb attacks have reduced the local population from 12,000 to 2000. Those who are most vulnerable, like the elderly, the women and the children, have been moved to safer places and in some areas they are sheltering underground. Apart from the aid that can be smuggled through the lines, nothing has reached this area for a very long time.'

I was approached by a young blind man with black hair and a pale thin face. Speaking perfect English, he told me that he had been arrested by Serb para-militaries and taken to the local police station. During the interrogation his tormentors would silently creep up on him. He had been detained for two days while his mother continuously begged for his release.

He assured me that there was no reason for his arrest but they continued to harass him in this way every couple of weeks. Eventually, he, his mother and his sister had left their village and travelled to Junik, where he now worked for the hospital. He wanted me to organise visas for himself and his family to go abroad but I explained that this was not possible.

'But you evacuate the sick and wounded children,' he said. 'We have seen you on television and read about you in newspapers. I'm only 21 and I am blind.'

'An official evacuation wouldn't be possible from here,' I said,' the situation is totally different.'

'But you managed to do it in Bosnia,' he said. I tried to explain.

'The only way to obtain an exit visa here is through the embassy in Belgrade. I understand how difficult things must be for you but I don't want to give you false hope. The only way out of here is across the mountains into Albania and for you, this would not only be extremely difficult but also foolish.' He agreed that he would not be able to attempt such a journey but gave me his name and a contact address, in case I could think of a way to help him in the future.

Due to the extensive media coverage, people tended to assume that I had some special means of getting people out of besieged areas. Of course that wasn't true; there was no Ivan Bagarić here; and unlike the larger aid agencies, we did not have unlimited funding and government support.

On our return to Junik, the driver stopped the car on the only stretch of road where I could get a signal and I quickly sent a message to Bill. Using the call sign 'Oscar Alpha' assigned to me, I told him that I had reached my destination. We arrived back at the chalet to find Lum Haxhiu waiting with three officers. Lum explained that he had made a call to Smolice, a small village about 30 miles away.

'The journalists have been refused access,' said Lum, 'but the Angel of Mostar is welcome.' One of the men, a commander, leaned towards me as Lum spoke, looking hard into my eyes.

'The area is very dangerous. The journey will have to be made across country as it is surrounded by Serb forces and you may have to walk part of the way.' I thought of my ankle but decided not to mention it.

'We have sick and wounded children living in the area who are seriously in need of medical treatment. We will send our own cameraman in with you and afterwards he will give you the film so that you have a record of what you encounter.' I nodded and after a short discussion between Rambo and the men, they left us alone. That night I lay in bed listening to the sound of explosions. I was awake for some time, wondering what the next day would bring.

We ate breakfast outside in the sun with Alberta and her family. She had heard about our forthcoming journey and was very concerned, insisting that I eat plenty, she was afraid I might not get another chance. After a meal of yoghurt, fried peppers and flat bread, we went to see the Italians but Rambo insisted that I keep quiet about the meeting the previous night.

When we arrived, they were in the process of interviewing a general who was reported to have been killed in the fighting. He told them that the KLA was being restructured and he didn't yet know what rank or position he would hold. I was surprised that he had agreed to talk to the journalists, especially as he was supposed to be dead. Though perhaps there was propaganda value in that very fact.

23 | THE PIED PIPER

THE FOLLOWING EVENING LUM Haxihu pulled up outside our house in an old Yugo and I climbed in beside him. Rambo sat behind us with a soldier carrying a small video camera. As he drove, Lum talked about his son who had fallen ill when he was just a few months old. He had taken the boy to see a Serb doctor who prescribed some medication but a short while later the baby died.

'An Albanian specialist told me that my son had been diagnosed incorrectly and that the medicine had killed him,' said Lum, his eyes fixed on the road ahead.

After a few minutes we came to one of the many check points set up by the KLA. Two soldiers waved us through with the victory salute. These checkpoints were placed every few kilometres along the route and after some discussion with a soldier at the third check point, Lum informed us that we wouldn't need to cover any ground on foot after all, as the soldiers had secured a route by road. Instead we drove at top speed along country lanes, often without lights as we passed through Serb-controlled territory.

We eventually reached a small village and Lum parked the car outside a house damaged by shelling. I followed Rambo down some dark concrete steps into a large cellar and in the candlelight I could see about 100 faces staring up at me, most of them children. Rambo explained that they were forced to shelter there beneath the rubble, afraid to go above ground for fear of shelling and snipers. The room was freezing cold and smelt of damp and upon sitting down we found that even the mattresses were wet. A baby was planted in my lap, gazing up at me placidly, a dummy protruding from his mouth. I wondered if he had ever known anything other than this dank cellar.

When I asked how they managed to eat, Rambo explained that whenever there was a lull in the fighting, the women would race upstairs to try and bake some bread in the stone oven outside. They were often forced back underground by gunfire or rocket propelled grenades and the bread would be ruined. As a result they were all thin and malnourished, their faces pale from lack of sunlight and their lips cracked and sore from the cold and damp.

Tears stung my eyes and I saw that Rambo was also crying for despite his macho appearance he was highly emotional, especially where his people were concerned. I felt so helpless sitting there in my clean clothes surrounded by the desperate faces. I looked up to find the soldier filming me and although I was aware of them all watching I knew I had to speak.

'I am here in a cellar beneath what used to be someone's home, surrounded by women and children living in the most appalling conditions. They are afraid to go out into the sunlight ...' As if on cue, a mortar exploded overhead, followed by rapid machine gun fire. One or two of the children and even some of the adults began to cry, although the baby continued to stare at me unconcerned.

'These people are being ignored by the outside world while they sit here, day after day, night after night, waiting and praying for NATO to save them.'

As we prepared to leave, the women gave me a hug and thanked me for coming. An old man took my face in his hands and kissed my forehead, causing the tears to stream down my face as I climbed the stairs. I knew that those frightened faces, their paleness emphasised in the candlelight, would continue to haunt me for a very long time.

We drove on to other villages, where each trapdoor led to another cellar filled with old men, women and children and as we entered I would hear the whispered Albanian words '*Angelli i Mostarit*'.

Finally, when it was completely dark, we arrived in Smolica. The village originally consisted of 70 homes but most had been destroyed. We went to one of the two remaining houses and were introduced to a family who welcomed us inside. Rambo offered to take a photo of Lum and I sitting together on the couch and I passed him one of my cameras. There was a knock on the door and some soldiers entered, all of them dressed in black. They were members of an elite commando unit who were using the house as their headquarters. I guessed they were members of AFRK (Armed Forces of the Republic of Kosovo) who were loyal to Ibrahim Rugova. Rugova, who had been President of Kosovo since 1991, had followed a policy of peaceful resistance to the Serbs until the massacres in Drenica earlier that year. Unlike the KLA, these men were professionals, moving in smaller groups and usually avoiding contact with outsiders.

There were a couple of regular soldiers staying at the house and one of them sat down beside me and asked if I could help his family. Ardi's parents were in Switzerland but the Serbs had refused permission for his sister and two brothers to join them. Their house had recently been shelled whilst the three children were inside and they had all been wounded, the boys quite seriously.

'Khalil, the eldest, has infected wounds where his arms were torn by shrapnel and Musa was badly burned. My sister wasn't really hurt but she can't stay here alone because I have to fight and cannot take care of her.'

I glanced at Lum who shrugged and said, 'If you think you can help them, if you believe you can get them reunited with their parents in Switzerland that would be fine,' he said.

'There are others who need help too,' said Ardi, 'I have a friend; an officer called Nik Hiseni whose child is in need of an operation.' I looked at Rambo who immediately nodded.

'We can take them out the way we came in,' he said.

We stayed up talking with the soldiers for a while and they told us that earlier that day a fifteen-year-old boy was shot by a sniper. I wondered what kind of monster could pull the trigger knowing he was killing a child. There were loud explosions and the rattle of machine gun fire; we were only about a mile from the front line. Fortunately, the immediate area was shrouded by trees making it relatively safe.

Early the next morning I was taken to Ardi's house to view the damage. We had to run as fast as possible to reach the house as the area was targeted by snipers. The commandos ran alongside me, shielding me from the bullets that ricocheted through the empty streets.

A shell had entered through the roof and shrapnel had exploded in all directions, ripping through wooden beams and becoming embedded in the walls. Once again I was shown the basement of a ruined house where people huddled together in fear. As we left, I saw a missile lying on the ground. It was about five feet long and according to the writing on the side, it was manufactured in Russia. The Geneva Convention banned this kind of artillery so I photographed it, intending to show the type of weapons being used against civilians.

When we returned to the command post, Lum arrived in a jeep and drove us to another village called Nec, where I was introduced to Nik Hiseni, the officer Ardi had mentioned. Aged about 30, he was about the same height as me and was wearing army fatigues and a camouflage cap. Nik's youngest daughter, Doruntina, was sixteen months old. She was suffering from a hernia and when I first saw her she was screaming in pain. She was a lovely baby with rosy cheeks and a mass of blond curls.

As I stopped to consider what I should do, another man joined us. His name was Hili Krasniqi, a good looking man in his late twenties with thick brown hair swept back from his face. Speaking English with a soft accent, he introduced me to his three-year-old daughter Marigona who had short dark hair and a small bow shaped mouth. Her eyes were dark and serious but she grinned with some energy. She had cataracts. Perched on my lap, she peered intently at my face and I could see the milky white patches over her pupils. Whenever the sun appeared from behind a cloud, she would squint.

'I took her to Russia in January for an operation,' said Hili, 'but she had a temperature and couldn't undergo the surgery. I was supposed to take her back in March but war broke out and it became impossible to travel. They tell me that unless she has the operation soon she will go blind. Please, can you help us?'

I told him of the risks, explaining that I had no ceasefire arranged, and no guarantees for their safety. I figured that I could probably arrange an operation once we reached the other side, but as for the journey, I was dependent upon the KLA.

'We are desperate,' said Hili. 'My wife and children are in danger here all the time so we are willing to take the risk.'

I suggested he discuss it with his wife, it was vital that she be made aware of the danger. He went off to speak with a young attractive woman with long dark hair and dark eyes. She was breastfeeding her baby, Arbresha. Their oldest daughter, Miranda, who was five, came and held my hand but Marigona tried to push her away.

Hili soon rejoined us and said that his wife insisted she would rather take a risk on the mountain than continue living in danger and watching her child go blind. He'd also spoken to Nik and his wife Hanna, who felt the same. Nik had gone to call to his parents in Switzerland on an army satellite phone and Lum indicated that we should leave. The families would join us in Junik later.

Valbona's mother, an elderly woman with wisps of grey hair protruding from a headscarf, came to kiss me and thank me for helping her grandchildren. She was crying and I felt wretched for I was being thanked for something I had not yet done.

The children waved as we drove off in the jeep, stopping only once at what seemed to be a farm building used as a mess hall for soldiers. I was offered some suspect meat, which I politely declined. It was 40 degrees outside so I drank some water instead. To my surprise, the journalists appeared, but before they could ask any questions I was whisked back to the jeep. On the way back to Junik, my mind whirled with doubts about the mission that I had just agreed to undertake.

We arrived in Junik to find a family waiting for us at the chalet. Hamez Shala was an engineer and his wife an architect but neither had worked for several years. Hamez began to cry as he told me how they had struggled to survive in recent years, both forbidden to work. When war broke out in March they desperately wanted to leave the area but it hadn't been possible. To make matters worse, Besa their two-year-old daughter was deaf; she couldn't hear shelling or gunfire and had to be watched all the time.

'I would prefer to jump into the nearest river with my family than to stay here under these circumstances,' he said. 'Please, will you help us?' I told him that I had no guarantees for their safety but got the now familiar answer.

'We'd rather take that chance than to continue living in fear,' he said.

I tried to explain that the evacuation had not been planned, that we would be dependent on others but he insisted that if I refused to help them, he and his family would perish. Despite my reservations I agreed to take them and they quickly left to gather some belongings from their home on the outskirts of town.

I was told to be ready by five pm so I dressed in a pair of jeans, a T-shirt and my waistcoat, which still held some of my kit. My other clothes, water, and toiletries I carried in my rucksack. Rambo arrived and we went to meet the others who were waiting on the edge of the town with some mules.

Ardi was there with a group of soldiers and three children. Khalil, who looked about thirteen, was tall and rangy with short brown hair and his arms were swathed in bandages. Musa, his eleven-year-old brother, was grinning broadly, despite the severe burns to his face. Lira, the youngest, was eight years old. She was wearing a grey spotted track suit and across her forehead was an angry looking scar. The three of them giggled as I attempted to greet them in Albanian. When Ardi was leaving he took my hand and I saw he was wearing a gold ring with a large red stone.

'I entrust you with their lives.' he said solemnly. 'When you reach the other side, please contact our parents in Switzerland so they can be reunited.'

He handed me a piece of paper with his parent's details and I put it inside my waistcoat. He hugged the three youngsters and as he walked away Lira slipped her hand in mine, reminding me of the great responsibility I had accidentally assumed.

Hili was saying goodbye to his family and Valbona was crying as he kissed the sleeping baby in her arms. Miranda, the eldest, was oblivious to the seriousness of the moment, gazing fondly at the mules being loaded with the meagre supplies the families had brought with them. Marigona just stood there peering up at me with a solemn expression on her face.

At that moment Nik arrived with Hanna and their three children. Dede, the eldest, was twelve, with a thick mop of blond hair. He stood quietly to one side while his sister Drita, a beautiful ten-year-old with long dark hair, hugged her father, tears rolling down her cheeks. Doruntina was crying so Hannah placed a dummy in her mouth to soothe her.

'Time to go,' called Rambo, starting up the hill. The Shala family walked alongside him. They carried no belongings. Hamez told me that a sniper was now operating in the area where they lived, so it had been too dangerous to collect anything after all.

Bekim was seated on one of the mules, a jacket draped across his wounded shoulder. He was escorted by his younger brother who was dressed in denim jeans and a T-shirt and carried a rifle. We were also joined by a large middle-aged woman dressed in black who was accompanied by Dino, her sixteen-year-old nephew.

As we prepared to move, the Italian journalists appeared. Gian demanded to know what was happening and when I explained he asked if they could join us. I suggested he talk to Rambo who clearly wasn't happy.

'You have to let us come with you,' said Gian; 'there is no other way out of here.' I took Rambo aside and eventually convinced him to let them tag along. They wanted a couple of mules to carry their equipment but they were told that they would have to wait until we reached the next village.

The soldier had been filming the group and when we passed he gave me the cassette, which I zipped inside my waistcoat together with the disposable cameras. The sun was shining and it was still quite hot as we set off up the hill. Apart from the soldiers, there were 26 of us in all and as we strode along the dusty road, I was reminded of a book I once read called *The Pied Piper* by Nevil Shute. The main character is an elderly man who travels to France on a fishing trip. Germany is at war with Europe and some guests at his hotel ask him to take their children to England. Their harrowing journey proceeds first by train and then on foot and they are joined by other children in need of help along the way.

24 | THE ACCURSED MOUNTAINS

ABOUT AN HOUR INTO the journey we stopped at a small village but there were no mules available for the journalists to hire. We sat down to rest and the mothers gave the children biscuits and water that they carried with them. Gian came over to tell me that mines had been dropped on the border by helicopters the previous night, so we would not be able to continue.

The information had come from two men who appeared to be very drunk so I was sceptical and asked to see the head of the village. I repeated what Gian had said about the mines but he was sure it was just a rumour; in Kosovo information was currency and people thrived on rumours. Gian had begun filming the group and suddenly Rambo shouted for him to put away the camera.

'It's still daylight and the Serbs can see us. Are you crazy? You are deliberately drawing attention to us!' He was shaking with anger, his face bright red and his fists tightly clenched.

'Okay, okay,' said Gian as he lowered his camera. 'But I think you're overreacting.'

Rambo looked as if he might punch him so I stepped in and tried to calm him down. Eventually he backed off but it was clear the two men had become enemies.

Rambo sent a messenger back to Junik with a note for Gani Shehu and while we waited I was approached by an elderly soldier called Chamed who was tall and skinny with a brown, weathered face. Chamed insisted that he knew for a fact that the rumour about the mines was simply not true; several of his colleagues had crossed the border the previous night. Half an hour passed before Gani himself appeared in a white jeep. I asked him what he thought we should do and taking me to one side, he lowered his voice.

'I do not think it is likely that mines have been dropped at the border but I cannot be sure,' he said.

'Where is our escort?' I inquired, noticing that the soldiers were no longer with us. His discomfort was obvious.

'They'll meet you en route,' he said, 'they have gone on ahead to assess the situation.'

I nodded, fully aware that the decision was being left to me. I returned to the group and told them what I knew.

'I can't guarantee there aren't any mines. All I can do is to cross the area ahead of you and if I make it across, you can follow in my footsteps. Those of you who would rather not take the risk must make your decision quickly. We have to get moving.'

'You're being totally irresponsible,' said Gian. I spun around to face him.

'Junik will soon be overrun by Serb forces. Surely these people have more chance of crossing the border than surviving a Serb offensive? They have to make their own decision. No one invited you to come; in fact you were the one who insisted there was no other way out. If it's safer to stay then why haven't you turned back?'

Rambo announced that the women wanted to continue. Valbona, who was just buttoning her blouse after breastfeeding the baby spoke confidently. 'We trust you and we will follow wherever you go.'

The other women nodded in agreement but Hamez Shala was obviously not sure what to do. He wanted guarantees, which I couldn't give. I told him that if he had doubts then he should take his family home. He said that he would prefer to do that but his wife wanted to go on. We were losing time and it would be getting dark before we reached the border. I had not forgotten how difficult the inward journey had been and I didn't relish the thought of trying to find our way through the forest in the dark. I was hoping to reach the border by nightfall where we could wait until it was safe enough to cross.

'It's time to go,' I said.

Amongst the group was a man in his forties called Sadedin who was helping to lift the children onto the mules and making sure the cumbersome wooden saddles were secure. The sun was rapidly disappearing behind the mountains and it was already getting a little cooler. The road soon narrowed to a track that led into the forest. Dusk was falling and the trees looked menacing as they towered above us casting long shadows. I noticed that Khalil flinched each time we heard the sound of an explosion and I put my arm around his thin shoulders to try and reassure him. He was leading the mule that was carrying his brother and sister and my heart went out to him. He was so young yet already he had experienced so much. He was now forced to depend upon a stranger, a foreign woman he didn't even know.

Rambo and I set off with the mule carrying Bekim and behind us rode Marigona, Miranda and Drita. Valbona and Hanna walked alongside them, carrying the babies. They were followed by Hamez and his family together with the widow, who was leaning on her nephew for support. I could just make out the figures of the journalists and Sadedin bringing up the rear.

Large drops of rain began to fall, spattering the leaves, slowly at first and then faster and heavier. Digging out my jacket from the rucksack, I handed it to Valbona who pulled it on over her shirt. The other women quickly attempted to cover the children but within minutes we were soaked. It was now completely dark and we could hardly see ahead of us. The rain became torrential and the ground became thick, slippery mud. Rambo stopped and shouted that we would have to turn back but we were one third of the way to the top and the thought of giving up now filled me with dismay.

'Can't we take shelter under the trees?' I asked. 'It might not last for long.' He shook his mane of wet hair.

'The children could die out here.'

I felt he was exaggerating. It was wet, but it certainly wasn't cold and I knew we would be safer in this weather. The border patrols would be holed up and the noise of the heavy rain would mask the sound of the mules. I pointed all this out and suddenly to my shock and dismay, Rambo seemed to break down.

'I can't do this any more,' he said, 'because I don't know what's best. I can't make decisions right now because I'm so tired. Please, let's go back.'

Without Rambo to guide us it would be impossible to carry on, so I reluctantly agreed. The whole procession turned around on the narrow path and with the mules slipping and sliding in a mixture of wet mud and clay, we retraced our steps. To my amazement I saw that the journalists were wearing large waterproof capes that covered them from head to toe, whilst the children were all getting soaked.

For what seemed like an eternity, we slipped and stumbled down the mountainside. It was dark and the rain was so heavy that we could barely see so we each held onto the person in front or grasped the tail of a mule. It was nearly midnight when we finally reached Gjocaj, the small village we had passed through earlier. We knocked on the door of an old farmhouse but nobody answered and we huddled together soaking wet and frustrated, desperate to get the children out of the rain. Finally, an old woman pulled back the heavy wooden doors and ushered us inside.

We must have presented quite a sight but she didn't seem surprised by our impromptu arrival. The women and children were taken inside and the men were led upstairs. Mattresses were placed side by side across the floor and once we had stripped the children of their wet clothes, the youngest were tucked beneath blankets on the makeshift beds. It wasn't long before they were all sleeping soundly, exhausted by their adventure.

I helped Khalil to remove his shirt and saw that the dressings on his arms were damp. The wounds were already infected and this would make things worse so I gently peeled away the wet bandages. He stood there bravely while I cleaned and covered his arms with sterile dressings that I carried in my bag. Musa was watching and when I had finished, he reached into a pocket of his jacket and gave me a KLA badge. I realised that I was being given what was probably his prize possession and so I thanked him with a kiss, bringing a sheepish smile to his anxious little face.

One of the women asked me what was going to happen. She said that they were all desperate to continue, afraid that if they gave up and returned to their homes, they might never get another chance to leave. As I prepared to answer her, the rest of the women and the older children gathered round to hear what I had to say.

'Well tonight, we had to travel through the forest in the dark,' I said, crouching down low and blindly feeling my way around the room. 'But tomorrow we will travel in the sunshine.' I stood upright. 'We will be like sunflowers with our heads held high.' The children began to march around the room with their arms swinging and the women responded by laughing and clapping their hands. For months their children had been forced to shelter in the dark, damp cellars away from the snipers, the rockets and grenades.

I realised that my clothes were soaked so I quickly changed into some dry jeans and a T-shirt. My shoes were also wet and I left them beside the door in the hope they might dry off a little by morning. I went upstairs and found the men were already lying down. Some were sleeping but Rambo gestured for me to come to his bedside. He apologised for having lost control and I patted his hand and assured him that it didn't matter.

'You were probably right anyway,' I conceded. 'At least the children are dry now and they'll get some rest. We'll leave early in the morning and try again.'

Rambo nodded and as I quietly headed for the door, I was aware of Gian watching me from his bed across the room.

Downstairs the children were all asleep and in the adjoining room I found their mothers were also in bed. There was a spare place for me so I swallowed a couple of pain killers before wearily lying down and closing my eyes. Everything was spinning around in my head and it wasn't until dawn broke that I was finally able to sleep.

We awoke to find the rain had stopped but heavy grey clouds cast their shadows across the landscape. A group of soldiers were lounging around outside, their mood jubilant as they told us how they had made a successful attack near the border the previous night. I immediately inquired about the mines and one of them assured me that the rumour was untrue. I asked whether any of them had been sent to accompany us but all I received in reply were shrugs. There seemed to be very little order or discipline within the group. As an army, the KLA were lacking co-ordination. We ate breakfast in the courtyard of the house, tearing freshly baked bread from a large flat loaf and dipping it into homemade yoghurt.

Hamez Shala came to tell me that although his wife would prefer to continue, he had decided that she and the children would return with him to Junik. He explained that because of the sniper in Junik they had no spare clothing and what they were wearing was still wet. He made me promise that once I reached the other side I would do what I could to arrange treatment for his daughter Besa.

'The doctors say that there is an operation that will enable her to hear. If you can promise to help us I will find a way for us to get to Albania. But I must be sure, I wouldn't want us to become refugees in Bajram Curri.'

I assured him that if they reached the other side; I would do whatever I could to help. As the mules were loaded, we watched them begin the journey back down the hill. As we prepared to set off I was surprised to see that one of the mules was unable to carry more than one child because Gian's rucksack was tied to the saddle. Rambo was already confronting him about it, so I didn't interfere.

We set off into the forest once again, the path becoming steeper as we climbed. Everyone seemed in good spirits and dappled sunlight was shining through the trees. The ground was wet and occasionally a mule would slip, frightening the children on its back. When one of the mules suddenly took off in the wrong direction, Rambo grabbed the reins, hitting the unfortunate animal on the nose. It reared away from him, nearly throwing the children off its back and I begged him not to hurt it again.

We had been travelling for a couple of hours and it was nearly noon, so having reached a clearing we settled down to rest. The children ate biscuits and drank some water while I wandered off to find a suitable place to send a radio message. Within minutes I made contact with Tony, one of the border monitors on the other side and quickly told him to inform Oscar Charlie Bravo (Bill Foxton) that we would reach our destination in about six hours. As I waited for an answer, the radio began beeping and I realised that the battery was flat. I had no spare batteries but it didn't matter as I wouldn't need to use it again.

Rafaelli joined me on a small plateau from where we could see the group resting beneath the trees. Some of the children were stooping to gather handfuls of wild strawberries, tiny explosions of sweetness. I tried to see if there were any signs of the refugees who were reported to be hiding in the forest but I was sure they would have seen or heard us by now.

Rafaelli asked if he could interview me and when it was over I asked him why the journalists tended to stay at the rear of the group? Why was it that each time I turned around they disappeared behind the trees as though they were playing hide and seek?

'They are professionals,' he explained, 'they are always prepared for an ambush.'

'Is that why they never help with the children?' I asked. 'Everyone else, including you, takes a turn in carrying a child.' He shrugged; obviously not wanting to criticise his colleagues.

It was time to move on, so we lifted the children onto the mules and set off once again. We clambered over jagged rocks and waded through rivers and streams. One of the mules was slipping and sliding as it tried to negotiate a steep bank and the children looked as though they might fall off so Rambo suggested that I sit behind them. He lifted me onto the large wooden saddle and I put my arms tightly around the two youngsters. The mule swayed and seemed about to lose its footing and as soon as we made it up the steep incline I immediately got down, not wanting to add to its burden any longer than necessary.

The journey was arduous, especially where there were rocky inclines that were almost too steep to climb. My calves were aching and my ankle was starting to cause severe pain. I looked around and found a perfect stick, thick and strong and just the right size. As I prepared to go on I could hear the widow's laboured breathing behind me. She was wearing backless shoes, even more inappropriate than my own and her excess weight was making things worse. I sighed and handed her my stick, wishing I hadn't been brought up so well.

En route to Albania. Top to bottom: Rambo; Marigona, Miranda and Drita; Dede after his mother and sisters had been captured; Hanna with Doruntina.

After a while it became apparent that Rambo was lost. Valbona explained that he was not the experienced soldier I had presumed him to be; in fact she said that this was his first visit to Kosovo in seventeen years. Gani had assured me that the soldiers would rejoin us for part of the way, but there was no sign of them. Rambo was convinced they would soon arrive and insisted we wait. An hour passed and still nobody came. No one seemed to know the way. Sadedin suggested that he and Rambo should scout up ahead to see if they could locate the right path.

Shortly after they left, Chamed, the old soldier from the village, appeared through the trees. He was carrying food for the children and as they gathered round him to eat, he assured me that he knew the way to the border and would take us across. Apart from the unimaginable relief, I was touched by the fact that he had decided to follow us.

As we waited for the two men to return, I played with Marigona while her mother sat breastfeeding the baby beneath a tree. I was hot and thirsty, having given away my water bottle, so I went to find a stream. Lying on the bank, I sipped the ice cold water from my hand and it was the most marvellous thing I had ever tasted. I splashed my hair and face and bathed my sore and swollen ankle in the soothing water. The mules grazed, taking advantage of the welcome break.

It was four o'clock by the time the two men returned. Rambo thought that we should wait until dusk before going on but Chamed and I disagreed. We both felt that it made more sense to travel this last section in daylight, the going was already difficult enough. We included all the adults in the discussion and the majority chose to move on immediately, not wanting to continue through the forest after dark.

This part of the mountain was the most difficult and the children were tired. Doruntina was in pain and she cried constantly as Hanna carried her along the narrow path. I gave her my dog tags to play with and they kept her distracted for a while. We were hot and our limbs ached from the relentless steep climb. When we finally reached the edge of the forest, I suggested that Rambo and the other two should keep their weapons hidden in case they were spotted.

Finally, at 6.00pm we came in sight of the ridge that spanned the border. We settled down beneath the trees to wait for nightfall and Gian asked me to explain what was happening for the benefit of the camera. Speaking softly into the microphone I said that we were waiting for darkness before attempting to cross the border into Albania.

'Do you not think that this mission is dangerous?' he asked, pointing the camera at my face. I watched Marigona as she carefully spread a small white cloth on the ground before sitting herself down.

'Yes, of course it's dangerous,' I replied 'but if these children remain in Kosovo they could die.'

Through the trees I spotted Rambo and was surprised to see that he was out in the open brandishing his gun. He had obviously seen something. Then there was the sudden, gut churning rattle of machine-gun fire. I caught a glimpse of the others racing into the undergrowth but somewhere behind me a baby was screaming. I turned and saw Hanna, who was crouched beneath a tree with her two daughters, and as mortars exploded around us and bullets whistled overhead I panicked, unsure what to do. I was afraid that if I told them to run they might get killed but I couldn't just leave them behind. Almost petrified with fear I finally scrambled across to where they were and pushed them to the ground. I managed to shield Drita completely while Hana lay across the baby, who was screaming in terror.

'Mama, Mama!' she called, over and over again and I felt wretched, cursing myself for putting them in danger. I had often come under fire in Bosnia but never when children were with me. They had placed their faith in me and I knew that I had failed them. Tears streamed down my face each time the baby screamed but all I could do was try to protect them and pray they would somehow be saved.

Whenever I attempted to raise my head, another burst of gunfire erupted close by so we were forced to stay where we were. Bullets ripped through the branches, splintering the bark above our heads and soon a helicopter gunship was hovering overhead. I would have to make a decision.

The only options were to run or to surrender. Running would almost certainly draw fire so I decided to surrender, for at least then the others might have a chance. I had to find the courage to get up, knowing that when I did so, I might be killed. Gesturing for them to stay where they were, I took a deep breath and slowly stood up.

25 | UNDER ARREST

I SHOUTED AS LOUD as possible, trying to make myself heard over the sound of the guns. *'Nema putzanja!* Stop shooting.' Amazingly, the guns fell silent. Leaving the cover of the trees, I walked out into the open calling in English 'Operation Angel, humanitarian, women and children!' A man's voice replied from somewhere up ahead.

'Put your hands up and come towards us.' I raised my hands in the air and saw a cluster of green helmets just beyond the ridge. One soldier raised his head slightly and gestured for me to approach. As I climbed the steep hill he became impatient, urging me to hurry up. When I was halfway up, he called for me to remove my waistcoat, which I dropped at my feet before continuing. They must have assumed I was armed, as I reached them I was grabbed and roughly searched and I was told to keep my arms raised until they were sure I presented no threat. I explained that I was accompanying a group of women and children and the first soldier ordered me to call them, assuring me that they would not shoot.

'Hanna, its okay, you can come out,' I called, not sure whether she would hear me.

The soldier shouted in Serbian and then in Albanian and at last I saw Hanna climbing towards us with the children. Once they reached the top, Hanna was searched whilst I was ordered to retrace my steps back down the hill, followed by three of the soldiers. I slipped and fell a couple of times as I was forced at gunpoint to move quickly down the steep grassy slope.

They insisted I walk on ahead of them while they took cover behind the trees, presumably fearing an ambush. After a few minutes, the one who spoke English jabbed at my back with his rifle and told me to call the rest of the group. I decided to use the opportunity to give the men a chance to escape.

'They say that there will be no danger if you come out. They know there are only women and children,' I called, my voice echoing through the forest. There was no response and suddenly the soldier removed a pistol from his belt and held it to the back of my head.

'Tell them if they don't give themselves up now, I will kill you!'

I was so completely overcome with anger that I was no longer frightened and I spun around to face him, my hands upon my hips.

'How dare you threaten me' I said, and cupping my hands to my mouth I shouted as loud as I could,

'Get away; run as fast as you can!'

I expected to feel a bullet slam into my skull but instead he gave me a shove and ordered me to collect the mules. One of them had escaped from where it had been tethered but the other two were standing patiently beneath a tree, still carrying the bags tied to their saddles.

I took their reins and led them back up the hill with the soldiers following behind. It was getting dark and as we approached the top, I saw that Hanna and the children were lying in a small bunker dug into the hillside and that they had been given blankets, food and some water. Doruntina was sleeping but Drita just sat staring straight ahead, tears streaming down her face. Hanna managed to smile at me reassuringly.

'Can I take my bag?' I asked the soldier, gesturing to the small blue rucksack tied to the saddle of one of the mules.

'No, wait,' he replied. I watched as they unloaded all the bags and emptied them onto the ground but I grew worried when I realised that one of them belonged to the journalists; inside was a box of slides and some camera film.

'That isn't mine,' I said quickly, moving towards the contents of my own bag. This one is mine.'

He glanced at me briefly and then collected the items together.

'They aren't mine,' I insisted, worried what the photographs might contain but he ordered me to move away.

I sat on the grass beside the bunker, feeling suddenly chilled. Whether it was the change in temperature, shock, or the after-effects of adrenaline in my system I don't know, but my teeth were chattering and I couldn't stop shivering. A blanket was thrown towards me, which I gratefully wrapped around my shoulders.

'What'll happen now?' I asked the soldier nearest to me. He shrugged.

'We are waiting to speak to our headquarters.'

'Couldn't you just let us continue across the border?' I asked. 'We haven't done anything wrong.'

'Do you have permission to cross?' he asked.

'No, but 15,000 refugees have crossed here recently. What difference would it make if we joined them?'

He just looked at me blankly.

'At least let them go,' I said, gesturing towards Hannah and the children.

'We will wait to speak to headquarters,' he said.

'Have you heard of Operation Angel? We delivered aid to Kosovo a couple of months ago and it was broadcast on Serb television.'

'We've been here a long time and we don't have access to television.' He then started speaking into a hand-held radio.

As I watched the landscape slowly being swallowed up by nightfall, I wondered if the others had managed to escape or whether they were still hiding in the forest. Somehow Hanna had become separated from her son Dede when the attack began and I hoped to God that he was with the others and not alone on the mountain. Now that I had time to think I was again overwhelmed with guilt, asking myself questions to which I didn't have the answers. Should I have refused to attempt the evacuation? Should I have left them to their fate? I was completely exhausted and sat for a while with my head bowed. Eventually one of the soldiers sitting nearby offered me a cigarette, which I accepted gratefully.

'What's happening?' I asked.

'No English' he said. 'Parlez vous Francais?' He told me that they were waiting for the military police to come and take us to Djakovica, the town where their headquarters were based.

Djakovica is the Serbian name for Gjakove, a large town mainly inhabited by ethnic Albanians. The area had recently been surrounded by Serb forces but it was one of the few places that still had electricity and water. I could hear the distant drone of an engine and saw a vehicle mounting the hill. It resembled an armoured personnel carrier but with windows made of plastic, which were flapping in the breeze. Hanna was ordered into the vehicle with the children and she glanced back at me, afraid we might be separated. Her English was limited, and I spoke no Albanian but I tried to assure her that I would do my best to stay with them.

Inside the vehicle were two benches running lengthways either side. Hanna and the children were seated alongside an army officer whilst I sat opposite between two military policemen. The engine strained as we bumped and rolled across the hillside but thankfully Doruntina was asleep. Drita was softly weeping and even in the dark I could see the fear on Hannah's face following ten years of oppression and violence. To make matters worse, both mother and daughter were doubtless thinking of Dede and wondering whether he was still alive.

I was cold and exhausted but most of all I was consumed with worry. A tear rolled down my face, which Drita must have noticed for all of a sudden she began to sob. Hanna tried to comfort her daughter but she pushed her away. Seeing this, the officer shouted to me above the roar of the engine.

'You must be strong, don't let them see you cry.'

I realised that of course he was right and I quickly tried to regain control. Holding back the tears, I wiped my face and tried to smile, which must have helped a little for Drita's tears soon subsided. We drove on across the rough terrain for about an hour before stopping in the middle of the countryside. The officer explained that our vehicle had broken down and we were waiting for a relief vehicle to arrive. He opened the rear door and lit a cigarette, cupping it in his hand to hide the flame.

'This area is controlled by the terrorists,' he said, referring to the KLA. 'Any moment now we could be targeted by snipers.' I responded with a shrug, hoping the others wouldn't hear.

One of the men offered me some roast chicken from his ration pack. First I offered some to the others. Hanna refused, as did Drita, and it was only when they agreed to accept sealed packs of Amita, a cherry flavoured drink, that I realised they suspected the food might be poisoned. Not having been raised in a country filled with hatred towards my people, I did not have the same paranoid concerns and gratefully accepted a piece of chicken.

After a while, another vehicle came along and we were transferred inside, this one even noisier than the last. Only two men accompanied us this time, including the English-speaking officer. The temperature had dropped considerably causing me to shiver and to my amazement, the officer draped his jacket around my shoulders. Hanna had brought a blanket with her from the dugout and she and the children snuggled beneath it on the bench. As we travelled through the darkness, I tried to sleep but the interminable grinding of the engine and the bumpy terrain made it impossible and I stared into the darkness, wondering whether the rest of the group was safe.

It was after midnight by the time we arrived at our destination; a large military base on the outskirts of Gjakove where rows of tanks and trucks stood in silhouette against the moonlit sky. Doruntina was still sleeping as Hanna carried her into the building where a cell awaited us. There were two sets of bunk beds at the side and in the centre were a table and some chairs.

Two men entered, both dressed in civilian clothes, one of them carrying a small video camera. I was ordered to join them at the table whilst Hanna and the children were taken outside. One of the men sat opposite me, his hard eyes focused on mine as the other man began to film.

'What were you doing on the mountain?' he asked. I explained briefly that I had come to deliver medicines to Kosovo and that having found children in need of medical help, I had agreed to evacuate them to Albania.

'We have hospitals here, why would they need to go to Albania for treatment?'

I shrugged in reply; loath to commit myself to an answer he would not appreciate.

'We killed two terrorists who were with you,' he said. 'They were firing at us.'

I was horrified, believing that he meant Rambo and Bekim's brother but I tried hard not to show it.

'There no terrorists with us,' I stated calmly, aware that it might be a ruse to obtain information. It was difficult trying to maintain that outward calm thinking of death of two young men and my part in it.

'How many terrorists did you see in Junik?' he demanded.

'None,' I replied truthfully, not considering the KLA to be terrorists. For more than an hour he questioned me, often repeating the same thing over and over.

'Why were you there? Are you working with the terrorists? Was it a planned operation? Are you a spy?' Throughout the interview the camera whirred.

I was tired and in the end I wasn't even sure if my answers were the same as when he first began the interrogation. He must have realised that we were just going round in circles for eventually he signalled to the cameraman that the interview was over. As he prepared to leave the cell he told me that the soldiers would be searching the mountainside for the people who had escaped.

'There are helicopters in the air and dogs on the ground. We will find them, of that you can be sure'.

A few minutes later I was taken into another room where all the contents of the baggage from the mules were laid out on a table. There was some money, mainly dollars and deutschmarks, clothing, nappies, some papers and passports and the slides and film left by the journalists. Also there were my two plastic cameras, the video cassette tape given to me by the KLA soldier and my hand-held radio.

'Please indicate which of these items belong to you,' said a soldier standing behind the table. I pointed to my belongings and asked if I could have them back but was told that I could only have the toiletries and clothes. I asked to use a bathroom and was taken past a number of guards to a washroom down the hall.

I was concerned for Hanna. The interviewer was now talking to her and of course I had no way of warning her of what had been said. I had not, for example, told him that three journalists accompanied us, hoping he would believe there had only been one, the photographer whose film they had in their possession. I was afraid that if they thought there were other journalists with the group they might make a greater effort to track them down.

The washroom was lined with old sinks and behind a partition was a hole in the floor. The smell of urine was so overpowering that I decided to wait, blessed with a strong bladder. I opened my sponge bag and proceeded to do what I could to remove the dust from my face and hair. The water trickled slowly from the tap but I was able to brush my teeth and scrub away some of the mountain dirt ingrained on my hands and feet. My shoes were still wet from trekking through rivers and streams, so I carried them and walked barefoot back to the cell.

When the interview with Hannah had ended, a guard delivered a tray of food and we were left alone. To my astonishment the tray contained four chocolate pancakes, four glasses of milk, some yoghurt, biscuits and several small cartons of Amita. It was hardly typical prison fare, especially at this hour of the morning. Once again Hanna was suspicious of eating anything prepared by Serbs but when she saw me eating with no immediate ill effects she too began to pick at the food.

Drita refused to join us, remaining curled up on the bunk with her face to the wall. In hushed voices we swapped information, although I couldn't be sure that we really understood each other. Speaking in broken English she told me that she had admitted there were three journalists with us. When asked about her husband she told them that he lived in Switzerland. Keeping an eye on the door, I removed Ardi's piece of paper and a pen and asked her to list the names of all the people who had been with us on the mountain. I knew that I might not remember all their names and I was determined to trace them later if possible.

We were exhausted and dawn was breaking but I did not sleep. My mind was filled with images from the mountain: Marigona with her dark eyes and cheeky grin and Rambo's tears mingling with the rain. I relived the interminable climb through the forest and the sound of mortars exploding and Doruntina screaming.

26 | THE INTERROGATION

IT WAS NOT LONG before the sun rose and a guard entered the cell and told us to prepare to leave. Hanna had fed and changed Doruntina, who was starting to cry. I suggested we ask for a doctor but Hanna was adamant that she would not have her baby treated by a Serb. Picking up our few belongings, we followed the guard down the corridor and went outside, where tanks and military trucks were parked in neat rows. Soldiers were milling around preparing for departure and as a vehicle pulled up alongside us, I saw that the English-speaking officer was sitting inside.

As we drove out of the base I was able to study him in the light of day. He was a tall, handsome man dressed in the green uniform and steel helmet of the army. We drove for some time with the sun beating down on the roof of the vehicle, making it hot and stuffy inside. The officer removed his flak jacket and offered it to me. His manner was gentle and it was hard to imagine him condoning the atrocities and ethnic cleansing perpetrated by the paramilitaries.

'There are snipers in the area' he said, 'These windows are plastic so I suggest you place this behind your head.' As Hanna saw him pass it across she must have known we were once again in danger, as she promptly crossed herself. I handed him the flak jacket. 'I'd rather it was used to protect the children.' He looked at me askance but nodded and passed it across to Hanna. I suggested she and the children lie down between the seats with the jacket placed over them.

'She is a Christian,' he stated. 'We are passing through a Christian area now and as you can see, none of the buildings have been damaged because they do not support the terrorists. They don't bother us and we don't bother them.' I said nothing, for most of the children wore plastic rosaries around their necks, yet some of their homes had been razed to the ground.

We arrived in a small village and were transferred to another armoured vehicle for the onward journey. It was very claustrophobic and the noise was almost unbearable so I was relieved when the vehicle finally stopped. As we got out there was the sound of a bugle call and I guessed it was an army barracks.

We were taken into a large square surrounded by long, low buildings. The officer gestured for Hannah and the children to follow him and Hannah looked worried. I begged him to keep us together but he said it wasn't possible. He did however assure me that we would be reunited later. I asked him to explain this to Hanna and although she looked sceptical she agreed to go with him.

I was taken across the square and shown into a long narrow room furnished with a boardroom table and a number of chairs. The soldier told me to sit down and wait and I was left alone for a while. When the soldier returned he handed me a strong Turkish coffee and as soon as I drank it, he brought another. After a while, a man came in and sat down opposite me. He explained that he had to take a statement and once again I would have to relive the events of the last few days. He asked some questions, mainly to make sure that he had the facts in order. I was offered yet another coffee but declined, for I could feel my pulse racing, though caffeine doesn't usually affect me at all.

I was then taken into a small prefab where I was told to sit down. To my relief it was air conditioned for it was now unbearably hot outside. There was a desk in front of me and sitting behind it was a middle-aged man with slicked back hair. My father would have described him as a 'crook in a suit'. Peering at me from over the top of a pair of reading glasses he asked where I was from.

'England,' I replied.

He then said something that I couldn't understand. Sitting beside him was the soldier who had taken my statement but when I looked to him for an explanation he just kept quiet, shifting uncomfortably in his chair.

'I'm sorry,' I said, 'My Serbian is limited, I don't understand what you are saying.' His face reddened with anger and suddenly he began to shout.

'Tell him,' I said to the soldier, 'That I only know a few words of your language.' The soldier tried to explain but the man banged the table, startling us both.

'He says that you are lying. That you speak the language fluently and he thinks you are a spy.'

I had a severe headache and was beginning to wonder whether this was going to develop into a full scale interrogation. Looking him straight in the eyes, I sighed and spoke slowly and clearly: 'My knowledge of Serbian is restricted to words such as *Dobar dan* (Good day) *Havala* (Thank you) and *Molim* (please). Oh, and *Nema Pucanja* (Stop shooting).'

His mean, beady eyes borred into mine; making my skin crawl. I was feeling nauseous, which might have been fear, but having been in more difficult circumstances than this, it seemed unlikely. He said something to the soldier who translated for me.

'Why were you carrying a radio?'

'In order to get assistance for the children once we reached Albania,' I replied.

'Who do you work for?' translated the soldier.

'A British aid organisation.'

'Where is your identification card?'

'I only carry a passport but this is the organisation I represent,' I said, pointing to the Operation Angel logo on my T-shirt. 'We brought aid to the State hospital in Pristina. You can check with Mrs. Teodorovic and Velco Popevic of the Yugoslav Red Cross. They know me, they know my organisation. We brought several tons of medical supplies and equipped the baby unit with incubators. We even had the support of the Mayor in Pristina. In fact we were supposed to return there last month but at the last minute our visas were refused. If you have access to a computer you can look on our website.'

If he bothered to check out the web site, he would see that I was telling the truth, for there were numerous pictures of our convoy being escorted across Kosovo by the Yugoslav Red Cross. The interrogator was quiet as he absorbed this information, then he rose and left the room.

'Would you like some more coffee?' asked the interpreter.

'No thank you, my head hurts and I feel a little strange. Some water might help though.' He ignored me, staring intently at the wall.

When the interrogator returned, he was accompanied by the Yugoslav (or as some states, including the US referred to it, the Serbia and Montenegro) army officer. The interpreter left the room without looking in my direction and the officer took his place.

'What were you doing with a radio?' he asked.

I told him that most of the aid workers carried them, to keep in contact with one another.

'Describe this mission,' he said. I explained how we had arranged to return to Kosovo with a second convoy but a week before departure, our visas were refused.

'We decided to deliver the aid to the refugees and health centres in and around Tropoje on the Albanian-Kosovo border.'

'What were you doing in Kosovo?' he demanded, impatiently waiting for the officer to translate.

'No aid is reaching the villages and there are sick children in desperate need of help.'

'You entered illegally. Why didn't you wait for permission?'

'I told you, our visas were refused. Sometimes desperate situations call for desperate measures.'

There followed a heated discussion between the two men and then scraping his chair noisily on the floor, the interrogator stood up and left the room. I massaged my temples, trying to ease the constant throbbing and when I looked up the officer was staring at me.

'Sally Becker,' he said softly, 'You are a very brave woman.'

I couldn't think of anything to say and we just sat there in silence until the interrogator returned.

'I feel very sick,' I told him, not sounding particularly brave. 'I really need some air.'

'First you will answer my questions,' said the man, glancing at some notes in his hand.

The interrogation continued for hours. Sometimes he would ask a question and before I could even reply, he'd ask another. At one point he told me that he knew I was connected to the terrorist organisation known as the KLA. He believed that I was spying on their behalf, or on behalf of the West.

'You were travelling with a group of soldiers who were smuggling arms in order to kill innocent Serbs!' he cried. Of course I denied it but he looked at me with disdain and said quietly, 'Your friend Hanna is the wife of Nik Hiseni who is wanted for terrorist activities. He is a murderer.' I thought of Nik, so quiet and unassuming and then remembered what Hanna had told me.

'But he lives in Switzerland,' I said.

'No!' he shouted, again banging the table with his fist, 'He is here in Kosovo, planning the execution of our policemen. He is a terrorist!' He then seemed to calm down again before continuing.

'As a British citizen you should understand. You suffer the same problem with the terrorists in Northern Ireland.'

His words reminded of a similar comment made by Milaslav Paic, an official who worked at the Yugoslav embassy in London. I had been asked to attend an interview regarding our first application for visas to Kosovo and after a lengthy discussion, Paic sat back in his chair.

'You are Jewish,' he had stated, his hands clasped in front of him,' Therefore you should understand our situation better than most.' I looked puzzled, wondering where this was leading.

'You have a similar problem with the Palestinians. The Israelis declared Israel to be a Jewish state but the Arabs do not accept it. They attack your people through terrorism and therefore they have to be controlled, for the security of your citizens.' I was concerned that by contradicting him, I might forego the permission I needed to enter Kosovo but I couldn't agree.

'I am British, not Israeli and just because I am Jewish does not mean that I support the way some Israelis treat their Palestinian neighbours. Oppression breeds violence. Discussion and compromise is the only way to secure a lasting peace.' The official's eyes had narrowed slightly as he leaned across the desk.

'The terrorists do not need to fight for Kosovo. The Albanians already make up 90 per cent of the population and they breed at such an alarming rate that within a few years there won't be room for any Serbs.' He then strode briskly from the room and I thought I might have ruined our chances. Instead, much to my surprise, the visas had been issued later that day.

Around the time of my interrogation at the army barracks, Nik Hiseni received a message from the Serb authorities informing him that they had his wife and children in custody. They warned him that if he did not come forward, they would be executed. Fortunately, he was familiar with Serb tactics and refused to comply.

The man repeated his questions for a while until finally he must have realised that he was getting nowhere. I was now slouched in my chair, barely able to pay attention and afraid that at any moment I was going to collapse. I desperately needed to lie down but he just kept repeating the same questions over and over again. It was only when I slumped forward, my chin on my chest that he finally gave up and left. The officer helped me outside and told me to sit down on the grass verge. I watched him walk away, wondering if I would ever see him again.

I noticed that a television crew was setting up nearby and Hanna was brought out to be interviewed. To my horror, they had placed the camera film, slides and the radio in front of her on a bench. With a great effort of will I forced myself to stand up and marched over to remove the items out of range of the cameraman.

'Those are nothing to do with her!' I declared angrily. At first they just stared in amazement and then the cameraman focused on me and proceeded to ask me some questions.

'I need a doctor,' I said, ignoring him. They tried to film me but I just kept turning my back to the camera. Eventually a man wearing a white coat with a stethoscope dangling from his neck appeared and offered to examine me. I tried to explain how I was feeling and he placed his hand on my forehead. 'No problem. You're fine.'

It suddenly occurred to me that perhaps the coffee had been drugged. This could account for why I was feeling so sick, light headed and strange. I remembered how quickly they refilled the empty cup and yet weren't interested when I asked for water.

'So what are you doing in Kosovo?' the doctor asked and I noticed he signalled for the cameraman to start filming. The journalists' equipment had now been moved and placed in front of me.

'You aren't a real doctor are you?' I said.

'Of course I'm a doctor – but what are you? Are you a spy?'

This time I turned and spoke directly into the camera, 'These are not mine,' I said, pointing to the equipment. 'I am not a spy; I am a humanitarian aid worker trying to save the lives of innocent children. This is Serbian propaganda.'

This obviously wasn't what they wanted to hear and without any warning I was grabbed roughly from behind and my wrists were placed in handcuffs which were so tight they cut into my flesh. I was then thrown into the back of a car and driven away from the barracks at top speed.

27 | A 'CONFESSION'

DRIVING THROUGH THE TOWN centre of Gjakove, I could see people staring into the car and some of them smiled or waved. Gjakove was predominantly ethnic Albanian and I was hoping that someone might recognise me and report that I had been captured. We pulled up outside a police station and I was taken inside and ordered to sit on the floor in the corridor. I was concerned for Hanna and the children, having assured her that I wouldn't leave them.

My presence was causing a stir and a group of armed men dressed in the purple blue camouflage uniform of the Serb paramilitary police appeared in the corridor. They were known to be the main perpetrators of brutality against the Albanians. Many of them were untrained civilians who had been given arms and authority by Milosevic when he first revoked the autonomy of Kosovo in 1989.

Sitting on the cold tiled floor with my back to the wall, the steel handcuffs biting into my wrists, one by one they swaggered past me, spitting and hurling abuse. My ankle throbbed and I had a pounding headache so leaning my head back against the wall, I closed my eyes and tried to shut out the sound of their voices.

Some time later I was escorted along the corridor and into a room where the handcuffs were finally removed. I rubbed my sore wrists, which were ringed with bloody welts. There were two men in the room, one was a policeman, the other a soldier. The policeman was holding Bill's radio and he told me to sit down, pointing to a chair near the door.

'Who is on the other end of this?' he asked, examining the walkie-talkie. He depressed the talk button causing it to bleep.

'Probably one of my volunteers,' I replied.

'Why isn't it working?'

'The battery is dead.' The soldier gave me a penetrating look.

'You were spying for the terrorists weren't you?' It was more of a statement than a question so I just sighed. After placing the radio on the desk, he came towards me. Bending down so that we were almost nose to nose he whispered the word 'terrorist' in my ear. I struggled to avoid the sour odour of his breath.

'Where did you get the radio?' he asked.

'Operation Angel' I replied as he leaned in closer.

'To whom does the radio belong?' he asked gently. I shook my head and sighed, wondering what to say. My ankle was aching and hoping to change the subject

I asked for some pain killers. He told me to show him where it hurt and then slowly and deliberately he began to crush my foot beneath his heavy boot. I tried to push him off but he slammed me back into the chair. Just as I thought I might pass out from the pain, the policeman intervened. I don't know what was said but a moment later my arm was almost wrenched from its socket as I was pulled from the chair and pushed back into the corridor.

Hanna was sitting on the floor with Drita and Doruntina and I was ordered to sit against the opposite wall. Hanna raised her finger to her lips, warning me that we weren't supposed to speak. I was in a great deal of pain but I didn't want them to know that I'd been hurt. Instead I focused on Doruntina as she toddled around in front of me. Drita's eyes were red from crying but now she just sat there quietly staring into space. I wanted so much to reassure her but even if I could have spoken their language, I didn't dare talk for fear of causing more trouble.

Hanna held up her wrists and crossed them to show that she too had been in handcuffs. I was relieved to see that she wasn't marked but I was outraged that they had done such a thing, especially in front of the children. Three of the men I had seen earlier came back down the corridor to glare at us and one of them slid his forefinger across his throat, causing his companions to laugh aloud. Fortunately, Drita hadn't seen the gesture but Hanna had and I saw the fear flicker across her face. After a while we were taken upstairs and told to sit on a bench on the landing. Hanna asked for a carton of milk for the baby, which was delivered.

We remained there until some time in the early evening when Hannah's aunt came to collect the children. She told me that she lived close by and would be taking care of them until Hannah was released. After they left, I was taken back downstairs to the reception area.

I was ordered to sit inside a glass enclosure on a broken chair and the only way to prevent it from falling was to balance using my feet. An old policeman sat opposite me in the cramped space. He was tall and stooped with thinning grey hair and some of his front teeth were missing. When I asked to use the toilet, he sent me limping down the hall. They had given me the rucksack containing my toiletries so I was able to have a wash at the small sink. My foot was swollen and bruised and when I gingerly began to clean the blood off, three of my toenails came away. I was very dehydrated so I drank water from the tap before returning to my seat in the small office.

I spent the rest of the night and the whole of the following day balancing precariously on the broken chair. There was no sign of food and the only water available was from the tap in the toilet. I thought of Hannah and hoped that she at least had somewhere to lie down. A German-speaking policeman had replaced the old man but apart from asking me where I was from, he largely ignored me. During the evening I returned from the bathroom to find another man in his place. He was in his mid-twenties with short cropped blond hair and blue eyes and as soon as I sat down, he began to ask questions in a mixture of Serbian, English and French.

Most of the questions were related to politics; my opinion of Milosevic, how come I didn't help Serb children. Why were Clinton and Blair supporting terrorists? I answered as best I could until we were interrupted by a commotion in the hall. Some of the soldiers from the previous day were pressed up against the glass, jostling for position. Behind them was a big man with dark hair and a straggly black beard. He was wearing a bandanna tied around his head and a long knife dangled from his belt.

'You were on television this evening,' he said, as he pushed past them and entered the room. 'They say you were spying for the terrorists!'

I explained that I was an aid worker on a mission to help some children but he sneered and demanded to know why I was carrying a long wave radio.

'You had pictures of the terrorist Haxhiu. You also had film of women and children and you were calling for NATO to help them.'

It became apparent that the video tape I was carrying had been broadcast on television so I didn't bother defending myself, knowing it was pointless when the evidence was so obviously damning.

'You were filmed leaving Junik with the terrorists!' he shouted. The soldiers began to mimic a chant used by Albanians in support of the KLA, '*UChK*'! *UChK*!'

The crowd increased until there must have been 50 or 60 men surrounding the glass enclosure and they all joined in the chant. Some carried RPGs on their backs and grenades hung from the webbing on their chests. They were wearing black jumpsuits and many had long hair and beards. One of the men was carrying a Heckler-Koch machine gun and he looked as though he would kill me given the chance. They might have been Arkan's volunteers – he was rumoured to be operating in Kosovo. Arkan was the nickname for Zelko Raznatović, the notorious leader of the Tigers, a paramilitary force who were alleged to have committed atrocities against the Muslim population in Bosnia (and later proved to have done so).

'All those children died on the mountain because of you,' said the young policeman.

At first I thought I had misheard him but he said it again.

'They were all killed because of you.'

I was so crushed by his words that when some of the other men began to crowd into the office I hardly noticed. The man with the bandanna jabbed his gun into my stomach, calling me a spy and although it was painful, I was not scared and in fact I would have welcomed the bullet.

After a while they grew bored and gave up, leaving me alone. I removed the last cigarette from the pack I carried in my waistcoat and closed my eyes as I inhaled. Tears were running down my face and I couldn't stop them, didn't try to.

Some time later I was on my way back from the washroom when I saw Hanna sitting alone in the corridor and hurried past, hoping she hadn't noticed my swollen eyes. I was physically and mentally exhausted and leaning against a table, I rested my head in my arms. Suddenly there was a resounding crack close to my ear and looking up I saw that the young policeman had smashed his stick across the table.

'No sleeping!' he cried.

I sat there all night long and whenever I inadvertently dozed off, I was woken by the crack of his stick on the formica close to my ear. I had an unbearable head-ache but was forced to stare into the neon strip light overhead, feeling wretched and wishing I could stop the thoughts that threatened to overwhelm me.

The old policeman was back on shift again the next morning and he seemed concerned by my appearance. I asked him whether I could have a cigarette but he didn't smoke and asked a colleague for one on my behalf. A few hours passed before I was taken upstairs and told to pick up the phone. Watched by two men in civilian clothes, I was put through to David Slinn, the First Secretary of the British embassy in Belgrade.

'We've been trying to find out what happened to you, Miss Becker,' said Slinn, 'Are you alright?'

'Do you have news of the people I was trying to evacuate?' I asked him. 'I've been told they were killed.'

'That's not true. A call was made by a journalist who had been with your group and apparently, they are all safe and well.'

At first I was unable to speak.

'Are you sure?'

'We received a message from an Italian news service that everyone is fine. No one was hurt.'

'Thank you,' I said, 'Thank you so much!'

'There was a family with you. Do you have any information about them?' I told him they had been brought to Gjakova with me and that the children were staying with their aunt.

'Their mother is still downstairs,' I said. Once again he asked if I was all right and I told him that apart from some pain in my legs, I was fine.

'It's possible you'll be moved from there soon, but don't worry, we'll find you. I'll try to visit you tomorrow. Do you have a message for anyone at home?'

I asked him to tell them I was fine and not to worry. We ended the call and I headed for the door. Hearing they had all survived, all the guilt and remorse that had weighed so heavily on my shoulders was suddenly gone and I practically floated down the stairs.

The old policeman had brought me a pack of Serbian cigarettes; the tobacco was rough and they had no filters but I was very grateful and thanked him profusely. He didn't speak any English but he made it clear that I shouldn't say anything.

That afternoon, Hanna and I were ordered into a car with two policemen and were driven through the town at high speed, as though they were expecting an attack. As we drove through the busy streets, I told Hanna that Dede was safe. She didn't know whether to believe me and I couldn't speak enough of her language to explain how I knew. The car stopped outside a small café where people were sitting drinking coffee in the sunshine and I found it strange to see life going on as normal.

We were ushered into a small office where a young woman sat typing while another woman, middle-aged with dyed red hair, was dictating to her. She reminded me of Rosa Klebb, the evil colonel in *From Russia with Love*. The policemen joined us and we all sat down. I was asked if I wanted a drink from the café and taken aback, I tentatively requested a cappuccino. I began to relax for the first time in days, sipping the delicious foamy coffee and smoking a Marlboro Light given to me by the one of the policemen. They were chatting to Hanna in Albanian and I asked how come they spoke her language.

'We are Albanian,' one of them said.

'*Shum mir!*' I said, 'Good!'

They laughed but Hanna looked slightly uncomfortable, her eyes darting towards the woman with red hair. I was given a piece of paper to sign that I couldn't read, written in Cyrillic but a pen was passed to me and I was ordered to put my signature at the foot of the page. At first I hesitated but seeing that Hanna had complied I thought I had better do the same. The woman made a short speech but when I looked to Hanna for an explanation she began to cry and placed one wrist across the other.

I immediately tried to make the woman understand that Hannah was innocent and offered to serve double my sentence if they would release her. To my surprise the redhead nodded and made a short speech. Glancing up at me she then said '*Trideset dana!*' (Thirty days.)

Hana looked shocked but at the same time she thanked me, explaining that they had agreed to accept a fine for her release so she would not be going to prison after all. I had been tried and sentenced in a foreign language without the presence of a solicitor and although I was unhappy at the idea of being locked up for a month, I was very relieved that Hanna would now be free to join her children. We were driven back to the police station and I just had time to touch her hand before we were parted.

A short while later I was pushed into the back of a jeep alongside two soldiers and a civilian driver. We drove south across the lush green landscape towards Prizren, a large, picturesque historic city, taking the long route to Lipljan prison to avoid KLA-controlled areas. (Most of the predominating Albanian population was forced or intimidated into leaving the town during the Kosovo war.) One of the soldiers dropped his heavy rifle on my foot during the journey. He apologised, so perhaps it was an accident. It was nearly three hours before we arrived at our destination, which to my amazement looked nothing like a prison at all.

The place resembled a hotel complex with neat lawns and flowerbeds. The officer who came to collect me from the main gate had dark, wavy hair and a surly face. Her uniform was blue and she wore a pale blue shirt and a navy cap. A shiny black baton hung from her belt. 'I saw you on television,' she declared triumphantly as she escorted me along the path. I kept quiet, thinking that for once it might be wiser to say nothing and as we approached the main entrance I could feel the hot sun beating down. Birds were singing and the air smelt of roses; appearances can be deceptive.

28 | LIPLJAN PRISON

15 JULY 1998; BY the time I began my sentence many small towns and villages had been surrounded by Serb forces. The recent offensive had resulted in many deaths and a quarter of a million people had now been displaced. The KLA, although still active, were losing territory and despite a call from the International community for Milosevic to halt the offensive, Junik was falling to the Serbs.

We entered a reception area leading into the women's block. Opposite the entrance was a staff room manned by two prison officers. Along the corridor was a washroom comprising a sink area, a small room with a plastic bowl for laundry and a Turkish-style toilet, which also doubled as a shower. There were two dormitories, one to the left of the washroom and the other directly opposite but the majority of the prisoners were housed upstairs.

I was ushered into the staff room where an attractive woman in her late thirties began to register my details. She was quite officious while my surly escort was present but as soon as she left, the atmosphere changed completely. I was to find out later that she was Albanian, one of only three officers still employed by the prison. The rest of the staff were Serbs.

Selima, who was pregnant, had worked at the prison for the past fifteen years. We communicated in my limited Serbo-Croat as she took notes of my name, date of birth and so on. I had to hand over my earrings, a ring and some of the items from my sponge bag, such as my razor, perfume bottle and scissors. They already had possession of my passport and money. The walkie-talkie, plastic cameras, videotape and some of my papers had been confiscated by the police.

I was shown into the first dormitory where amongst the row of beds was a child's cot. As I proceeded to unpack a spare T-shirt and underwear, the grim-faced officer returned and told me I had a visitor. I was escorted across the grounds to a larger building near the main entrance and was shown into an office where a pleasant looking Englishman rose to shake my hand. He introduced himself as David Slinn, First Secretary to the British Embassy in Belgrade, the man I had spoken to on the phone. He was tall and good looking with dark hair and glasses and I guessed him to be around 30. I was relieved to see him and it was a pleasure listening to his refined British accent. Beside him sat a young woman employed by the prison to monitor our conversation and Surly also stayed with us throughout the visit.

'So, how are you?' asked David.

'All the better for seeing you,' I replied. 'Thank you for coming.'

Although I had been held since Thursday, he told me that it was not until Saturday that they learned of my arrest. As soon as the news came through, Colonel Crossland, Defence Attaché to the British Embassy, had raced from Belgrade to Junik in a diplomatic car.

'We were led to believe you were being held by the KLA, although that didn't make much sense,' he said. 'When the Colonel stopped to pick me up from my hotel in Pristina, a reporter from Sky suddenly announced that you were actually in the hands of the Yugoslav police. We tried very hard to get further information but it wasn't until Sunday that I was able to make contact with you in Djakova.'

I had spoken to Colonel Crossland back in March when I was trying to obtain visas for the first convoy to Kosovo. I had agreed to deliver a large number of shoeboxes filled with aid that had been collected by his local charity and although he was very helpful, he had voiced his doubts about our securing permission to enter Yugoslavia. Shortly after we returned from Kosovo in April, having successfully delivered aid to both sides of the conflict, I received a fax from him with the words 'Well done!' scrawled across the page. I asked David to send him my regards.

'Actually he drove me here and is waiting outside in the car.'

We proceeded to discuss what had happened to me following my arrest and he assured me that my treatment in the prison would not be on a par with the brutality of the paramilitary police. He told me that one of the Italian journalists had informed their TV station in Italy of what occurred on the mountain. They had received the call from a satellite phone in Junik the day after we were ambushed and he assured me again that none of my group had been hurt and all had been accounted for. He also told me that he had spoken to Duncan and my family, who sent their love.

'Your arrest and imprisonment has been broadcast internationally and the fact that you were convicted without a proper trial and without an interpreter or lawyer present, may give you the right to appeal if you wish.'

I assured him that I certainly wanted to appeal; I had another convoy arranged for September and therefore a great deal of work to do. I also wanted the chance to highlight the situation in Kosovo and to begin tracing the families who had managed to cross the border.

'How are you physically?' David asked. I told him I was ok but from some pain and swelling in my legs.

'I'll have a word with the prison governor before I leave,' he said 'and I'll visit you again as soon as possible. You'll also get a visit from Bob Gordon, the British Consul in Belgrade. He'll bring a list of lawyers for you to choose from.'

'How will I pay for a lawyer? My work has always been voluntary so I don't have an income.'

'Your father said that he will cover any costs incurred. Please don't worry. By the way, I have been asked to do an interview for Sky television tomorrow morning, so I'll be able to confirm that I've seen you and that you're well. Is there anything else I can do for you? Do you need anything brought in?'

I asked him for some clothing and a few books to help pass the time. He said that Bob Gordon would bring them on his visit and with that, he stood up and prepared to leave. We shook hands and I thanked him before being led away.

I returned to my room in the women's' quarter to find that I was being moved into the dormitory across the hall. Although the room was large there were only four beds, two at either end. Plate glass windows overlooked the front of the building and although the windows weren't barred, fixed to the exterior walls were wrought iron railings that would prevent anyone attempting to escape.

I was told to collect supper from the hallway where a large vat of soup was set on a table alongside several hunks of bread. The soup was a vague reddish colour, watery with a piece of fatty meat floating on the surface but I was starving, having had nothing to eat for three days. I returned to the dormitory and sat down at a long wooden table in the centre of the room. Dipping the dry bread into the soup, I ate whilst studying my surroundings. There was a stack of lockers against the wall and hanging beside them was a long list of prison rules written in Cyrillic which I couldn't understand.

When I had finished eating, I returned my bowl and spoon to the hallway, surprised that my door remained unlocked. A short while later I was joined by my cell-mate, Zoya. Although she was Albanian, she spoke a little Serbo-Croat so we were able to communicate, she spoke slowly and used her hands a great deal. We had to whisper because one of the rules was no talking. Zoya was in her late forties, short and solid with a large shiny round face, pale skin and a mane of long straight black hair and dark eyes. She spoke with a slight lisp as her two front teeth were missing and as we talked she kept glancing nervously at the door.

She told me that she was serving a five-year sentence for manslaughter. Her husband had been violent towards her and eventually she snapped and killed him with a knife. She spoke about it quite calmly and without any shame. Her two children, both in their twenties, were living in Saudi Arabia.

'Only three years left and then hopefully I will join them,' she said, proudly handing me a photograph of her grandchild. Opening her locker, which contained a couple of shirts, a pair of leggings and some toiletries, she pulled out a box and invited me to help myself to her stash of biscuits, chocolate and boiled sweets. I asked her where she got them and she explained that once a week the prisoners would make a shopping list and order things from the local shop. Having already sampled the prison fare, I welcomed this news.

At precisely 10.00pm, an officer came to the door and told us to get ready for bed. I quickly used the wash room opposite and climbed into the bed I had been allocated. After a few minutes, the officer returned and wishing us goodnight, she closed and locked the door. I noticed that Zoya was very friendly and polite to the officers, almost deferential, and I wondered whether she genuinely liked them, or whether it was fear. I had many more questions to ask her but almost immediately after the lights went out, she began snoring heavily on the far side of the room.

I lay awake for a quite a while, listening to the drone of military aircraft flying overhead and the distant thump of explosions. Having spent time with the people of Kosovo, seeing how they were living below ground in fear of their lives, I was able to visualise them all too clearly, imagining their anguish as the planes flew overhead, the children wide-eyed with fear. I thought of Marigona and the others, wondering how they were. I hadn't slept since leaving Junik and this was the first time I was able to lie down, so it wasn't long before I fell into a deep exhausted sleep.

At 6am an officer banged on the door, which gave us an hour to wash, dress and prepare for the day ahead. Breakfast arrived in the form of two hard boiled eggs, a hunk of bread and a cup of incredibly sweet syrupy black tea. Zoya didn't want any breakfast, she worked in the staff canteen over in the main building and would eat there. At eight o'clock someone came to collect her and she padded out of the room, her open sandals clacking on the floor.

I could hear some of the prisoners cleaning the washroom and hallway. One of the women smiled nervously as she passed my open door and I returned her smile, making the symbol for 'free Kosovo'. She looked delighted and after checking to make sure the officers weren't watching, she returned the salute. She then disappeared into the washroom to tell her companions. There were five of them, ranging in age from 17 to 40 and they all began to wave at me from across the hall.

I wandered across to the window and saw a group of male prisoners dressed in blue overalls. They passed by in single file, their heads bowed but when one of them suddenly looked up I caught a glimpse of his face. He was battered and bruised and I noticed he was limping badly. There was an angry shout and he quickly averted his gaze.

The temperature was already rising rapidly despite the hour, and the sun, magnified by the glass, was increasing the oppressive heat inside the room. I had just opened both windows to let in some air when an officer appeared at my door shouting in anger. I couldn't understand what she was saying but guessed she wanted me to move away from the window. I quickly complied and she pointed to one of the chairs that were placed around the table.

'Stay there,' she barked as I sat down.

Sitting on the hard wooden seat, I wished I had a book or something to occupy myself. After about an hour, by which time I had studied every detail of the room, she reappeared and took me into a courtyard at the rear of the building. To my surprise I was left alone so I had a look around. Lipljan prison housed both male and female inmates in separate two-storey buildings overlooking a central courtyard. Neat flower beds lined the perimeter of the courtyard, which was enclosed by a high wall. I went and sat down on the grass, making the most of being outdoors. The sun shone brightly and I could hear birds singing overhead. The smell of the freshly watered flowers hung in the balmy air and once again I found it hard to believe that I was actually in prison. I could see the women waving from a window on the upper floor of the building where I slept and I waved back. An officer came out and made it clear that this was forbidden. She beckoned me back inside and handed me a broom, a bucket and a washcloth and told me to clean the other dormitory.

I swept and cleaned the floor as best I could until an officer came to inspect my work. She was in her early twenties with short fair hair framing a baby face.

'Again' she said in English, 'This is no good!'

I began to sweep the floor for a second time while she stood over me. I don't know what I was doing wrong but she became angry and began to shout. I held my hands out palm upwards to show that I didn't understand what she was saying but she suddenly took hold of the broom and shoved it against my chest. Her attitude annoyed me and I shook my head and leaned the broom against a wall. She seemed a little surprised as I strode past her and when I entered my room I could hear her complaining loudly to someone in the office.

There was no clock in the room and my watch had been confiscated so it was only when I was told to collect a bowl of soup and the inevitable bread that I guessed it was lunchtime. The day dragged on with nothing to do, nothing to read and no one to talk to. It was only six weeks since I'd been at Windsor Castle meeting the Queen.

During the afternoon the senior officer appeared at my door to announce that I was being taken to visit the doctor. The officer, an attractive woman with dark hair and impeccable makeup, took me to another building where the surgery was based. I was told to undress but as I did so, I noticed that there were two male officers watching me from the doorway. The doctor, ignoring my protest that the examination should be conducted in private, listened to my breathing and checked my blood pressure. He then examined my ankle ,which was badly swollen. As he poked and prodded at the site of the bruising, I flinched.

'Where did this happen?' he asked.

'At the police station,' I replied, which didn't seem to surprise him, or for that matter to bother him unduly.

A middle-aged woman with dyed orange hair entered the room. She was wearing a white coat and smiling broadly, she said that she would be coming to see me the following day. I was given some pain killers and escorted back to the women's quarters.

The medication had to be left in the office but Selima assured me that it would be available when required. While I was there, I remembered Zoya telling me about the shopping list. I told Selima I would like to buy some things and she agreed to take my order which included two cartons of cigarettes, a box of matches, some fruit and two bars of chocolate.

The next morning I had a visit from Dragan, the Chief Prison Officer. He wasn't much older than me and we were about the same height and to my surprise he spoke perfect English.

'So, how are you?' he inquired. 'Are they treating you well?'

I shrugged and nodded.

'If you have any complaints, please don't hesitate to say.'

I told him that I was unimpressed with the prison doctor allowing people into the room while I was undressed. He seemed embarrassed and assured me that it wouldn't happen again. I asked him whether I would be allowed to contact anyone in the UK and he told me that I could write a letter or fax which would have to go before a panel of judges. He then stood up, shook my hand and left with the senior officer following behind.

I ate supper at about seven that evening; more soup and bread. Later I was joined by Zoya who had finished working in the kitchen. She was bursting with excitement and as soon as it was safe to talk, she told me that news of my arrival was all over the prison.

'You are famous!' she cried gleefully. '*Angelli i Mostarit*.' She stood gazing at me in disbelief. 'You are on television and radio. Serbs call you "The Terrorist" and Albanians call you "Daughter of Mother Theresa". She stopped talking suddenly and leapt to attention as two officers appeared in the doorway. Both were a little overweight with dark curly hair and I thought they might be twins until I was told that one was Serb and the other Albanian.

'I saw you on television,' said the Serb with an ironic smile. The Albanian looked a little uncomfortable.

She noticed some crumbs on the floor beneath the table and told Zoya to clear them up. Zoya immediately ran to get a dustpan and brush, which I tried to take from her as the mess was from my own supper but she insisted on doing it herself and the officers didn't object. After they left, I asked her why she was so afraid of them and she mimed being beaten. I asked her if she had ever been hurt by any of the officers but she said no, she never disobeyed orders. We continued to talk softly until it was time for bed and one of the twins came to lock us in for the night. It was the Albanian woman and as she said goodnight she smiled warmly before softly closing the door.

Hours passed before I was able to sleep. The room was hot in spite of the open windows and the mosquitoes made a meal of me. As I scratched at the maddening bites I recalled a quote by the Dalai Lama: 'If you think you are too small to make a difference, try sleeping with a mosquito.'

I lay there listening to the loud snores from across the room and worrying about the forthcoming convoy scheduled to leave Britain in September. There was so much to organise. We had to find sponsors to cover the costs of insurance, fuel and ferry crossings, and there were interviews to conduct with prospective volunteers as well as funds to be raised for the purchase of medical supplies. I had no idea whether Duncan would realise that I still intended to proceed with the mission and these thoughts spun round and around in my head until I finally fell asleep.

In the morning when Zoya left for work, I was told to wait until the other women prisoners had showered and taken exercise before I too could wash. Preferring not to use the open toilet as a shower, I filled the plastic washtub with water and stripped off my clothes. Having also washed and dried my hair I felt clean and fresh and whilst the women came in to do their chores, I was taken outside. Several male faces were pressed up against a window that overlooked the courtyard. I held up my fingers in the victory salute and was rewarded with a dozen smiles.

I had no idea how long the prisoners had been at Lipljan but since 1989 many of the adult population of Kosovo Albanians had at some time been arrested. Some of them may well have been sentenced for criminal behaviour but I suspected that the majority were political prisoners or members of the KLA.

Hour upon hour was spent in the room where I was made to sit on one of the hard wooden chairs, staring at the walls. I would have preferred to lie down on the bed where it was a lot more comfortable, but that was forbidden. The hours passed slowly with nothing to break the incredible monotony. I was wondering if I might go crazy with boredom when an officer came to tell me that I had a visitor.

Bob Gordon, the British Consul, was waiting for me in an alcove near the staff room. He was sitting between his interpreter and a male prison officer and I was invited to join them. He was of medium build with short grey hair and spectacles and I guessed him to be in his late forties. He was more reserved than David Slinn and after inquiring about my health he showed me some press cuttings from the British newspapers that headlined my arrest. They stated that I had been in the process of smuggling a refugee family across the border; no mention of the fact there were many other children with me, some in need of treatment. When I pointed this out he said he would inform the press.

'But why hasn't it been mentioned? David Slinn certainly knew about it for he's the one who told me the others had escaped. In fact he said he was going on Sky news to talk about it.' Bob shrugged.

'I've also been on Sky, he said, 'and BBC Radio. So has your partner Duncan Stewart and members of your family.'

'Well it would help if they at least knew the facts,' I said. 'Mike Mendoza is the spokesman for our charity, please tell him and he will deal with it.'

He gave me a pen and paper on which to write the number and then handed me a pile of books. Not one of them would have been my chosen reading material but I was grateful for something to while away the time.

'David said he would get me some clothes,' I said, 'I only have one pair of jeans and two T shirts. Did you manage to bring anything?' I asked hopefully.

'Sorry,' he said, 'I forgot but you can have them next time.' He asked my size but I wasn't sure, having lost quite a few kilos. My belt had been confiscated and my jeans were slipping down over my hips. He passed across two names he explained were lawyers the Embassy recommended. I asked their nationalities and was told that one was a Serb and the other Albanian.

'Well I think I would prefer to be represented by an Albanian under the circumstances.'

'That's up to you,' he replied, 'They are both very good.'

'When will I meet him?' I inquired, hoping it wouldn't be too long. I really didn't know how I would cope with sitting on a chair doing nothing hour after hour and day after day.

'Within the next few days, I would hope.' I asked if he would leave the cuttings so I could read them properly but he said that he didn't have permission, returning them to a file inside his briefcase. We shook hands again and he assured me that he would return again soon.

I was taken back to my room and ordered to sit on the chair but at least I could read. However bad the books were, it was better than staring into space. I opened the most interesting of the three and lost myself until Zoya returned that evening.

I'd received the items requested on my shopping list and signed a piece of paper that would allow them to take the money. I had $400 that had been confiscated by the police and returned with my passport, plus £50 that my father had sent through the British embassy. I gave Zoya some chocolate, bananas and a carton of cigarettes. She was thrilled and immediately put everything into her locker. I asked whether she had any money to buy things, but she said she didn't. She hadn't had a visitor since her arrest two years previously.

'How do you cope?' I asked.

'I don't think about it, I just do it.' We feasted on fruit and chocolate and chain smoked until bedtime.

One evening I heard a dreadful scream from the room above. I looked at Zoya for an explanation but she placed a finger to her lips. The screaming continued for about 20 minutes, interspersed by a constant rhythmic thump. The screams were heartrending and although I couldn't understand the words it sounded like someone was begging for mercy. I knew that it might be foolish to interfere but I couldn't bear the thought of doing nothing. Zoya tried to stop me but I shrugged her away and crept out into the corridor. All of a sudden the screaming stopped and I could hear the sound of footsteps descending the staircase.

There wasn't time to return to my room so I hid beneath the staircase as baby face and a big broad officer with curly blond hair appeared in the hall. They were red faced, sweating and breathing heavily and in their hands were the long black truncheons that they usually wore on their belts. I realised that they had shared the task of beating the prisoner and from the sounds we heard, they had obviously put in a great deal of effort. As soon as they entered the office, I slipped back into the room where I found Zoya in bed, feigning sleep. Lying in bed that night, I imagined I could still hear the poor soul screaming.

The following morning when I opened my door I saw a young woman shuffling towards the washroom; her legs a mass of purple bruises. She was obviously the victim of the beating I had heard the previous night and I saw her eyes widen

Liplyan prison, July 1998.

with fear as an officer appeared in the corridor. The technique they had used is known as falanga, which involves a series of blows to the soles of the victims' feet, causing severe pain and swelling, which can lead to kidney failure. I desperately wanted to help her but I knew that it would only make things worse. It was horrible, knowing there was nothing I could do. I toyed with the idea of sending a letter or fax to Amnesty International but I knew that it would be pointless, the letter would never be sent.

That afternoon I was told that I had a visitor. I was shown to the alcove directly opposite the office where a man sat waiting. He was about 50, with greying hair and dark eyebrows. A young woman was with him, holding a notebook and pen. The man introduced himself as Azem Vllasi, a lawyer who had been appointed as my legal representative. He told me that he had decided to represent me free of charge for he admired and supported my work.

Vllasi, an ethnic Albanian and onetime leader of the League of Communists, became President of Kosovo in 1986 but was toppled in 1988 and replaced by appointees of Milosevic. The local population responded with a series of demonstrations and strikes and a state of emergency was declared. As a result, the newly appointed leaders were forced to resign, but under threat of force, Kosovo's legislature passed an amendment allowing Serbia to assert its authority over Kosovo. Vllasi was arrested by the police and charged with 'counter revolutionary activities'. He remained in prison until 1990.

When Azem spoke to me, I detected a twinkle in his eye and I supposed that from a politician's point of view I was an interesting case. He asked me to recount my experiences of the last few days in order to ascertain exactly why I was arrested.

I had to provide some background information in order to explain my reason for crossing into Kosovo without a visa and while I spoke, the woman took notes. Only when I reached the point where I had been sentenced, did Azem interrupt me.

'You weren't put on trial. This will give us the grounds for an appeal. Don't worry; you will be out of here shortly.'

As they rose to leave, I told him about the woman upstairs who had been so badly beaten. Although I saw concern in his eyes, he merely nodded and I realised that this was nothing new.

A few days later Vllasi returned but this time to my surprise and delight, he was accompanied by Marta of the Mother Theresa Charity. I hadn't seen her since our mission to Kosovo in March and I could hardly believe that she was now here, inside the Serb-run prison. As we hugged each other, I noticed Azem was carrying a newspaper, which he spread open on the table. I could see my name and recognised the words *Engelli i Mostarit* but the article was written in Albanian so I wasn't able to read it. Marta translated but as I listened to the words I was filled with dismay. The article was a gross exaggeration of what I had actually said and when I complained, Marta explained that the woman who'd accompanied him on the previous visit was a journalist.

My words had obviously been twisted for political purposes and I was livid. Marta reached for my hand and tried her best to reassure me but her sympathetic tone and gentle touch seemed to dissolve my self control. Hot tears pricked my eyes and trickled down my cheeks as the intense stress of the past couple of weeks finally took its toll. She pulled me close and held me as the tears streamed down my face. Finally, when I felt able to speak I turned to Azem.

'How could you let this happen? It's bad enough knowing that my mission has been the subject of propaganda by the Serbs but to see the Albanians doing the same? It isn't right.'

Azem tried to assure me that it wasn't as bad as it seemed but I was sure there would be repercussions.

'Please, just do your best to get me out of here. It's terribly frustrating, being shut away like this. People are suffering and there's nothing I can do about it.' He nodded and patted my arm.

'We will soon have an appeal date' he said.

An officer came to announce that the visit was over and I gave Marta a quick hug.

'Stay strong,' she called after me as I was led back to the room.

That night and most nights thereafter I could hear the sound of jets roaring overhead and the sound of distant explosions as the bombs found their targets. I imagined the women, children and elderly huddled together in the damp cellars; cold, hungry and frightened.

I was visited by the Serbian Minister of Justice, Dragoljub Jancović, who was accompanied by a number of journalists, which came as a shock. When they entered my room I was ordered to sit down while he and the others remained standing. Speaking to me through an interpreter, he wanted to know whether my treatment in the prison was satisfactory. I nodded and he asked whether I regretted my decision to commit an illegal act by violating the border without official permission. I explained that I had applied for permission but this had been refused and I also reminded him that 15,000 refugees had crossed the same border within recent weeks. He became agitated and I realised that his questions were for the benefit of the press; yet another attempt at propaganda. I decided to take the opportunity to get my own point across. I went to stand up but Surly, who was directly behind me, forced me back down onto my chair, keeping a restraining hand on my shoulder.

'I am sick of hearing the planes flying overhead to bomb innocent civilians. I am not eating and I am not drinking in protest against this war!'

As my words were translated I saw the Minister's face darken with anger and he quickly left the room, dutifully followed by the journalists.

Refusing to eat wasn't difficult, especially as watery soup and bread seemed to be the staple diet but the daytime temperature had now reached 44 degrees, so refusing liquid was harder. Within the first two days I began to dehydrate and my legs began to swell but without a newspaper or radio, I had no idea whether I had managed to get my message across. In fact the protest had been broadcast round the world and there were reports that I was in danger of imminent circulatory collapse.

A couple of days later I was handed a letter from Duncan faxed from Britain. He was extremely concerned by my decision to refuse liquid and warned me that without water my body could suffer irrevocable damage and I would die within days.

Bob Gordon came to visit me for a second time that week. He carried some more newspaper cuttings, which again failed to convey the facts. I asked him why it still was not clear that my mission involved more than one family and that some were in need of treatment. He shrugged as though it was unimportant, causing me to wonder whether the disinformation was deliberate, though I couldn't think why. He tried to persuade me to stop the protest, insisting that I had achieved my aim.

'Milosevic hasn't withdrawn his troops and I can still hear the planes flying overhead,' I said. 'Why hasn't a ceasefire been enforced?'

Dragan, the Chief Prison Officer, came to see me again but this time he was alone. He inquired about my work and we had quite a long discussion about the war. He seemed genuinely interested in my views and we spent at least an hour in deep conversation. He talked about his family and how keen he was for the war to end. When it was time for him to go, he asked whether I had any complaints about my treatment.

'I would really appreciate being able to move around more, and perhaps to lie down occasionally,' I said. 'Sitting for so many hours on a hard wooden chair is pretty uncomfortable.'

'You may do as you wish. I will inform the staff immediately.'

As he was leaving he handed me a letter with OSCE printed at the top. It was from Bill Foxton and when I read it, I felt a great deal better. He assured me that my protest was being heard around the world and he wanted me to know that he and the rest of his team were immensely proud of me.

That same afternoon I was visited by the prison nurse with dyed orange hair. She explained in broken English that I must allow her to take some blood. She wasn't overly gentle when it came to the needle but she made me laugh and I grew quite fond of her over the next few days. She was concerned that I was suffering from kidney damage and wanted me transferred to hospital but I assured her that I was fine. I had lost a great deal of weight but apart from a constant ache in my lower back, I felt ok. Zoya did her best to persuade me to drink, not really understanding my reasons for the protest. I appeased her concern by offering her the remaining fruit and chocolate, which she promptly deposited in her locker with a gleeful smile.

David Slinn came to see me and this time he was accompanied by a beautiful young woman, tall and willowy with dark wavy hair. Bukurie Gjonbalaj – who called herself Bili – was an interpreter for the British embassy. Bili, an ethnic Albanian, who was rumoured to have close ties with Hashim Thaci, would later marry Michael Steiner, Chief of UNMIK (United Nations Mission in Kosovo). Concerned for my health, she and David urged me to stop the protest but I didn't yet feel I had accomplished my aim. Towns and villages across Kosovo were burning and innocent people were still dying.

29 | AN UNEXPECTED VISITOR

ON THE FIFTH DAY of refusing food and water, I was returning from the washroom when I collapsed. The prison doctor was called and he entered the room accompanied by the nurse. He told me that if I didn't drink immediately I would be evacuated to hospital in Pristina where I would be force fed. Ignoring him I addressed the nurse instead.

'I really am fine,' I assured her. 'I was exercising in the yard this morning and probably overdid it.' She took my blood pressure, which caused some concern and she advised me to lie down and rest. The doctor left the room, muttering under his breath. David and Bili arrived and both seemed concerned by my appearance.

'Sally you are very important to the Albanian people,' said Bili, taking my hand. 'If you continue with this protest you might die!'

'Your people are dying all the time because nothing is being done to help them.'

David pulled up a chair beside the bed. 'If you really want to help, you need to stay well.'

I collapsed once again during their visit and this time I awoke to find myself attached to a saline drip. The doctor was standing beside me and although it might have been my imagination, I thought I detected a smirk on his face.

The following day I was visited by the British Ambassador Brian Donnelly, who was able to talk to me alone in my room. I proceeded to tell him about the violent attack on the female prisoner but he pointed to the ceiling light which hung overhead and I guessed he was concerned that the room might be bugged. He informed me that my father was on his way to the prison. He and Duncan had applied for visas at the Yugoslav embassy in London but although Duncan's application was refused, my father's had been accepted.

I was surprised that he should come. My father wasn't a staunch supporter of my work. He never really understood why I was prepared to take risks for people I had never met and assumed that when my work in Bosnia ended, I would return to being an artist. Instead, I had gone to Chechnya to try and help people trapped in the war-torn city of Grozny. By the time I turned my attention to Kosovo, he had given up trying to dissuade me.

When he entered the room, tears pricked my eyes, but my father wasn't a sentimental man so I bit my lip and gave him a quick hug.

'You've lost weight,' he said. 'You look a bit gaunt.'

He was holding two bags. One was filled with clothes, books and letters from friends and the other contained six large bottles of water.

'Why have you brought the water?' I asked curiously.

'Duncan said you're in danger of severe dehydration and kidney failure. You have to drink lots of water.' I smiled.

'Dad, there is plenty of water here, that isn't the problem. I was protesting against the war!'

My father, almost six feet tall and well built, sat down heavily on one of the chairs.

'Never mind all that,' he said impatiently, 'just drink the water.'

I asked him why Duncan's visa had been refused.

'I have no idea,' he replied, 'though to be honest, I think he was somewhat relieved.'

His comment did not surprise me for being a doctor with a very large practice, it was difficult for him to take time off. He would have to rearrange appointments and quickly find a locum, which was never easy at short notice.

'Bob Gordon picked me up in Belgrade last night and drove me down to Pristina,' he said, 'I'm staying at the Grand Hotel.'

I smiled wryly, for Duncan and I had stayed at the rundown concrete construction in April with our volunteers. The rather imposing hotel, built by Albanians but used mainly by Kosovo Serbs, was rumoured to serve as a base for Arkan's paramilitaries. While we were there we had to watch what we were saying as apparently all the rooms were bugged.

I told him he looked tired and he said me that artillery fire had kept him awake all night. In order to bring the bags in, they first had to be inspected by the Governor. My father had bought him a bottle of Chivas Regal and as he handed him the box, he asked whether I was a good prisoner.

'You see that list,' said the Governor, pointing to a sheet of paper on the wall. 'Those are the prison rules and your daughter has managed to break every one of them.' Nevertheless he allowed all the items through without even checking them.

'What a nice chap he is,' said my Dad, 'and what a lovely place!' Taking into account the possibility that the room was bugged, I didn't bother to shatter his illusion.

He left a short while later, promising to return the next day. I noticed that amongst the letters from friends and family, there was another from Duncan. Unlike the previous letter, which had been curt and to the point, this one contained words I would always treasure. He wrote how pleased he was to hear that I had allowed myself to be rehydrated, assuring me that this would not lessen the impact of my protest. He also told me how much he loved me – something he hadn't said for a very long time. That night as I lay down to sleep, I realised that for the first time in two weeks there were no planes flying overhead.

The following day I was escorted to a secluded rose garden close to the main gates where my father was waiting. We were seated at an elegant table and served with coffee in china cups. Bob Gordon appeared, together with the Senior Officer and told us that a film crew from the BBC was waiting at the gate because the Governor had apparently given permission for them to interview me.

'Yes, of course,' agreed my father until he saw the look upon my face.

'I don't think it would be appropriate in this setting,' I said abruptly.

'Why? What do you mean?' asked my father.

'There are similarities to Theresienstadt,' I replied, knowing that he would immediately understand.

My father, an authority on the Second World War, had told me about a particular Nazi concentration camp in Czechoslovakia where the conditions were terrible and only one in eight prisoners survived. When the Red Cross requested permission to inspect the camp the Nazis agreed, but they delayed the visit for several months. In the meantime Jewish labourers were ordered to transform the edifice from a dirty, dingy camp to a bright sunny, cheerful Jewish 'town'. The prisoners planted flowers and cleaned and painted so that when the Red Cross representatives eventually toured the camp, they passed playgrounds, gardens and newly painted dwellings.

'This place, it's not real.' I said, gesturing around the idyllic setting. 'The sweet smelling roses, the coffee and cakes served on delicate china. The prisoners are actually fed on watery soup and suffer brutal beatings. Some of them have been here for years without a trial. If I agreed to be interviewed here, I would be endorsing the worst kind of propaganda!'

'I didn't realise,' said my father.

Bob went to tell the Governor that I had declined the interview and when he returned he was smiling.

'You have been pardoned by Milan Milutinović, the President of Yugoslavia,' he declared. 'You'll be released this afternoon; as soon as they have arranged transport to the Macedonian border.' I could hardly believe it.

'But the appeal ... it hasn't been settled yet. How come they're letting me go?'

'They obviously realised that the sentence was unjust,' said my father. 'Anyway what difference how or why. Just be glad you're getting out of here!'

Bob explained that I would have to be escorted to the border by police

Jack Becker.

because I was being deported. There was only one flight from Macedonia each day so we had to hope that I would reach the airport in time. We sat there waiting anxiously for around two hours while Bob made endless calls on his cell phone.

When the final permission came through, I was rushed to my room in order to pack my belongings. I gave most of the new clothes to Zoya for although they wouldn't fit her, she had promised to hand them on to the others. I also left her some perfume and writing paper, makeup and toiletries and by the time we were finished, her locker was overflowing.

Before I left, I went to the office where Selima and the other Albanian officer were on duty. They were surprised but obviously delighted to hear the news that I was leaving. I asked them to transfer the remainder of my money to Zoya's account. As I said goodbye, large tears rolled down Zoya's cheeks and I gave her a hug, wondering how she would survive another three years in that place.

The senior officer arrived to escort me to the gate and as we left I looked up at the windows where the female prisoners gathered to watch my departure. Letting the officer overtake me, I quickly turned and waved to the faces pressed up against the glass.

The officer walked me to the main gates where Bob and my father were waiting and it all felt unreal. Dragan and other members of the staff were standing in line to say goodbye but Bob hurried me along. He told me that there wasn't much time before my flight was due to leave and we had a long drive ahead. My father sat beside me in the back of the police car whilst Bob followed behind us in a jeep. Our driver and his female colleague did not seem to speak English so I chatted to my father throughout the journey. We drove at top speed along narrow country roads and several times we almost crashed as oncoming vehicles passed by with only inches to spare. When we finally reached the Macedonian border, we were both very grateful to get out.

Bob came alongside us and lowered his window to tell me that I had to walk through customs and meet him up ahead. I handed over my passport to the customs official, who marked it with a stamp. Across the top I saw that I was denied entry into Kosovo for the next three years. As my father attempted to join me, he was stopped at the checkpoint by the passport official.

'If you step across this line you will enter Macedonia,' declared the man.

'But I would like to accompany my daughter to the airport,' said my father, a little confused.

'Well' said the man, 'that's fine but you will need a visa to return to Kosovo.'

'How long will that take?' he asked, explaining that he'd left his suitcase in Pristina and his return flight was from Belgrade.

'Three months.'

We had no choice but to say goodbye on the spot, so keeping his feet firmly in Kosovo, he leaned across and kissed me goodbye. I watched him return to the police car and as soon as he got inside it sped off down the road.

Bob was concerned that time was running out so I began to hurry, not wanting to spend the night in Macedonia. My face had been all over the news and for Serbs, I was currently public enemy number one. Bob also drove very fast but much more safely and we arrived at the airport with minutes to spare. He hurriedly escorted me to the check-in desk where I thanked him profusely for all his help.

There was no direct flight that day and I would have to change three times before eventually arriving in London. I was still quite weak and the journey was long and tiring. Family and friends were waiting to greet me at the airport but first I had to negotiate my way past the television crews and newspaper journalists. I hugged my mother, who was crying and then saw Duncan, his blue eyes twinkling as he smiled.

'Welcome home Miss Becker,' he said.

My father had been whisked back to Pristina where he had been told to wait for Bob Gordon. As the police car pulled up outside the Grand Hotel, the woman addressed him for the first time since picking us up from the prison.

'What did you think of his driving?' she asked, nodding towards her colleague.

My father was so surprised that she spoke English that he was actually lost for words.

30 | ANOTHER MISSION

I AWOKE TO FIND that Mary Banks had sold her story to the press. The *Daily Telegraph* wrote:

> Mary Banks, a coach driver with the expedition convoy, said: 'We are worried stiff that she might take other convoys to Kosovo. If she does, volunteers could end up getting killed. She is a very foolhardy woman. When we came home and later saw her on British television after her so-called jail ordeal it just stuck in our throats. She unnecessarily put our lives at risk.'
>
> Mrs Banks is joined by Dawn Jackson, from Reading, Jenny Wheately, from Brighton, Alison Scheffel from Liverpool and Madeline Brown from Wantage, Oxon, in complaining about the trip.
>
> The women, all travelling aboard a coach, claim they suffered a perilous journey in which their vehicle climbed a 10,000ft mountain over 12 hours, while being shot at by snipers.
>
> Mrs Banks said: 'We could have lost our lives about 30 times on that track, which was barely wide enough to hold the coach. The girls were traumatised and screaming all the way. One of them passed out.

Another article, headlined 'Carry On Kosovo', was spread across two double pages in the *Daily Mail*. It was basically a send-up of the whole mission and included further quotes from Banks who again implied that I had taken the convoy into Kosovo. A similar story was repeated in one form or another by most of the British media and a cartoon appeared across half a page of one of the broadsheets in which I was depicted swinging from a rope while figures tumbled into the ravine. Mark Cutts was quoted as saying 'It was one of the most inexperienced groups I have ever found in a situation like that.'

He conveniently omitted to mention all the work we had done on behalf of the UNHCR. He also stated that the UN had been forced to organise a special evacuation for Dawn, Alyson and Jenny. Many of the volunteers were angered by the allegations and made statements to the contrary. Pat Bravington said:

> We are very distressed at the allegations being made against Sally. She took care of us to the best of her ability. She never put us in any danger and she had even arranged for the Chief of police to escort us over the mountains.

Towards the end of August I was invited to appear on *Hard Talk*. The studio in which the interview took place was designed in the style of an interrogation room and was very intense. Tim Sebastian was a seasoned interviewer who had challenged presidents, prime ministers and kings, so it was daunting to be sitting opposite him with a camera in my face. The programme was made for BBC World, so this was my chance to highlight the war. I was therefore frustrated when Tim raised the subject of Mary Banks; it seemed to be a terrible waste of airtime.

I was also asked to appear on the BBC's political programme *Breakfast with Frost*. Huw Edwards was hosting the programme and with me on the sofa was Milisav Paic from the Yugoslav embassy in London. He disputed the evidence of atrocities committed by the Serbs and refused to accept that there was a continued offensive against ethnic Albanians. I talked about the suffering of women and children living in cellars beneath the rubble of their homes, but he simply denied it was happening.

Early one morning someone called me from BBC Radio 4's *Today* programme to set up an interview straight after the news. As one of Britain's most respected radio programmes – practically revered by the middle classes – I thought this would enable me to talk about Kosovo. Instead, Mary Banks came on the line.

Whilst I was forced to defend myself against the allegations, I was prevented from talking about the things that really mattered. In addition to this, the embassy had never corrected their mistake, leaving the press to believe that I had crossed the border to help one family. There was no reference to the fact that Junik was surrounded by Serb forces and no mention of the women and children I had been trying to help.

I was hoping to try and find them during our next mission to Albania and Coxy had already started recruiting volunteers. We received a number of calls from production companies who wanted to make a documentary about my work but I turned down all the proposals, disillusioned with the press. Following a meeting with Belinda Giles, the founder of Soul Purpose Productions, Mike Mendoza suggested I reconsider. He assured me that she was sympathetic to our cause and intended to make a serious film about my work.

The producer was Paulette Farsides, a small, olive-skinned woman with black shoulder length hair and, it seemed to me, a patronising manner. She was accompanied by her co-producer Juliana Rufhas, a fair-haired young woman with a slight German accent. Over lunch at Victoria station I told them of my plans to trace the children and how I was hoping to bring them to the UK for medical treatment. Paulette told me that the film would be commissioned by *Witness*, a programme on Channel 4 and knowing the series dealt with important world issues, I agreed they could join us.

I was invited to attend a demonstration against the war in Kosovo that would take place in Trafalgar Square, to speak alongside Vanessa Redgrave and Bianca Jagger. The event was attended by about 5000 people, mostly ethnic Albanians who waved flags and carried banners bearing the words FREE KOSOVA. Corin

Redgrave invited me to join him on the march to Downing Street where we delivered a letter to Prime Minister Tony Blair.

Whilst I was away some of the volunteers had virtually taken over our house, which had caused Duncan a great deal of stress. We were also at odds on the subject of children. I was hoping to have a child of my own one day but Duncan already had two grown-up daughters and wasn't planning to have any more. In addition to this, the constant publicity that surrounded my work was beginning to intrude on our personal lives. Although we were both loath to admit it, we eventually agreed that our relationship was no longer working and it was time to go our separate ways.

As the date of departure approached, I received a fax from Bill Foxton who was still based in Bajram Curri. The area had become more dangerous so the aid organisations had pulled out, despite the recent influx of refugees. The volunteers were made aware of the situation but this only seemed to make them more determined to help.

I flew to Tirana ahead of the convoy and was met by Pierre Maurer, a member of Bill's staff, who drove me to the Hotel Rogner in Tirana. Pierre was a bear of a man from Switzerland with short fair hair and a close cropped beard. With his French drawl and his eye for a pretty woman, he had quite a reputation as a Casanova. As we booked in at the reception desk, he told me there had been a serious incident in Bajram Curri and for the moment our mission was on hold.

The brother of Fatmir Haklaj, the local clan chief, had been stopped in Vlora with a car filled with arms and ammunition. He was arrested, and as a result the OSCE staff were being held hostage at the hotel. They were told that they

Convoy.

The Shogun would be hijacked and painted red. (Courtesy Martha Grenon)

Coxy prepares lunch.

would be killed if they tried to leave and negotiations were currently taking place between the OSCE in Tirana and the Albanian Minister of Justice.

Haklaj, who was head of the Rapid Deployment Unit in Bajram Curri, had been chief of Police until he was demoted for killing nine people in revenge for the assassination of one of his brothers. He killed one man for each of the bullets he found in his brother's body; blood for blood, as expounded in the Kanun, an ancient code of law especially popular amongst the tribes of northern Albania.

Waiting for me at the reception desk was Hili Krasniqi and Nik Hiseni but I did not recognise them at first as they were dressed in civilian clothes. Somehow they had heard I was coming and had brought their families to see me in Tirana.

'Where are they?' I asked, desperate to see them all.

Hili smiled and took my arm and the three of us left the hotel. We crossed the main road and walked through a spacious park where there was a large café. As soon as we entered, Marigona ran towards me and leapt into my arms, where she remained all afternoon. I remembered Drita trembling in fear as I tried to protect her from the bullets, yet she and Dede gave me a hug and thanked me for helping them. I had spent the past two months feeling entirely responsible for what happened on the mountain but they obviously didn't feel the same.

Dede told me how he had searched for us after the ambush and finding my dog tags on the grass he assumed we had been killed. They had hidden in the forest overnight whilst the Serbs continued to search for them with dogs and helicopters and as soon as it was light they made their way back down the mountain. When Hannah was released, they attempted the journey again but this time they had Hili and Nik to help them. Upon reaching Albania they were taken to a refugee camp in Shkodra run by a local priest.

I offered to buy them all lunch, insisting they order anything they wanted. Valbona clutched my hand in hers and every now and then Hanna would give me a hug. We spent a wonderful afternoon together, watching the children eating, laughing and running around in the park. Although they were still pale and thin they were much more relaxed, no longer living in fear of their lives.

Hili told me that his house had been destroyed when the Serbs attacked their village. He showed me photographs of the devastation and tried to describe how it had looked before.

'When the war is over, we'll go home and I'll rebuild it.' He said.

When the time came for us to leave, I explained that I was trying to arrange a medevac for the children. Duncan had managed to convince the Nuffield group of private hospitals to provide treatment for up to 50 patients. In addition, a local businessman had offered the use of a former hotel to house the families of the children for up to six months. As they said goodbye, I had to peel Marigona's arms from my neck and watched her squeal in anger as she was carried away.

I was telling the film crew about the refugees when a message came through that the recent crisis was over. Haklaj's brother had been put on a ferry at Koman and had just arrived in Bajram Curri, so the staff of the OSCE had now been released.

That evening we were joined in the hotel by Ismet Shamolli, who told me how worried he had been when I was captured. We ate in the hotel dining room, entertained by a group of musicians who were dressed in traditional ethnic Albanian costumes; white caps and white shirts with red and black waistcoats and black trousers tied with a sash. To my delight, they dedicated a haunting song to me. Later we strolled past the opera house where buses passed by, filled with pale-faced young men on their way to fight in Kosovo.

The film crew followed me to Durres, one of the most ancient cities in Europe, where I was due to meet the convoy arriving from Britain. The port was filled with vendors selling cartons of Amita, the sweet cherry drink sold throughout Kosovo. Others were peddling an assortment of nuts, cigarettes and cheap plastic toys. We were almost deafened by the sound of people shouting and cars hooting. While Rob the cameraman began to film the vehicles disembarking from the ferry, we were jostled by gypsies begging for a few Lek and scruffy young men in search of a deal. Children with dirty faces and unwashed hair approached us for food and I handed them some biscuits and fruit that I carried in my bag.

When the vehicles eventually cleared customs I was joined by Liz Dack in the Shogun. There were four 7.5 ton trucks and a Mercedes mini bus, a Carrols truck from Seaboard and Mary McDermott's trusty old camper van. Together, she and John Cox had catered for the volunteers as they drove across Europe. Coxy, who reminded me of the sailor who appeared on Players cigarettes, was travelling with Janey and Rob Penny, his sailing companion. Sailing was Coxy's passion and one time Duncan had joined him on his boat. They were happily sailing along the East Sussex Coast when a wind whipped up, forcing them much farther than was originally planned. It was touch and go for a while but eventually they were swept onto a beach and Duncan arrived home soaked to the skin. This was Coxy's second mission with Operation Angel, having joined us when we took aid to Kosovo in April.

Whilst I was serving my sentence in Lipljan, he worked extremely hard, collecting aid and holding fundraising events at The Norfolk Arms in Steyning. The pub's landlord, John, was also on this mission. Coxy had recruited him together with some of the other volunteers, including a lovely couple called Bernie and Susie. Bernie Sullivan worked for BskyB, who gave him a satellite phone for the trip. This would enable our convoy to be in direct communication with the outside world, even in places as remote as Bajram Curri.

Bernie and Susie shared the driving with Bill Parkes, a calm and softly spoken man who proved an asset to the mission. Roger Hall, a policeman, was travelling as Mary's co driver in the camper van. We were also joined by Keith Carney from Dallas, Texas, who was Operation Angel's director in the US. There was another

American called Martha Grenon, a talented photographer who knew the region well. The group was smaller than previous missions and therefore better organised.

We headed straight to the border town of Kukes, 125 miles from the capital. The streets were lined with concrete buildings sprouting satellite dishes like fungus on the façades. We were taken to a secure compound where the volunteers were finally able to rest. Night had fallen so it would be dangerous continue as bandits operated in the area, eager to relieve the vehicles of the aid. Even in daylight we would need an escort for the convoy. My vehicle was carrying very little so it was agreed that Liz and I would continue on to Bajram Curri, from where we would arrange an escort.

I agreed a price of $50 for two men armed with Kalashnikovs. They reminded me of the two villains in *101 Dalmatians*, their beady eyes scanning the road ahead. They told me to drive fast in order to reduce the chance of being stopped, but the road was very narrow with sheer drops on either side. I did my best to keep control of the vehicle but it was extremely difficult around the hairpin bends, especially in the dark.

After a while Liz nudged me and pointed at some shadows looming up ahead. The bright headlights reflected in their eyes and as they came closer we could see they were wolves. Running alongside us with the full moon shining overhead, they remained with us throughout the six-hour journey and then loped off into the night.

When we reached the hotel Ermal, an armed guard opened sleepy eyes and grudgingly gave us a key to one of the rooms. We carried our belongings upstairs and exhausted from driving all day and most of the night, we slept fully dressed. Later that morning we waited for Bill to return from a border patrol. Since the hostage incident, the Presidential Guard had been stationed outside the OSCE office and we had to show our ID before we were allowed to enter.

Pierre Maurer was there and when I told him about the wolves; he looked sceptical. Bill greeted us warmly and ordered coffee while I explained that the volunteers were still in Kukes. He offered to send one of his drivers to escort the convoy back to BC.

Durim was about six feet three with curly black hair and designer stubble. He wore a denim jacket and tight black jeans and carried a rifle and a Russian Tokarev pistol. He suggested he take along a friend, who turned up in a red Nissan Patrol. Curtains obscured the rear windows and like many vehicles in the region, the number plates had been removed. The two men would drive to Kukes and escort the convoy back to Bajram Curri.

'Alessandra Morelli of the UNHCR is also in Kukes awaiting an escort. She is expected to leave there today so your vehicles could tag along behind her,' said Bill. He made the necessary calls on his sat phone as there were still no landlines in BC and mobile phones were useless.

In the meantime, he brought us up-to-date. With the escalation of the war, many journalists were coming to BC and Fatmir Haklaj had organised, in the

Durim, the convoy's armed escort.

words of Julian Borger for the *Guardian*, 'the comprehensive fleecing of the foreign press corps as it has endeavoured to follow the KLA into Kosovo'. The BBC and other press had left the dusty town with only their clothes. With most of the aid agencies now gone, the situation had deteriorated and refugees were left wandering around desperate for food and clothing.

We had waited for several hours, giving Durim time to reach the convoy, when Alessandra Morelli made a surprise appearance. Her hair was a mess and she looked fraught, complaining that she and her staff had been forced to make the journey by themselves.

'All we had to protect us was an unarmed driver in a vehicle fit for the scrap heap!' she cried angrily, as she marched around Bill's office.

When we judged it was time to leave, Bill sent two of his staff to accompany us. Armando Foresti, a local man, was slightly built with fair hair and a nervous disposition. The other man was Arben Miloti, a young man from Shkodra with thick dark hair and deep-set eyes. The sun was still shining when we drove out of Bajram Curri, planning to meet the convoy half way.

We had hardly left the town when two men wearing black balaclavas appeared from behind some bushes at the side of the road. They leapt in front of our vehicle, firing their guns into the air and forcing me to screech to a halt. Pulling open the doors they tried to yank us from our seats and I realised they were after the vehicle. Knowing the volunteers would be coming down the same stretch of road I was desperate to warn them. As I reached for the radio one of the men hit me with his rifle. I saw a brief flash of light and found myself lying on the ground as the Shogun disappeared in a cloud of dust. Fortunately, I was still clutching the walkie-talkie and immediately tried to make contact with the volunteers.

'This is Angel One to convoy, I repeat, Angel One to convoy! Do you read me, over?' I cried, hoping the signal would reach that far. While I waited for a response, a small car came chugging down the road and we waved for it to stop. Armando, still shaking with fear, demanded they take us to Bajram Curri.

Back at the hotel, I felt a little groggy and there was a large bump on the side of my head. While we were waiting to hear from the convoy Bill insisted I go to the hospital to check for concussion. The doctor who examined me suggested I rest but of course that wasn't an option. The convoy was on its way into town and so far we had not received any response to my messages. Bill had a superior radio with a much greater range, so he tried calling Durim.

'Yes Oscar Charlie Bravo, go ahead, over,' a voice replied.

I spoke to Coxy and told him what had happened but just as he relayed the information to the others we heard the sound of gunfire coming from the radio. I was panic stricken thinking someone might have been shot.

In actual fact the shooting had come from the convoy's armed escort. Durim was walking ahead of the vehicles, firing his rifle in the air to deter any bandits that might be lying in wait. I sighed with relief at the news, but stood there watching anxiously until they eventually came into sight. The volunteers seemed largely unperturbed but Paulette and Juliana looked strained and pale. They had obviously been traumatised by the event and both went straight off to their room while their cameraman joined us for a drink.

The volunteers had taken the rooms along the top floor where I found Bernie preparing the satellite phone. It was in a small case, which he opened and attached to the laptop. Within a few minutes he had transmitted a report to our webmaster, together with a number of photos. I was very impressed. Computers hadn't been around for very long, at least not in the public domain and although I had sent pictures before, it certainly had not been possible from such an isolated place.

After dinner, we joined Bill on the terrace where he regaled us with amusing stories. He had a very dry wit and would punctuate his remarks by waving the metal hook that he wore in place of his hand. 'Bajram Bill', as he was known, was unique both in looks and personality. He was a dreadful flirt and although he wasn't exactly George Clooney there was something very attractive about him. He told us that he was married and had two grown-up children, but for the past three years had been living with a German woman in Bosnia. According to Bill, the relationship had recently ended because he was not prepared to commit.

The next morning I went to see the UNHCR who had scaled down their operation and moved their office to the Hotel Ermal. Only one resident member of staff remained, a local woman called Albana. I explained that I was trying to trace the children from the mountain in order to arrange their onward journey. She told me that most refugees were housed in the Cultural Centre opposite the hotel, so I went to see the man in charge.

After checking the list of names, he informed me that Khalil, Lira and Musa were already on their way to Switzerland where they would be reunited with their parents. Although disappointed that I had only just missed them, I was delighted to know that they would soon be reunited with their parents.

During the distribution of medical equipment to the local hospital, a tall, dark haired man limped towards us with a small boy at his side. The boy had a mop of thick brown hair. Just five years old, he was seriously hurt when his home was destroyed by fire in Kosovo. His face and arms were badly burned and although the wounds were beginning to heal, he could not use his fingers. Liz explained that the burns were causing his hands to claw; he needed plastic surgery or he would soon be permanently disabled. We told them to come to the hotel where we would collect all their details.

In the meantime the OSCE had arranged for Pierre Maurer to escort us to the UN warehouse in Tropoje, which was still the central distribution point for humanitarian aid. Pierre had a PhD in Political Science from Bradford University and had written a book about Tito. He was very familiar with the Balkan region and was a close friend of the famous film maker Emir Kusturica. As a research Fellow at the School for Yugoslav Studies at Bradford University, Pierre was also fluent in Serbo-Croat. He adored women and it was impossible to have a serious conversation with him when a pretty woman was around. He was also a successful businessman having introduced Swiss cigarettes to the Balkans and as a result he was very familiar with the major smugglers of the region and had experience in dealing with hard men.

As we drove along the muddy track, a call came through the walkie-talkie demanding the convoy to stop. I could hear raised voices and somebody mentioned a gun. Walking towards the rear of the convoy I could see Roger and Mary arguing with a man who was sitting in a car alongside the camper. He was pointing his gun at Roger and looked angry enough to use it. According to the man, Roger had nudged his wing mirror as they passed him on the narrow road. Pierre appeared and calmly suggested that I offer the man a few dollars for the damage. After a few tense moments, he grudgingly accepted.

Tropoje sits at the foot of the Shkelzeni Mountain, which is 2800m high. Since the escalation of the war, there had been a tidal wave of refugees flooding into the town, only ten kilometres from the border. Many were being housed by the locals, who were already living well below the poverty line.

When we pulled into the car park there was a large crowd of people milling around and I was concerned to hear that the warehouse had recently been targeted by looters. After a meeting, we decided to distribute the aid ourselves rather than leaving it in the warehouse. The refugees were told to form a line while Elizabeth and Riki wrote down their details. At the same time the volunteers started to rearrange the aid into individual boxes according to their needs. Each box contained a selection of clothing, food, cooking equipment and bedding.

Prenda Ismaili, formerly a local teacher, was employed as an interpreter for the UNHCR. Prenda, in her thirties I thought, tried to convince me that we should leave the aid in the warehouse but I refused. Firstly, I didn't want the aid to be stolen and secondly, I was reluctant to leave it with the UN.

Prenda started shouting and Paulette quickly told Rob to start filming. Not wanting yet another public row with a UN official, I tried to reason with Prenda, explaining that we just wanted to be sure the aid reached the refugees. She continued to insist that we leave it in the warehouse but she had no real authority so we began to distribute the boxes to the people on our list. During the distribution, a man came to see me and explained that he was responsible for the refugees in Bajram Curri, who were also in need of help. He gave me a list of their names and I told him we would keep back some aid.

The distribution was difficult, with people pushing and shoving and doing their best to carry away more than their quota. Many of those waiting in line were desperate, for now that the aid agencies had pulled out most things were scarce. One old woman staggered away with a very large container of goods, only to return for another. It was on her third trip that Liz noticed and confronted her. The woman shrugged and grinned but she still didn't give up, sneaking round the back of a vehicle and helping herself.

Pierre and the local police were very helpful, holding the crowds back long enough for the bulk of the aid to be handed out before we prepared to leave. I was in the process of turning my vehicle around as the other drivers were closing their doors and revving their engines, when suddenly there were several loud gunshots. I turned to see a group of men brandishing rifles, obviously intent on getting the rest of the aid.

'Angel One to convoy,' I called over the radio, 'move out! Everybody move out now! Over.'

It was mayhem as several of the drivers began trying to manoeuvre their vehicles out of the car park and onto the road. Pierre and his driver had driven a few yards ahead, waiting for us all to follow. Guns were still firing as we sped off down the road but no one was hurt and the vehicles were unscathed. Pierre, who seemed completely unperturbed by the drama, assured me they were just trying to scare us, hoping we would abandon the aid. We returned to Bajram Curri and later I found the man from Tropoje with his list of refugees. By the end of the day we had distributed all of the aid and the vehicles were now empty.

The following day I was sitting on the terrace when a shadow loomed over me and looking up I saw Rambo. He was dressed in a T-shirt and jeans; no weapons in sight and he looked like any ordinary guy. As we sat there chatting in the afternoon sun he told me that following the ambush, Gian and Rafaelli had immediately headed back to Junik, leaving Fausto and the rest of the group behind. The widow could barely walk and had to be virtually carried down the mountain on Rambo's back. He then rounded up some soldiers and went back to collect the others who were waiting in the forest. Bekim was currently in a hospital in Tirana and would soon be discharged but he had lost the use of his arm.

One afternoon I was walking through town when a man called my name. I turned around to see Chamed, the old soldier from the mountain. He took me to meet his family who were living in an apartment block nearby. Over glasses of squash, he told me that he had remained in Junik for another three weeks until the town finally fell to the Serbs. He had two children in their teens, a son and a daughter. His son was hoping to study to become a doctor so I suggested that we send his details to the Halley Stewart Trust, who might be able to help.

Having read of my release from prison, Hamez Shala arrived in Bajram Curri. He came to the hotel to remind me of my promise to try and help his two-year-old daughter Besa and we suggested he fill out an application form, which we added to our growing list.

Shortly before the convoy was due to leave, Bill informed us that the chief of border security had organised a party on our behalf. Sheep were being slaughtered across Albania for the beginning of the Muslim festival of Ramadan and I felt guilty at the thought of an animal being killed especially for us. Bill laughed but assured me that the one we would be eating had slipped in a crevasse and would have died anyway.

We drove for about two hours along a narrow dirt road running parallel to the Valbona river. The valley is bordered on both sides by spectacular mountains and some of the peaks were still covered in snow. We eventually stopped in the village situated high in the Dinaric Alps and piling into a one-storey shack with a few tables and a bar. We feasted and danced until dusk.

Security was getting tighter and one day while we were having lunch, a group of armed men rushed onto the terrace. They wore uniforms and masks, part of the Rapid Deployment Team, brought in to impose law and order in the town. We were told to lie face down on the ground while they searched the hotel for a missing felon but eventually they left empty handed.

Our volunteers had adopted a stray puppy, a sandy-haired mongrel which they named Angel and much to the disgust of Halil, the puppy lived beneath the terrace of the hotel. One evening a wedding was taking place and there was the usual parade of vehicles around the town. As they passed by the hotel, beeping their horns and firing rifles in the air, Angel went off to investigate.

One of the drunken guests was firing his rifle from the back of a truck, when suddenly there was a scream and a curse as he shot two of his own fingers off by mistake. Angel, who had learned to take advantage of any opportunity for a snack, promptly ate them. The unfortunate wedding guest was rushed to the hospital, where the doctor suggested they try to locate the fingers. The dog was immediately taken to a vet and forced to vomit, but the chewed and partly digested fingers were not fit to be reunited with their owner; Fortunately Armando had the foresight to get Angel out of there before it was too late.

A short while later Paulette announced that she and the film crew were leaving. I was surprised, for they had led me to believe that the documentary was about the evacuation of the children, which wouldn't happen until November. When I asked her about it she said they were working to a deadline and needed time to edit the footage; but it seemed to me that all they had filmed were a series of mishaps.

31 | BLOOD AND RAIN

MÉDECINS SANS FRONTIÈRES AND the ICRC had pulled out, leaving many children without appropriate medical treatment. Having done what Daniel Enders suggested and arranged the hospital beds in Britain, we sent word around that any children in need of medical help should contact Operation Angel at the Hotel Ermal.

In order to assess those who came seeking assistance, we had to convert one of the rooms in the Ermal. Liz was in charge of the assessments and she examined each child before deciding who would be included in the medical evacuation. Those who could be treated in Albania would be referred to the hospital in Tirana.

Halili and his father arrived at the hotel and while they proceeded to fill in a visa application a nineteen-year-old boy arrived. He was tall and thin with a shaven head and wild dark eyes. He told us that he had been arrested and tortured in Kosovo where the police had sat him on a chair and interrogated him with methods that could only be employed by a sadistic madman. They had systematically driven a nail into the back of his head and although the wound had now healed, he was obviously still traumatised by the experience and his mind was not functioning properly. Liz immediately prepared another application.

Choosing whom to help was not an easy task because some of the parents would exaggerate their child's problem in order to get visas. This was understandable but as much as we wanted to help them all, we knew that our applications had to be restricted to medical emergencies and their families. Apart from the pressure caused by a constant influx of prospective patients, the psychological strain on Liz was immense; refusing treatment meant condemning the child to remain in Bajram Curri through the winter.

The details of those we accepted had been faxed to Duncan, who passed them on to the Home Office. The authorities wanted each medical case confirmed by UNHCR, so I told Allessandra Morelli of our plans and requested her support.

'We have nothing to do with medical evacuations. You will have to make a request to the ICRC.'

I promptly called the ICRC, who told me that medical evacuations were the responsibility of the UNHCR. I had encountered this situation in Bosnia and despite the fact that fifteen years had passed, it seemed nothing much had changed. I sent a fax to the British Home office explaining the problem.

Many Kosovans came to the Ermal seeking information from the OSCE, one of the few organisations still with a base in Bajram Curri. Amongst them was the widow who had been with me on the mountain. She had been reunited with her daughters and was hoping they could travel abroad but I had to explain that we were only dealing with paediatric medical cases. I expected her to be angry but instead she shrugged and gave me a hug.

Liz and I were getting some supplies from a local shop when I spotted my Shogun on the main street. The vehicle had been sprayed with red paint but there was a small dent in the rear bumper that I recognised instantly. Before Liz could stop me I approached the man sitting in the driver's seat, a local gangster called Petrit. He was a big, burly man with shoulder-length black hair and dark glasses. Around his neck were several very thick gold chains. Leaning into the open window, I said, 'You are driving my car!'

He grinned disdainfully and gunned the engine but just as I was contemplating grabbing the keys, Liz appeared beside me.

'Don't!' she hissed.' He's probably armed.'

I chose to heed her warning and watched him tear off down the road in a cloud of dust. I had one more task to complete, which involved a trip to the British Embassy in Tirana. Having received all the visa applications, they now wanted to interview some of the parents. We arranged to travel with the OSCE and would meet Hili, Nik and the others in Tirana.

One at a time the refugees entered the room where the British Consul waited to question them. When the interviews were over, he assured me that there would be no problem with regard to issuing the visas and we could expect to receive confirmation from the Home Office within a few days.

After the refugees returned to Shkodra, I went to meet my colleagues at the Hotel Rogner. Stephen Nash, the British Ambassador was having coffee with Demetrios Plaits, the Greek Chargé d'Affaires and they invited me to join them. Demetrios was interested in hearing about the planned evacuation and when I had finished explaining, he offered the use of a Greek Air force plane to carry the children and their families to Britain. I was delighted and could hardly believe my good luck when Daan Everts, Head of the OSCE in Albania, offered to arrange the transport of our patients to Tirana.

Everything seemed to be falling into place and back at home our volunteers had completely refurbished the hotel. My brother Eddy and his friend had cleared out the old furniture while my mother and my aunt helped some of the volunteers to scrub and clean the place from top to bottom. Eileen, a woman with boundless energy, spent every free moment there until it was spotless. Windows and doors were fixed and the walls were painted. A new kitchen was installed and Mari's husband put in new sinks and toilets. My cousin, who lives in Israel, donated money to buy enough food for six months and we were given beds and covers, tables and armchairs.

Keith Carney had managed to secure visas for some of the patients to travel to the United States. He had also arranged hospital beds and surgeons to carry out the operations; three of which involved open heart surgery. Besa Shala was on the list and she and her family were flown to a specialist clinic in Dallas, where she would be fitted with cochlear implants.

2 November was Bill's birthday. He was 55 years old and he invited me to celebrate with him at a local restaurant. After a couple of large whiskeys, Bill decided to tell me what happened on the night I was captured by the Serbs.

'We were at the border waiting for you to cross when we heard the sound of a fire fight and saw a helicopter hovering overhead. The UN and some EC monitors were there too but after a while they left. I stayed there for most of the night though, hoping to God that you'd eventually appear. When you didn't come I was devastated, thinking that you must have been killed.'

Bill then reached across the table for my hand and told me that he had fallen in love with me. Before I could respond the waiter appeared and he ordered a bottle of local red wine which we drank with the meal. Afterwards when we made our way back to the hotel we were both a bit tipsy and as we crossed the street he looked up and suddenly started to laugh. When I asked what had tickled him he pointed to the large statue of Bajram Curri that overlooks the main square, and I realised why he was so amused. The figure of the soldier holding his rifle stood out in stark relief against the moonlit sky. By the time we reached the hotel entrance I was laughing so much that I walked straight into the glass doors. Bill laughed even louder, especially when I pointed out that he might wake the armed night watchman who was sleeping in the foyer. We crept past him and stumbled towards the stairs, both of us giggling like children. That night we became lovers and although it was probably just another war romance for Bill, at the time I thought that I had found my soul mate.

The day of departure approached and final preparations were put into place for the evacuation. The OSCE would ferry the children and family members to Tirana where the British Consul would issue the final documentation. Demitrios called to let me know that the Greek Air Force plane was on standby to fly the children and their families to Britain and I received confirmation that the St John's ambulances would be awaiting our arrival at the airport.

On the day of departure, I was called into Bill's office. He looked completely bewildered as he handed me a fax from the British Embassy in Tirana and I had just finished reading it when Liz entered the room.

'All visas have been refused.' I told her, hardly able to believe my own words. 'Jack Straw has issued a statement to the press announcing that we have not fulfilled the necessary requirements.'

'But we've sent them all the medical histories, x-rays, Doctor's diagnosis and the rest. What more could they need?' asked Liz with dismay.

'Apparently each application should have been supported by the UNHCR but Alessandra Morelli assured me in this very room that their support was not

Liz Dack.

required. Straw also states that the cost to the British government would be £400,000, which is nonsense.'

'I'm going to my room,' said Bill, leaving me, Liz and two members of staff in the office.

None of the reasons issued in the statement made sense. The Greek Air force had offered to fly the patients to Britain and St John's Ambulance brigade would transport them to their destination. The medical treatment and aftercare would be carried out by staff at the Nuffield Private Hospitals; at no cost to the NHS. The visa applications were for a maximum of six months and we had arranged accommodation, food and transport for the whole of that period. The cost to the British government would actually be nil.

The statement concluded with Straw saying; 'The British government has already made it clear to Ms Becker that the focus of UK aid for the Kosovo crisis is on winter supplies and healthcare, channelling its funds entirely through projects based in the region.'

When Bill came back to the office he looked deeply upset. He told the staff to try and make contact with the people on our list to inform them that the mission had been cancelled and without another word he went back to his room. Later he told me that he had been overcome by the 'black dog', a term coined by Winston Churchill when referring to his depression.

I was called to reception and descending the stairs with a heavy heart, I found a small crowd of people waiting with their luggage. Amongst them were the children, smiling expectantly as I approached. Having to tell them that they would not be leaving after all was one of the hardest things I have ever had to do.

That evening Liz and I went downstairs to the bar adjacent to the hotel. Sitting at a table was Durim, Armando and a couple of friends and they had obviously been drinking for quite a while. We were invited to join them and I ordered a glass of Skanderbeg, the local brandy, which I drank straight down causing me to splutter. Durim told me that a soldier from Kosovo had been admitted to the hospital. There had been a border incursion by armed gunmen who had shot him in the chest.

'He was asking for you,' said Durim.

I went to the hospital and found the soldier with his chest bandaged. He looked pale and very weak but at least he was conscious. A woman moved aside so that I could see him.

'Thank you for coming,' he said, his voice just a whisper. I saw that he was wearing a gold ring with a large red stone and realised it was Ardi, the young man who had entrusted me with his siblings. 'I wanted to thank you for helping us; the children are with our parents in Switzerland. They are very happy.'

I went to find the doctor who told me that he would shortly be evacuated to Tirana where they had better facilities.

'Do you think he'll survive?' I asked. The doctor nodded.

'But the war is over for him.'

The following afternoon Liz and I decided to write a letter to Tony Blair, appealing the decision made by Jack Straw. We went to the Mona Lisa restaurant, a place where we had often taken our volunteers. There were several men inside but although the local women would rarely go to a bar, they were used to seeing us around and barely looked up as we entered.

For two or three hours we sat writing and rewriting the letter and when at last we were satisfied with our efforts, we decided to leave. With the curfew in place, it was forbidden to be out after dark so we set off back to the hotel. It was pouring with rain and the street was deserted but I caught a glimpse of Armando beneath an umbrella hurrying home.

Like everyone else, we were tired of the hotel food, so when Bill was given permission to use one of the rooms as a kitchen, we were all delighted. He would scout around for whatever he could find locally and conjure up some tasty dishes. That evening we had been promised roast lamb and all the trimmings, providing there was electricity.

As we approached the hotel car park, dusk was falling and the street lights came on, casting a sodium glow. This was a good sign as it meant the hotel had power. A man was standing beside a lamp post and I saw he was dressed in army fatigues, his face obscured by a black balaclava. He was holding a gun that glinted in the lamplight. As I threw myself into the shadows, there was a searing hot pain through my thigh.

When the man disappeared I gingerly touched my leg which felt wet, blood mingling with the rain. I wasn't sure whether I was dreaming until Liz appeared in front of me clutching the side of her face.

'What happened?' she asked, her voice trembling.

'It's my leg,' I said, my teeth gritted in pain.

Liz rushed into the hotel to get help and eventually found Bill in the kitchen. He was holding a glass of whisky and when she rushed towards him crying,' Sally's been shot!' it shattered on the floor.

32 | NOBODY'S ANGEL

I WAS VAGUELY AWARE of voices but they sounded muffled and distant. An army truck seemed to appear from nowhere and I thought I was hallucinating. Bill hauled me onto the back of the truck and he and Liz leapt in beside me as the vehicle lurched onto the main street. We hit a pot hole and I was thrown around, causing a fresh gout of blood to pour from my leg. I heard Bill's voice saying that the bullet might have severed the femoral artery and if so, I only had minutes.

When we reached the hospital I was carried to the emergency room but there was no light and someone was dispatched to find a bulb. As the doctor examined my leg, I heard Bill's voice again.

'Thank God, it's a 'through and through.'

The bullet had passed through my thigh and come out the other side. An antiquated machine was brought to my bedside and an x-ray was taken. The doctor then began to remove the debris from the wound, which caused excruciating pain. I was given an injection of morphine and as the medication started to take effect, Bill told me he was leaving.

'I have to send a report,' he said. 'Anyway the dinner might be ruined.'

There seemed to be a great deal of noise around me so I hauled myself up to see what was going on. The room was filled with people. 'What's happening?' I asked, wondering again if I might be hallucinating. The doctor smiled.

'They have come to see the Angel of Mostar,' he said.

That evening I was supposed to be attending a charity ball in London held by the Celebrity Guild of Great Britain. They had decided to make a special donation to Operation Angel and Duncan and my mother were there to receive it on my behalf. They were sitting in the banqueting hall surrounded by celebrities when a phone call came through to say that I had been shot.

When the wound had been thoroughly cleaned I decided to leave the hospital – I was obviously the target and they had no security. The morphine had left me relatively free of pain so I was able to make my way slowly down the stairs. Outside I found Durim waiting to drive me back to the Ermal. Liz was waiting in Bill's office with Andrea, a German woman who worked for the OSCE. Tall and athletic with short blond hair, she was studying to be a nurse. Liz helped me into a chair while Andrea was busy setting up a saline drip.

Duncan Stewart and Sally's
mother at the charity ball.

Liz's face was badly
bruised where the other
man had hit her with his
gun but she insisted that
she was alright. I sat down
beside her and was listening
to them speak when all of a
sudden it felt as though my
body were shutting down.
Darkness was closing in and
I could not move or speak. It
occurred to me that I might
be dying but there was
no way to let them know.
Fortunately Liz happened to
turn to me and realised that
something was wrong.

'She's going into shock!'
she cried, and they quickly
tried to insert a canula into
my arm. My veins had constricted and no matter how hard they both tried, they
couldn't get the needle in. Andrea suggested they try to insert the canula into my
neck and when at last the drip was in place I immediately began to recover. If
they had not acted quickly my vital organs would have been affected and I would
probably have died. Strangely enough, I wasn't concerned at the time; the terror
came later when I recalled how close to death I had actually been.

With the drip stand in tow, they helped me down the corridor to my room and
as soon as I lay down on the bed I began to drift off to sleep. A short while later
I was woken by Bill as he entered the room with a plate of lamb, potatoes and
vegetables. When I realised it wasn't a joke, I politely suggested he take it away, for
having just been shot, I really wasn't hungry.

During the night the pain in my leg intensified as the effects of the morphine
began to wear off. Liz decided to increase the dose but she explained that it
would have to be injected into my buttock. I wasn't able to turn onto my side so
eventually Liz called Bill in to help her. I caught a glimpse of him standing in the
doorway and a moment later there was a needle in my backside. At least the deed
was done.

I awoke the next morning to find two men standing beside my bed: the
Albanian Minister of Health and a doctor. They asked if I minded them taking a

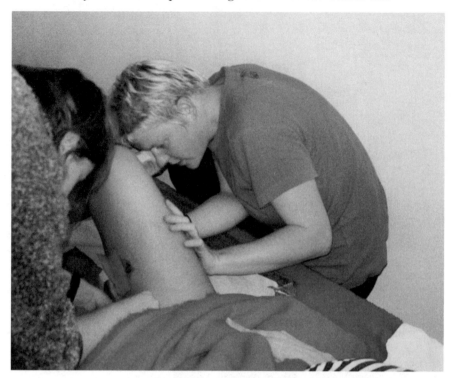

Liz and Andrea tend to the bullet wound.

look at the wound and Liz removed the dressings from my thigh. Although the entry wound looked relatively minor, no bigger than a ten pence piece, the exit wound was a gaping hole, at least two or three inches in diameter and the slight movement had caused it to bleed heavily, immediately soaking the bed sheets. The men explained that they had been sent by President Meidani, who had arranged for a helicopter to fly me to Tirana.

'Can we take the children with us?' I asked. He shook his head.

'I'm sorry, no, that won't be possible.'

'Then I have to decline your offer I'm afraid, I can't leave without them.'

Looking dismayed, he spoke to his colleague for a few moments before turning back to me.

'The doctor says that the wound is infected. You need specific antibiotics and treatment in sterile surroundings. In Tirana you will have the best possible care.'

I told them that although I was grateful for their offer, I didn't feel able to leave.

'I have promised to try and help these families and if I go they will think I abandoned them. At least while I'm around they still have some hope.'

They eventually gave up trying to persuade me and politely said goodbye.

Bill called the British Embassy and made a request for antibiotics and sterile dressings and as soon as they came, Liz and Andrea started cleaning the entry and exit wounds in my leg.

We had a visit from the local Chief of Police who wanted Liz and I to make a statement about the night of the shooting. His hair was cut in the style of Elvis Presley and he wore tight black bell bottom trousers and platform shoes. We told him that our attackers were wearing masks and he wrote something down.

'Did you see what they looked like?' he asked, causing us to stare at him in dismay. Sherlock Holmes he was not. Liz was prepared to stay with me in Bajram Curri and although I would have loved her to stay, I felt she had done more than enough already. The OSCE had been inundated with calls from the media so by going home she would also be able to use the media interest to highlight the plight of the children. Bill arranged for Liz to be driven to Tirana and as she prepared to leave we were both quite upset. We'd been through a lot together and I was going to miss her very much.

'I'll do my best to make them listen,' she assured me.

Mike had arranged a press conference upon her arrival in Britain but although the coverage was widespread, it was not what we hoped for; they were more interested in details of the shooting than the plight of the children.

A few days later I received a letter from the President of Albania.

Dear Miss Becker,

I am glad to hear the good news coming from Tropoje that your health keeps improving and that actually your condition is not life threatening. Considering this a grave act which 'you good lady did not deserve' I am convinced that the generous and patriotic region of Tropoje has given and will give you the occasion to access that it knows to respect guests, and that ugly act which aims to take your life is alien to the tradition and mentality of this region.

Just like my people I have followed with much admiration your activities to aid the people in need due to the anachronistic wars fomented by sick minds amidst Europe; once in Bosnia, yesterday in Kosovo and today in Albania.

Your determination to continue this activity deeply affects me personally and believe me, that my compatriots, wherever they are, will highly value this thing.

True Albanians know to evaluate friends and I wish you a speedy recovery and success in the realisation of your vocation, which has inspired, and continues to inspire, many people in search of a better and fairer world.

President Rexhep Meidani

Back in Britain, the press had a field day. 'Nobody's Angel' and 'Fallen Angel' read the headlines. Lyndell Sachs, a spokeswoman for the UNHCR, criticised my attempt to arrange medical treatment for the children, saying: 'We are more concerned with building the infrastructure in Kosovo to benefit a greater number of people.'

Bill was inundated with calls from the press and he dealt with most of them on my behalf. I made an exception for Lorraine Kelly because she had been so supportive in the past, but to my disappointment she brought up all the nonsense that had been published by the press.

Channel 4 broadcast the documentary and when Mike called me to say how biased it was, I decided to resign. I was fed up with the sniping and the constant criticism from the UN and the press. With my credibility at zero there seemed little point in continuing to represent the charity. From now on I would have to work alone.

FROM . Office of Republic of Kosova   PHONE NO. . 28312   Nov 18 1998 09 28AM P0
18/11 '98 09:39   S0

REPUBLIC OF KOSOVA
Government of the Republic

Phone: +49 228 955 K50
Fax: +49 228 354 536

To **Sally Becker**

OPERATION ANGEL

Bajram Curri
via fax 00871 761 280 174

Dear Sally,

It was with great sadness and a feeling of shame that I received the news of the terrible deed of those who threatened your life, the life of the 'angel'.

The greatness of your work seems to be in the fact that nothing can stop you.

Wishing you a speedy recovery, I look forward to seeing you soon

Sincerely yours,

Bujar Bukoshi

Dr. Bujar Bukoshi
Prime Minister

A note to Sally from Dr Bujar Bukoshi, the Prime Minister of Kosovo.

33 | BAJRAM BILL

IN ORDER TO AVOID infection, Liz and Andrea had been cleaning and dressing the wounds in my leg several times each day. Now with Liz gone and Andrea often busy patrolling the border, there was no one around to perform the minor surgical procedures necessary for my leg to heal, so Bill Foxton, who was trained in field medicine, offered to take over.

Five or six times a day Bill patiently dug away at the wounds. It was difficult for him to be gentle with a hook in place of a hand but he carefully removed the threads of material that had been blasted through my leg on the point of the bullet and were now making their way to the surface. He also had to snip away necrotic tissue from the cavity to avoid the risk of gangrene and I would grip the metal rungs of the headboard whilst gritting my teeth.

With Liz's departure, Bill insisted I be moved closer to the office where the Presidential Guard remained on duty throughout the day and night. The room was very small and contained a single bed and a chair and there was a permanent bad smell in the air, though I was never able to identify the cause. Perhaps it was me. At night I could hear the sound of mice scurrying across the floor.

An old man trekked for miles across the frozen landscape to bring me some homemade yoghurt, and when he held my hand and told me that he would gladly have taken the bullet on my behalf I was moved to tears. Some of the children came to visit me and amongst them was little Halili, the boy who had been badly burned. He stood beside my bed and smiled and as I looked around at their faces, so innocent and full of hope, it made me even more determined to stay.

One afternoon there was a loud commotion outside in the corridor and two men entered my room, both of them heavily armed. One was the infamous Fatmir Haklaj, tall and slim with curly fair hair and a bushy beard. He was dressed in camouflage pants and he carried an Uzi sub machine gun, a Makarov pistol and two RPG 7 rockets. His bodyguard, Feriz Kernaiar, a convicted killer, was cradling a rocket launcher. To my relief, Bill Foxton and Beni came in behind them. Fatmir started shouting and gesticulating whilst I lay there helpless on the bed unable to understand a word he was saying. Finally when he finished speaking, he turned to Beni and grunted.

'He says you are much respected throughout Albania and Kosovo for all you have done,' said Beni. 'He wants to assure you that no Albanian would take up arms against you, for you are the symbolic daughter of Mother Theresa.'

'Thanks,' I said, thinking it might be wise to leave it at that.

'You have his protection and his guarantee that you will come to no further harm, and if you ever need his help, you only have to ask.'

I was just debating whether to tell him that my Shogun had been hijacked, when he turned on his heel and left, followed closely by the bodyguard.

Although I was starting to move around more, my leg was quite stiff and the slightest movement would cause the wound to bleed. Fortunately, the British embassy in Tirana continued to send a regular supply of dressings and antibiotics so the treatment could continue.

It was snowing and the roads were icy but I wanted to visit the children so Durim took me in his car. We stopped at a small house where Halili and his family were living in one room. I gave his father a few hundred dollars thinking it would help to get them through the winter but he decided he would use the money to take his family abroad. A few months later I received a message to say they had turned up in Britain and his son was having treatment.

With nothing much to do while my leg was healing, I spent a lot of time sitting in the office, the only room in the Ermal that was heated. The OSCE were now the only organisation using the hotel and two new members had recently joined the team. One was a Pole, Krysztof Tomkowski, an authority on cinema, and the other a lieutenant-colonel from Bulgaria.

Bill had managed to find a television and someone had hung a satellite dish outside the window. Whenever there was electricity, we would huddle around the gas fire and watch the news; or we'd light a few candles and talk late into the night. Nursing a glass of whisky, Bill would amuse us with tales from his army days, which began when he first left school. As soon as he was old enough he joined the Foreign Legion, serving in France and Algiers before escaping across the desert with a couple of friends; the journey was hell and one of his friends didn't make it.

In 1969 he enlisted with the British Army, serving with the Royal Green Jackets. He was brake man for the IRGJ British Bobsleigh Team during the 1972 European Championships and the following year he served as a company intelligence Sergeant in Belfast, where he was mentioned in dispatches.

Later Bill joined the Sultan's Armed Forces in Oman where he rose to the rank of Major. One night he told us about an incident that happened during this period. He was returning from an operation with sixteen soldiers and two other Frontier Force officers. They were travelling in a Sky van towards the Raysut airstrip when at 4500 feet the pilot collapsed. Grabbing the joy stick, Bill, who happened to be sitting in the co-pilot's seat, took control of the aircraft while his two colleagues tried to revive the pilot. The pilot's legs were jamming the rudder and the aircraft went into a spin. The Beluchi soldiers could see what was happening and started to panic as the aircraft descended. Warning lights were flashing and a siren was wailing and the officers tried to prepare everyone for a crash landing. Fortunately, someone thought to retract the flaps and Bill was able to level out and fly towards an airfield. Having never flown an aircraft before, he started to consider how to land the plane but one of his fellow officers managed to resuscitate the pilot, who took over at the last minute. Bill and his two colleagues were awarded the Sultan's Commendation for saving both the aircraft and all those on board.

It was during his time with the SAF that Bill lost part of his left arm when destroying a 60mm unexploded mortar round after a training exercise. Bill was eventually fitted with a prosthetic limb and he added various attachments. There was one he called his 'war arm', which was made of solid steel and another where the hook was studded with diamonds – for special occasions. After the injury Bill returned to duty as Deputy Force Welfare Officer and subsequently received an MBE for services to disabled Omani soldiers.

When the war broke out in Bosnia he joined the ECMM and spent two years in the Bihac pocket, which was often isolated by Serb forces surrounding the area. After the war he lived in Sarajevo and continued to work for ECMM as a training officer. It was around this time that he had apparently crawled through a minefield to save a Serbian child in the Vrbas Valley. Tony told me the story but when I asked Bill to confirm it, he simply smiled. Bill eventually transferred to the OSCE and in 1998 he became Head of Office for northern Albania. It was rumoured that he also worked for British Intelligence but this was never verified, although certainly the CIA were very active in the region.

I had begun to use Bill's en suite bathroom instead of the old Turkish style shower/toilet on the floor below. One evening after the water went off, I was struggling along the corridor with a bucket to pour into the sink. All of a sudden the lights went out and I could hear the sound of footsteps creeping up behind me. I almost jumped out of my skin as a voice suddenly yelled loudly in my ear and caused me to drop the bucket. Water spilled across the floor and I slipped, yelping with pain as something sharp suddenly caught me from behind.

'Oh dear, it's all gone wrong.' It was Bill. He explained that after the electricity went off, he had warned the others to keep quiet while he crept out of the office to make me jump. His joke went further than he had intended because as he reached out to stop me from falling he caught me with his hook. Andrea tended to the bleeding tramlines on my back while Bill apologised and tried not to laugh.

When I felt fit enough to travel, we drove down to Tirana. Bill and Andrea were on leave, so we booked into the Rogner and spent three days living in style. The beds were soft and comfortable and the rooms were heated, unlike the Ermal where it was freezing cold. In the evenings we ate in the palatial dining room, feasting on steak and sautéed potatoes and choosing mouth-watering desserts from the trolley. I had forgotten how pleasant it was to eat from china plates and drink wine and water from crystal glasses. Bajram Curri had been my home for over two months so the break was much appreciated.

Bill stays until dawn.

During the day I visited some of the embassies in Tirana, requesting help for the children still awaiting treatment. The embassies of Czechoslovakia and Greece had offered visas for the refugee families still waiting in Bajram Curri and Liz Dack had managed to arrange for a British paediatrician to travel to Albania to help those who could be treated at home.

I received a message from Keith Carney letting me know that most of the patients who had gone to the States were now being treated. Besa Shala was still waiting for the cochlear implant, but the device, surgery and subsequent speech therapy would be very expensive. Keith was doing his best to raise the money and in the meantime the family had applied for their visas to be extended.

On the day of our return to Bajram Curri, we were driven to the ferry in Koman, which would take us to Fierze in the north. A group of Albanian men were lounging around in a haze of cigarette smoke and they cast suspicious glances in our direction as we headed towards the stairs. I was feeling slightly dizzy as we climbed the rusted staircase and assumed that it was due to the long car journey. Moments later I felt myself falling and then everything went black.

Somehow Bill managed to get me into a cabin and I awoke to the chugging of the engines as the ferry made its way across the lake. He was nowhere to be seen but sitting beside the bed was Prenda, the UN interpreter. I hadn't seen her since that unfortunate day in Tropoje. She hugged me warmly and apologised for what happened when we first met.

'If I'd known who you were, I would not have interfered,' she said, 'I'm so sorry.' I was surprised when she began to cry and I took her hand and assured her that it didn't matter. She pulled some papers from her bag and showed me an article she had written in which she had likened me to Edith Durham, the remarkable and flamboyant Englishwoman who had spent the early part of the century travelling through the Balkans. I was flattered; Edith Durham was revered by many Albanians.

The dressing had come away from my leg, leaving the wound exposed and bleeding. It was obviously infected and would not be helped by the fact that I was lying on a dirty blanket stained with oil. With Prenda's help, I hobbled to a covered enclosure on the deck where of all people I found Avdyl, the caretaker from the tent above Padesh. He greeted me warmly and ever the gentleman, offered me his seat.

The ferry made its way through a series of spectacular gorges and interconnected lakes that were formed when the Drini valley was dammed in the 1970s. Passing between the high mountains, we occasionally caught a glimpse of some hardy peasants climbing the steep, half-hidden pathways to their solitary homes. Apart from the breathtaking scenery, it was a great pleasure to travel by water rather than by road across the rugged terrain.

Two hours later the ferry docked at Fierze, where Durim was waiting to take us to Bajram Curri. Wagon and Trailer had cleaned my room, though it still smelled a little strange. The mice, perhaps in search of food, had relocated to the OSCE office where the staff often ate.

Marigona and her family were still living in the refugee camp alongside Nik, Hannah and their children. As Christmas approached, Coxy and Janey packed up

Major Bill Foxton.

Andrea and Pierre share a light
moment.

Limping home.

all the food, clothing, bedding and toys that had been donated or bought for the hotel in Brighton and transported it across Europe. When they arrived in Shkodra, the aid was distributed between the 150 refugees living in the camp.

Despite daily debriding of the wound and large doses of antibiotics, my leg was severely infected and Bill was concerned about gangrene. I was feeling constantly sick, which we put down to the large doses of antibiotics. Bill told me that his superior, Tim Isles, who was based at the OSCE headquarters in Tirana, was being leaned on by the British government to get me out of the country and he explained that if I was to fall into a coma I would immediately be evacuated.

Nik had family in Switzerland and once he got exit visas for his wife and children he would be taking them there. Marigona was now four years old and without an operation to remove the cataracts, her eyesight would be irreversibly damaged. I decided to go to Britain and arrange things from there.

Duncan came to meet me in Tirana and we flew home together. Although he was now in a relationship, we were still very close and I knew he would do everything he could to help Marigona. My parents were waiting at the airport with some of the volunteers and I hobbled down the walkway and gave my mother a hug. The press were there as always and the photo ended up in *Hello* magazine.

The next day I was taken to the Sussex County Hospital and examined by a trauma specialist. Although the wound in my leg was still infected, it turned out that the constant nausea was also due to the fact that I was pregnant. An ultrasound scan confirmed that despite large doses of antibiotics and painkillers, the baby appeared to be fine.

When I called Bill to tell him that the news he sounded delighted and said he would be honoured to father my child; but in actual fact he was still with his wife. He asked me to conceal his identity for the sake of his family and although this meant I would have to bring our child up alone, I reluctantly agreed.

We made a new visa application to the Home Office on behalf of Marigona and included a letter from Christopher Lui, an ophthalmic surgeon who had agreed to operate free of charge. It took some time but finally we received confirmation that she had been granted permission to come to the UK; on condition that she came alone.

On Valentines Day I was packing my bags when a dozen roses were delivered to my door, together with a small enamelled box. Engraved across the top were the words 'Forget Me Not' and inside was the flattened 9mm bullet that Bill had dug out of the pavement after I was shot.

34 | 'I AM THE BABY YOU RESCUED'

MIKE MENDOZA HAD BEEN commissioned to make a film about the refugees in Shkodra and although he had been involved with my work for many years it would be the first time he would join me on a mission.

Shkodra is an ancient city on the shore of the Shkodra Lake in north-west Albania. An important cultural and economic area, it is the centre of Albanian Catholicism and at the same time the pre-eminent city of Sunni Islam in the country. The city was built in the shadow of Rozafa castle, which clings to the rocky hillside. A famous legend surrounds it, dating back to Ilyrian times.

Three brothers had set about building the castle but no matter how hard they worked each day, when night came the walls would fall down. A wise old man advised them to make a sacrifice so that the walls would remain standing but they could not decide whose life should be taken. Eventually they agreed that whichever of their wives brought the lunch the next day, would be buried in the wall of the castle. They each promised not to tell the women of their plan but the two older brothers broke their promise. Only the youngest man kept his word and the next afternoon, as the brothers waited to see who would come, Rosafa, wife of the youngest brother, arrived with a basket of food. When he told his unfortunate wife that she was to be buried in the castle wall so that they could finish building it, she did not protest. She agreed to be sacrificed on condition that they would leave parts of her exposed; her right eye so that she could see her infant son, her right hand so that she could caress him, her breast in order to feed him and her foot, to rock his cradle.

Crossing the spacious square in the centre of the town, I noticed that the fountain was filled with tyres though no one seemed to know why. We passed the Al-Zamil Mosque, which stands in the shadow of a Catholic church and making our way through the heavy traffic of old cars and bicycles we tried not to breathe in the diesel fumes and dust that polluted the spring air. In the older part of town, we walked through narrow streets past colourful houses with fading façades and broken shutters. The shabby store fronts were virtually empty, and blowflies buzzed around the rotting fruit and vegetables displayed on the market stalls.

When we entered the compound I could see Marigona playing with her sister in the mud. She didn't notice me at first as her eyesight had deteriorated but as soon as I came closer she raced into my arms. With the children clutching my hands, we headed towards the unfinished building that had been their home for several months.

There was a terrible stench for the refugees had only two toilets and rainwater was leaking through the roof, dripping puddles across the floor. Marigona led me down the corridor to a small, dark room which was no more than ten feet by six. There were two sets of bunk beds against the exposed walls and the family's belongings were kept in bags suspended from a washing line. When we entered the room I almost stepped on Arbresha who was playing on the concrete floor.

Valbona was delighted to see us and threw her arms around me, talking animatedly until she remembered that I could not speak Albanian. Miranda, proudly sporting her two new front teeth, was immediately sent off to find her father, who appeared a few minutes later with Nik and Hannah. More hugs were followed by coffee and Nik told me that he had finally managed to secure the exit visas for himself and his family.

Although they were concerned about Marigona travelling without them, Hili and Valbona decided she should go. Bill had managed to arrange for Beni to accompany us as her interpreter and on the day we were leaving he joined us at the camp. Most of the refugees had turned out to see her off and being so young, I expected her to cry. Instead, she gave her mum and dad a hug and jumped straight into the car.

Within days of arriving in Britain, Marigona was admitted for surgery at the Sussex Eye Hospital but she was naturally very frightened and kept getting out of bed. At one point she raced into the corridor crying for her mother. My heart ached for her; she looked so small and vulnerable and had already been through

so much. With Beni's help, we eventually managed to convince her to go back to her room where she was given a pre-med and then wheeled into theatre.

The operation went well and after two weeks of treatment she was ready to go home. Upon her arrival at the airport in Tirana she raced across the concourse to her parents, able to see them clearly for the very first time.

Marigona arrives in Britain.

Sally becomes a mum.

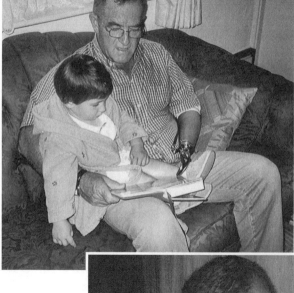

Bill with his daughter in 2003.

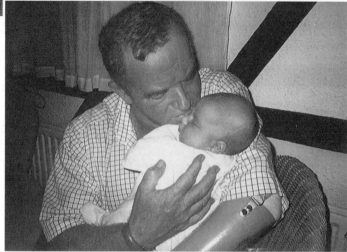

First kiss.

In the meantime, Serb forces continued to wage war against the ethnic Albanians and NATO finally responded with a series of airstrikes. The bombing campaign, which began on 24 March 1999, lasted ten weeks and involved 1000 aircraft that flew over 38,000 combat missions. By the end of May over 500,000 people had become refugees but Operation Allied Force was deemed a success, eventually restoring peace to Kosovo. Bill was awarded an OBE for his work in Albania and he wore his 'best arm' for the ceremony at Buckingham Palace.

On 19 July 1999, our daughter Billie was born. My sympathy for the mothers caught up in the war, forced to choose whether to place their faith in a stranger, or struggle for survival amidst the bullets and the bombs, was redoubled.

With a new-born baby to care for, I did not have much time on my hands but I wanted to continue helping the victims of war. In September I returned to Kosovo to establish a centre which would provide counselling for women and children suffering from trauma. The project was funded by One to One Children's Fund and continues to function today.

In 2001 Slobodan Milosević was arrested and pleaded not guilty to charges of abuse of power and criminal conspiracy. He was put on trial at The Hague where just a few months before the verdict was due, he was found dead in his cell from a heart attack.

During the Second Gulf War in 2003, I was watching a report on GMTV about a 12-year-old boy called Ali Abbas. Ten days into Operation *Iraqi Freedom* he had lost both arms and suffered 60 per cent burns in a coalition attack on Baghdad. The attack had claimed the lives of his parents, a brother and 13 other family members. Trapped in a hospital in the centre of Baghdad, the doctors were calling for Abbas and other wounded children to be evacuated and the UN described the situation in Baghdad's hospitals as 'critical'.

The story went on for days, with pictures of Ali beamed around the world but nothing was actually being done to help him. I could not understand why the British Goverment had not arranged to fly him out. There were certainly plenty of helicopters available and Kuwait was just across the border. One evening I was watching a documentary about Michael Jackson and knowing that he did a great deal for charity I decided to contact his close friend Uri Geller to ask for his help. Uri told me that Michael was currently facing some personal problems, otherwise he was sure he would have been willing to support the mission in some way.

I also sent a message to Heather Mills McCartney – whose charity had done a lot to help amputees – but received no response. Finally I got so frustrated I decided to try and arrange the evacuation myself. I contacted Downing Street and was put through to the Prime Minister's office. Someone took my details and surprisingly I received a call back just a few minutes later. The man I spoke to wanted to know all the details of my proposed plan and I explained that I was hoping to reach Baghdad and arrange a helicopter to evacuate the children to Kuwait.

When I finished speaking there was silence at the other end of the phone and for a moment I thought we'd been cut off.

'I think I should inform you that your journey would be a complete waste of time. As soon as you reach the Iraqi border, you will immediately be turned back.' I was confused, I was sure that the border I was planning to cross was manned by British soldiers.

'Precisely!' said the official. 'And they will be given strict instructions that under no circumstances will you be allowed to enter Iraq.'

A couple of days later the newsreader declared that Ali Abbas had finally been evacuated –on a helicopter to Kuwait. The clinic that made prosthetic limbs for Heather Mills McCartney had offered to treat him in the UK and he would soon be on his way to Britain.

In the meantime, Ibrahim Rugova and Hashim Thaçi agreed to work on creating provisional institutions of self-government until Kosovo's final status was decided. Rugova was elected as President of the Republic and he remained in office until his death from lung cancer in 2006.

That same year war broke out between Israel and Lebanon and I travelled to the border to help. In between delivering aid to the frail and the vulnerable, I was based at Hanita, the kibbutz where I stayed in my youth. Once again I found myself dodging katushya rockets that were fired into Israel from just across the border and although 30 years had passed, it seemed nothing had really changed.

On 17 February 2008, Kosovo's parliament unanimously endorsed a declaration of independence from Serbia and thousands of people swarmed onto the streets of the capital Pristina. The city centre erupted with the sound of fireworks and celebratory gunfire as Hashim Thaci, the Prime Minister of Kosovo, made a speech.

'We have waited for this day for a very long time. From today, we are proud, independent and free.'

The following year I was watching the news when Bill Foxton's image appeared on the screen. I had not seen him since 2003 but we had kept in touch by email. He was Country Director for a German NGO in Kosovo until 2007 and then he moved to the central Afghan Province of Bamiyan, where he managed humanitarian aid projects on behalf of Caritas.

According to the report Bill had invested his life savings in two Austrian-based hedge funds, both of which had been closed and the funds reinvested with Bernard Madoff, the notorious American fraudster. As a result of Madoff's ponzi scheme, Bill was facing bankruptcy. On 10 February, he set off to a small park near his home in Southampton carrying a semi-automatic pistol. Once there, he sat down on a bench and shot himself through the head.

Bill was a brave man with an adventurous spirit who always lived life on the edge, and had he been killed by a bomb or a stray bullet in some war-torn country, I would not have been surprised. But I was profoundly shocked that he had chosen to die alone on a park bench in Southampton.

Although Billie barely knew her father, she always hoped that one day he would be waiting for her when she came home from school. It broke my heart when I had to tell her that her dream would never come true.

A short while after his death Bill's son came to see me and I told him about Billie. I was surprised to learn that Bill had actually been married twice and that Will and Sarah were the result of his first marriage. Bill had left their mother Helen when they were very young so they both knew what it was like to grow up without a father. They immediately welcomed Billie into their family and she has loved them ever since.

I have often wondered what happened to the children I brought out of Mostar and although I only had a handful of names, I decided to do a Google search and to my surprise I received a response.

'Hi Sally, It's Selma!!!'

In between numerous operations Selma continued her studies and she had just graduated from Pace University in New York. We stayed in touch and when she recently got engaged to be married, Billie and I were invited to her wedding.

Maja lives in Florida where she runs a successful business and Hangar, the company that designed her prosthetic leg, offered to fly me and Billie to the States for a reunion. When I arrived at the airport I was greeted by a woman from *Good Housekeeping* magazine and she asked me how it felt to be reunited with one of the children I rescued. I was about to answer her when all of a sudden I caught a glimpse of Maja walking towards me with a big smile on her face and for once I was lost for words.

Senad remained in the West Midlands and he graduated from Leeds University with a Master's degree in computer science. He created a website for me so that I can easily be found, should any of the other children wish to make contact.

Through the website I received a message from Marija Topolovic, one of the children I brought out of Nova Bila in February 1994. She too was living in the US and someone had shown her the article that appeared in *Good Housekeeping*. The magazine had mentioned the website, which includes a series of paintings I created after the war. Amongst them is the scene in the helicopter when her mother lit a candle in prayer.

I was working at my computer one afternoon when I received another message. 'I am the baby you rescued.' Elmir's sister Lela was just seven days old when she and her brothers had been wounded when a tank shell hit their apartment. She said that her family would love to see me, so I decided to return to Mostar for the first time since the war.

Wandering through the narrow streets, it was hard to believe that the snipers were gone, especially as some of the buildings were still pitted with shrapnel and bullet holes, incongruous amongst the colourful awnings of the sidewalk cafes and department stores.

Sally and Billie with Maja at the airport.

Vava came to meet me and although he had put on a little weight, he had not really changed much at all. Over a drink, we talked about old times and he recalled the first time we met.

'I wondered who was this mad woman so willing to cross the front line,' said Vava, laughing at the memory. He told me that after the war ended he returned to teaching children at primary school but he still continues to write. He is also becoming well known for his paintings and has had many exhibitions of his work.

Lela and Elmir live in a house their father built on the outskirts of Mostar after the war. After plenty of hugs and kisses, Sendzana handed out glasses of homemade pomegranate juice while her husband Mohamer talked about the war. He recalled the day when the anti-tank missile ripped through their fourth storey apartment injuring him and the children and he spoke of their heartbreak at losing their eldest son.

Elmir still bears the scars from the shrapnel but although he lost the sight in one eye, he is able to drive and is training to be a car mechanic. Lela who is almost nineteen, is studying for her exams and plans to work in IT.

Having tried without success to contact Zoran over the years I was surprised when he turned up at my hotel. He lives on the east side of Mostar near Žena BiH, the women's shelter that was founded by his friend Azra Hasanbegović. In

Reunited with Lela and her mother.

2011 he received the Dusko Kondor Civil Courage Award, which was granted in commemoration of Professor Kondor to 'those brave people who risked their own lives by standing up to negative authorities and acting according to their own values.'

Erna Cipra became President of the Jewish community, who continue to work alongside their Muslim, Serb and Croat neighbours in an effort to reform and improve the unique relationships they had prior to the conflict.

Although Hafid has an apartment on the West side of Mostar, he rents it out, preferring to live on the East side of the city. He took me to visit Higijenski, the public health laboratory that served as a makeshift hospital during the war. The brickwork is no longer painted red and the bullet holes are gone but as we entered the compound I half expected to see my old ambulance parked outside the door. Going down into the basement was like stepping back in time, and I stayed alone in the corridor for a while, recalling those who had died there. I could see Medina's little face and wished with all my heart that I could have saved her.

Hafid explained that Dr Malović, the anaesthetist, had suffered from a break-down during the war so he had taken over as director of the hospital. I asked him whether he received any kind of recognition for his work – he and his colleague had carried out over 1700 operations over a period of eleven months, an astonishing feat – but Hafid shook his head. When he was asked to reflect upon his feelings about the war, he said that he is still haunted by the memory of the dreadful things that were done to the children so he is not yet able to forgive.

I contacted Ivan Bagaric, who became a Member of Parliament in the Croatian government and we arranged to meet on the Bulevar, the street that runs through the centre of the city, once Mostar's front line. He walked towards me with his arms outstretched and called out in English, 'My Angel!'

We talked about the divisions still in place across the region and he told me that the only way things would ever really change was if Bosnia-Herzegovina became part of the EU. He believes that is the only way to ensure a democratic process that would correct the present injustices and provide equality for all.

'This is vital, for without equality the state of BiH will not survive and that will generate ongoing conflict in the heart of Europe.'

I was also hoping to find out what happened to the patients who were evacuated during Operation Angel in December 1993, and Oliver Harvey, a chief feature writer from the *Sun*, offered to help. Those who hadn't come to Britain were flown to Italy or the United States but it was possible some had returned to Mostar. This time Billie came with me and as we drove along the banks of the Neretva my old 'war stories' began to take on new meaning for her. Oliver spoke to the concierge in our hotel and within minutes he found Amel, the boy who was still in a coma when we brought him out of Mostar.

Amel was living with his family in a small house on the hillside just above the city. Selma's father Mirsad, who runs a small antique shop in East Mostar, called them to ask if we could pay them a visit and they agreed. It was a miserable day and was raining quite hard as we pulled up outside the small house. Amel's mother greeted us warmly and invited us inside.

They explained that when he was rescued, he and his mother, who had also been wounded, were flown to Italy. He remained in a coma for several months and when he finally regained consciousness he was paralysed. His mother never left his side, helping to exercise his limbs and even moving his tongue every day until eventually he was able to speak. He told us that when he awoke he could recognise letters and words but he just couldn't say them. He slowly regained some feeling in his body and is able to walk but as a result of the extensive injuries, he never regained full use of his right arm.

He and his mother spent a year in the hospital before returning to Bosnia. Life was very hard for them because he was sent back without any medication or aftercare. He suffered from epilepsy as a result of the damage to his brain but recently his father had taken him to a hospital some 50 kilometres from

Mostar, where they prescribed him medication that has changed his life. He is able to use a computer and as we were leaving, he asked if he could add me on Facebook. A few minutes later I received a notification that he was subscribing to my updates.

As we drove back down the hill, the call to prayer issued from the minaret of Karadjoz-bey Mosque, competing with the bells of the Catholic church across the river. Oliver, a seasoned journalist (who didn't mind me pointing out his strong resemblance to Borat) has reported from places like Libya and Afghanistan. He went to Africa with Bob Geldof and wrote a book about Live Aid. Despite his wide experience of hard times in hard places, he was obviously moved by the stories of Amel and the other children of Mostar whose lives were changed forever by the war.

We visited Stipe and Erna Rozic and as we pulled up outside their apartment, Erna was leaning over the balcony just as she used to. When we walked into the apartment she took Billie's face between her hands and laughed aloud with delight.

After the war Damir had studied to become a doctor and went on to specialise in nuclear medicine. He is based at the White Hill Hospital in West Mostar and is married with three children.

Sadly the city remains divided, with the majority of Croats living on the west side of the river, Muslims and Serbs in the east. Poorly targeted international assistance, lack of international coordination and suspect foreign investment by western companies have cemented the ethnic divide. Residents pay taxes to parallel ethnic governments that administer separate infrastructures, public services, healthcare and police. The schools are segregated, apart from the School of Nations where children from both sides study beneath the same roof – but even there, Muslims attend in the morning and Croats in the afternoon. Lela and her friends watch movies, listen to iPods and surf the net; but they rarely cross the river after dark.

In Mostar there are graveyards where there used to be parks and row upon row of headstones. I watched as a man laid flowers at the grave of two young boys, probably his sons. I visited Sarica Harem, the graveyard where five-year-old Damir Greljo is buried and placed a small bouquet of flowers at the foot of his grave. Etched into the headstone, which is fringed with daffodils, is a portrait of the beloved little boy.

Yet despite the damaged buildings and the graves, parts of Mostar are thriving and tourists flock there in the summer. The narrow cobbled streets are from a middle-European fairy tale, and people who once ran past the snipers in terror now linger over coffee in sidewalk cafes. Stari Most, the bridge destroyed by shelling in 1993, has been restored to its original magnificence, a symbol of unity in an otherwise divided city. As I strolled across the bridge the sun was shining and a young man prepared to dive into the river, just as his father might have done before the war.

EPILOGUE

IT WAS NOVEMBER 2009. There was a murmur of anticipation amongst the guests as they sipped champagne and waited for the bride and groom to appear.

The doors opened and my daughter squeezed my hand as the newlyweds entered the opulent ballroom. The bride was dressed in an ivory satin gown and her blue eyes sparkled beneath the glittering lights of a crystal chandelier.

'She's beautiful,' said Billie and Selma's mother caught my eye … and smiled.

When I look back on the role I played in the Balkans conflict, there are more questions than answers and I suppose there always will be. I never knew why I was given permission that was often denied to others. I never untangled the web of misinformation and misunderstandings that bedevilled so many missions and I have never discovered what happened to £1 million of aid secured in a UN compound in Metković. I do not know what caused the breakdown in communications between the British government and the UNHCR on the issue of visas and I still don't understand why the British press withdrew their support.

I certainly never set out to become so embroiled in the Balkans conflict; it just happened that way. Each time I

Selma and Lenis, the bride and groom.

would find myself making a promise that I felt I had to keep. Each time I found myself thinking, 'Why the hell did I do that?' and each time I grew more afraid, knowing what honouring that commitment would entail.

I greatly regret the fact that the UN found it necessary to be obstructive towards me rather than working alongside me. I am sure that together we could have achieved so much more. Individual officers, soldiers and politicians said supportive things to me in private that they could not say publicly. But the whole is greater than the sum of its parts and for me, the whole represented everything that is bad about bureaucracy: inflexible, impersonal and lacking in imagination. Perhaps it doesn't matter that I have no answers to my questions: truth, as we know, is the first casualty of war.

Although applauded for my actions, I have also been subjected to a great deal of criticism. I have been accused of being foolish and naïve, and no doubt at times I was; but perhaps in part it was my naivety that enabled me to proceed. For had I done as the UN insisted and made applications for visas and hospital beds prior to each mission, some of the children might not have survived.

INDEX

Page references in *italic* refer to captions. Those in **bold** refer to the colour section.

ABC News 72, 128
Abuzayed, Karen 93, 125, 131
AFRK (Armed Forces of the Republic of Kosovo) 167
Agim 79
Albania 142, 144, 146, 148, 151, 156–57, 161, 164, 174, 176, 177, 181, 184, 212, 215, 222, 223–24, 231, 233, 235–36, 240, 243, **12**
Alberta 163, 165
Alma-a-shaab 15
American Jewish Joint Distribution Committee 34
Andrews QC, Bob Marshall 91
Ardi 167–70, 182, 227
Ashdown MP, Paddy 121, 122
Atijus, Dr Vladlena 27–28, 35, 36, 43, 50, 84
Austria 16, 39, 40
Bagarić, Brigadier Dr Ivan 35, 40, 41, 42–3, 47–8, 49–50, 52, 54, 55, 65–7, 68, 69, 72, 76, 78, 82, 83, 86, 88, 96, 111–14, 115, 120–21, 123–26, 164, 249, **2**
Baghdad 17, 243
Bajram Curri 144–46, 147, 148–49, 151, 156–58, 174, 213, 215–18, 221–22, 223–25, 231, 235–37

Banja Luka 42
Banks, Mary 142–43, 144, 145, 146, 149, 211–12
BBC 46, 48, 52, 54, 70, 89, 91, 92, 95, 101–102, 104, 200, 208, 212, 218
Beadle, Jeremy 90
Becker, Carol 12, 14, 97, 228, 229, 239
Becker, Billie 242, 243, 245, 246, 248, 250, **16**
Becker, Eddy 89, 224
Becker, Jack 12, 13, 14, 207, 208, 209, 239
Beeny, Yolanda 91, 97
Begkoyian, Genevieve 104–109
Bekim 164, 170, 172, 181, 221
Belgrade 164, 191, 194–95, 207, 209
Benabou, Albert 33, 43, 60
'Big Rod' 83, 86–7
Bilaslavo, Fausto 157–58, 221
Blair, Prime Minister Tony 190, 213, 227
Boban, Mate 87–8, 110, 115, 117, 123
Borger, Julian 218
Bosnia-Herzegovina 10–12, 14, 16, 17, 18, 19, 20, 23–5, 27–9, 33, 40, 42, 44, 47, 53, 57, 65, 68, 70, 78, 81, 87–9, 91–6, 100–102, 109, 111, 113, 117–18, 121, 123, 125, 130, 132–33, 135–36, 142, 154, 158, 160, 162, 164, 177, 190, 206, 219, 223, 231, 235, 248–49

Bowden MP, Andrew 91
Bowen, Jeremy 52, 61, 88
Bravington, Pat 143, 145, 211
Breakfast with Frost 212
Britain 15, 18, 23, 26–7, 29, 33, 61, 70, 79, 83, 84, 87, 88, 89, 94, 95, 109, 111, 116, 120, 136, 144, 151, 153, 163, 199, 204, 212, 216, 222–26, 228, 231, 234, 239, 241, 244
Brown, June 136
Brown, Madeline 211
Bugojno 87
Bukoshi, Prime Minister Dr Bujar 2, 232
Busova a 132
Capljina 26–7, 35
Carney, Keith 216, 225, 236
Central British Fund for World Jewish Relief 34
Chamed 171, 176, 221
Channel 4 212, 232
Children's Aid Direct 148
Christine 148
Christopher, Warren 11
Churdo, Peter 125
Cipra, August 67–9
Cipra, Erna 67–9, 247
Cirielo, Rafaelli 156–58, 160, 175, 221
itluk 28, 31, 35–6, 41, 50, 52, 69, 72, 82, 83, 84, 124
Clancy, Tim 66–8, 72–3, 76, 78–9, 82, 85, 119
CNN 53, 123
Collins, Michelle 136
Cox, John 212, 214, 216, 219, 237

Croatia 10, 11, 18, 20, 22, 24, 34, 40, 43, 70, 72, 93, 95, 102, 109, 128, 132
Crossland, Colonel John 195
Cutts, Mark 149–50, 211
Dack, Liz 66, 143, 148, 150–51, 216, 219–21, 223–25, *226*, 227, 228–29, *230*, 231, 233, 236
Dack, Simon 69, 91
Daily Mirror, The 70–1, 104
Daily Telegraph, The 65, 211
Danielle 44, 81, 83–4, 86
Dayton Peace Accords 134, 135
Decani 142, 161
Demić, Amel 75, 79, 96, 120, 248
Demić, Emir 80
Devereaux, Colin 136
Diamond, Anne 91
Djakovica (Gjakove) 161, 180–81, 188, 191, 195
Dommie 29, 44
Donnelly, Brian 206
Dowdney, Mark 104, 108, 117, 118
Dragan 198, 204, 209
Drenica 139, *140*, 167
Drita 170, 172, *176*, 177, 179–80, 182, 189, 215
Droce, Azem 47, 57
Durim 217, *218*, 219, 226–28, 234, 237
Durres 144, 216
East Mostar 37, 42, 44, 47, 49, 52, *53*, 54, *58*, 61, 64–6, 77, 79, 81, 84, 87, 93, 94, 109, 112–13, 115, 124, 248, **5**
Eddo 51, 72–3
Edge, Bob 146, 148, 150
Edwards, Huw 212
Ellis, Bernard 12, 26–7
Elvis 72–7, 78, 128
Enders, Daniel 151–52, 223
Eubank, Chris 91
European Community Humanitarian Organisation (ECHO) 148

Evening Argus 69
Everts, Daan 224
Farsides, Paulette 212, 219–20, 222
Fegan, Mick 102, 110–11, 116
Ferris, Roger 91, 97
Fierze 144, 152, 236–37
Figgins, Phil 150–51
First Gulf War 18, 123, **1**
Foa, Silvana 32, 65, 109
Foresti, Armando 218, 222, 226–27
Foxton, Major Bill 150, 152, 156, 164, 175, 205, 213, 233–35, *236*, *237*, 239, *242*, 244–45
France 16, 20, 24, 92, 100, 136, 170, 234
Fraser, Lady Antonia 91
Geller, Uri 243
Geneva Convention 31, 168
Ghali, Boutros Boutros 66
Giles, Belinda 212
Gillette, Lynne 24, 26
Gjonbalaj, Bukurie ('Bili') 205, 206
Gjonggecaj, Halil 148, 222
Gordon, Bob 195–96, 200, 204, 207–10
Gornji Vackuf 45
Grdani Brigade ('The Crazy Ones') 29
Grebenar, Fra Franjo 106, 108, 127–28
Greljo, Damir 68, 249
Greljo, Elmir *62*, *68*, 69–70, 91, 246, **7**, **8**, **16**
Greljo, Lela 68, 245–46, *247*, 249, **16**
Greljo, Sendzana 69, 74, 246
Grenon, Martha 217
Grozny 206
Grude 42
Guardian, The 218
Gulf Peace Team *16*, 17
Haklaj, Fatmir 213, 215–17, 233
Halili 223, 233–34
Hall, Roger 216, 220

Halley Stewart Trust 91, 131, 221
Handzar, Mirsad 64, 68, 72, 73, 75, 248
Handzar, Selma *58*, 59, *62*, 63–4, 68, 245, *250*
Handzar, Mirza *58*, 59, *62*
Hanita 15, 244
Hard Talk 212
Harvey, Oliver 248
Hasanbegovic, Azra 131, 246
Haxihiu, Lum 162, 165, 166–69
Hayruddin, Mimar 56
Herceg-Bosna 87, 132
Herzegovina 10–11, 18, 31, 41, 43, 133
Higijenski 57, *58*, 247, **5**
Hill of Crosses 20, 22
Hiseni, Dede 170, *176*, 179–80, 191, 215
Hiseni, Doruntina 168
Hiseni, Hannah 169–70, 172, *176*, 177, 178–82, 183, 186–87, 188–92, 215, 237, 241
Hiseni, Nik 167–70, 186, 215, 224, 237, 239, 241
Holbrooke, Richard 162
HOS (Croatian Defence Force) 45
Hoxha, Enver 146
Hulme, Jerry 81, 83, 116, 118, 131–32
Hum 31, 72
HVO (Croatian Defence Council) 11, 22, 23, 25, 26, 29, 35, 39, 40, 42, 50, 51, 69, 75, 78, 80, 116, *117*, 119, 133
Independent, The 65
International Council of Jewish Women (ICJW) 71, 87, 124
International Red Cross 20, 25, 42, 52, 66, 74, 78, 101, 152, 208
International Rescue Committee (IRC) 51
Iraq 17–18, 244

Isles, Tim 239
Ismaili, Prenda 220,
    236–37
Israel 15, 18, 39, 43, 51, 75,
    76, 186, 224, 244
Italy 20, 24, 25, 93, 102,
    120, 136, 195, 248
ITN 50–1, 59, 118, 127
Izetbegović, Alijah 10, 66
Jackson, Dawn 211
Jackson, Michael 243
Jacobs, Dr Nick 131
Jagger, Bianca 94, 212
Jakupi, Artan 152, 154
Jakupi, Avdyl 154–56, 237
James, Heather 14, 89
Jancović, Dragoljub 203
Janey 146, 216, 237
Jewish Adult Cultural
    Society (JACS) 91
Jewish Aid and
    International
    Development (UKJAID)
    91
JNA (Yugoslavia Army)
    11, 161
Johnston, Brian 136
'Joycey' 143
Junik 152, 155, 160–62,
    164, 169, 171–72, 174,
    181, 190, 194–95, 197,
    212, 221
Jurić, Dr 124
Justine 91
Kajtaz, Edina 131
Karadžić, Radovan 10, 11
Kates, Peter 49–50
Kazazić, Maja 60, 94–5,
    6, 15
Kelly, Lorraine 142, 232
Kernaiar, Feriz 233
Khalil 167, 169, 172–73,
    219
Kisiljak 106, 109
KLA (Kosovan Liberation
    Army) 135, 152, 155–56,
    158, 161–62, 165, 166–68,
    173–74, 180–82, 185, 190,
    192, 194–95, 200, 218
Koman 144, 151, 216, 236,
    14

Konjic 133
Konjihoddzic, Hafid 61,
    73–7, 78–82, 88, 116,
    119–20, 124, 247–48, 8
Kosovo 10, 16, 135–43,
    144, 146, 149–52,
    154–58, 160–65, 167,
    171, 176–77, 179, 181,
    185–87, 188, 190, 192,
    195, 197, 200, 202–3,
    205–9, 211–12, 216,
    218–19, 223, 226, 231,
    232, 233, 243–44
Krasniqi, Arbresha 169,
    241
Krasniqi, Hili 168, 215
Krasniqi, Marigona 168–
    70, 172, 176, 177, 182, 197,
    215, 237, 239–40, 241
Krasniqi, Miranda 27,
    169–70, 172, 176, 241
Krasniqi, Valbona 169–70,
    172, 176, 215, 241
Kraus, Dr Ognjen 123
Kruš ica 43
Kukes 157, 217
Kuwait 243–44
La Benevolencia 34
Lang, Dr Slobodan 107,
    113–14, 120, 121, 123
LDK (Kosovo
    Democratic Party) 144,
    161
Le Carré, Lawrence 92,
    95, 101–3, 110
Lebanon 15, 244
Lipljan 192, 194–205, 216
Little, Alan 70
Ljubuški 85
Lumley, Joanna 141
Lynne, Dame Vera 95
Macari, Gloria 91, 97
Macedonia 10, 154,
    208–10
Madoff, Bernard 144
Major, Prime Minister
    John 37, 89, 107
Makarska 40–1, 103, 110,
    116
Malović, Dr Dragan 61,
    74, 77, 78–80, 82, 248

Mandlebaum, Zoran 31,
    33, 35–6, 38–41, 45, 87,
    124, 131, 246, 2, 3
Marie 143, 145
Marina 22–3
Marta 137, 139, 203
Martinović, Vinko ('Stela')
    45, 73 9
Mattson, John 152
Maud 143, 145, 146,
    149–50
Maurer, Pierre 213, 217,
    220, 238
Mayer, Laurey 71
McDermott, Mary 145,
    149–50, 216, 220
Médecins Sans Frontières
    78, 154
Medina 88, 247
Medjugorje 20, 22, 24, 27,
    28, 33, 35, 42–3, 50–1,
    54, 60, 65, 69, 72, 82,
    83, 87
Medjugorje Appeal 12, 24,
    31, 42
Meidani, President
    Rexhep 230–31
Mendoza, Mike 34, 91,
    102, 130, 136, 200, 212,
    231–32, 240
Meridian 95, 101, 104, 120
Metković 40–1, 110–11,
    113, 116, 120, 250
Micalessin, Gian 157–58,
    160, 170, 171–72, 174,
    177, 221
Mikulić, Vladimir ('Vava')
    66, 72–3, 76, 82, 87–8,
    112–13, 124–26, 127–30,
    246, 8
Mills McCartney, Heather
    243–44
Milošević, Slobodan 10,
    135, 188, 190, 194, 202,
    204, 243
Miloti, Arben ('Beni') 218,
    233, 241
Milutinović, Milan 208
Mira 133–34
Mita, Jak 136, 137, 139
Mladić, Ratko 133–34

Montenegro 10, 136, 154, 185
Morales, Colonel Angel 54, 64
Morelli, Alessandra 152, 217–18, 223, 225
Morris, Christopher 65, 70
Morris, Jonathan 69
Morris, Neil 91
Morrison, John *92*, 101, 110–12
Mostar 11, 20, 22–3, 26–9, 31, 33–5, 37–9, 41, 42–3, 45–6, 50, 52, 54, 55–6, 60–1, 64–5, 71, 79, 84, 86–8, 91, 94, 96, 101, 103, 110, 114, 115–17, 119, 124, 128, 131–32, 152, 154, 161, 165, 228, 245–49, **2**, **4**, **9**, **16**
Mother Teresa Charity 136, 139, 203
Musa 167, 169, 173, 219
Nash, Stephen 224
NATO 124, 133–34, 167, 190, 243
Nec 168
Need, Major 110–12, 113, 115, 120
Neretva, river 31, 56
Neum 42
Nova Bila 42–4, 47, 73, 83, 86–8, 93, 96, 103–4, 106–10, 113–14, 120, 121–25, 131, 245
Novi Travnik 87, 132
O'Grady, Paul 136
O'Shea, Brendan 117, 135
Omerargić, Nermina *58*, 60
One to One Children's Fund 243
Operation Angel 89–9, 102, 108, 110, 115, 118, 120, 127, 131, 141, *145*, 146, 178–79, 184, 188, 216, 223, 228, 248, **10**
Operation *Deliberate Force* 134
Operation *Irma* 37, 120

Orasje 42
Organisation for Security and Co–operation in Europe (OSCE) 148–52, 156, 205, 213, 215–17, 220, 224–25, 228, 231, 234–35, 237, 239, **13**
Overseas Development Administration (ODA) 51, 57, 60, 94, 107
Paddy 29, 44–5, 121, 124, 158
Padesh 154, *155*, 237
Paic, Milaslav 186, 212
Parkes, Bill 216–219, 222, 225–227, 228–232, 239
Pasalić, Arif 74
Patel, Mansukh 92
Paul 54, 55–7, 63–4
Penny, Rob 216, **11**
'Petrit' 224
Pinter, Harold 91
Plaits, Demetrios 224–25
Popkewiez, Andrew 91
Porter, Dr Mark 89, 91
Posušje 20–3, 24–5, 124, **1**
Potocari 133
Praljak, General Slobodan 51–3, 117, 119
Price, Katie 136
Prince Edward 141
Prince Philip 141
Princess Margaret 89
Pristina 136, 139, *140*, 158, 184–85, 195, 206–7, 209–10, 244
Prizren 192
Prlić, President Jadranko 132–33
Queen Elizabeth II 141–42, 198
Ragdoll Foundation 142
Rajkov, Jovan 61
Rama 42
Raven, David 136
Raznatović, Zelko ('Arkan') 190, 207
Redgrave, Corin 212–13
Redgrave, Vanessa 212
Redmond, Tony 175, 235
Rees, Evelyn 93

Rees, Peter 93
Rifkin, Malcolm 121
Riki 144, 149, 220
Rob 216, 220
Roger 72–4, 76–8
Romano, Haim 31–2, 36, 50
Rose, Ashley 92, 100–2
Rose, David 92, 100–2, 111
Rose, General Sir Michael 121–22
Ross McWhirter Foundation 89, *90*
Rozić, Damir 31, *32*, 33, 35–8, 45, 50, *62*, 84, 87, 124, 131, 248
Rozić, Erna 31, *32*, 33, 35–6, 38, 50, 84, 124, 131, 248
Rozić, Stipe 36–7, 76, 87, 124, 131, 248
Rufhas, Juliana 212, 219
Rugova, President Ibrahim 135, 144, 161, 167, 244
Sachs, Lyndell 130, 231
Sadedin 172, 176
Sadler, Brent 53, 60, 63, 65
Sadrija, Abedin ('Rambo') 155–59, 160–65, 166–67, 169–70, 171–77, *176*, 181–82, 221
Sarajevo 11, 27, 34, 37, 42, 52, 55, 60, 66, 76–77, 96, 103–6, 115, 121, 123, 125, 134, 235
Scheffel, Alison 211
Schulz, Andrea 228–29, *230*, 233, 235, *238*
Scott, Selina 83
Sebastian, Tim 212
Second Gulf War 243
Second World War 10, 14, 28, 33, 39, 208
Sefo, Dr 35, 50
Selima 194, 198, 209
Serbia 10, 11, 18, 21, 185, 202, 244
Shala, Besa 169, 174, 222, 225, 236

Shala, Hamez 169, 172, 174, 222
Shamolli, Ismet 144, 216
Shehu, Gani 161–62, 171
Shkodra 215, 218, 224, 239, 240
Sir Halley Stewart Trust 91, 131, 231
Široki Brijeg 66, 124
Sky News 65–6, 69, 200
Slinn, David 191, 194–195, 200, 205–6
Slovenia 10, 18
Smolice 165
Sorensen, Leo Bang 46–48, 49, 52, 54, 57, 63
Spain 17, 19
'Spanish Captain' 43, 49, 66, 69
Split 20, 30, 34, 45, 69–70, 85, 104, 110, 115, 120, 123, 128, 130, **8**
Srebrenica 133–34
St John's Ambulance 225, 226
Stewart, Dr Duncan 24, 25, 89, 90, 91, 92, 93–7, 101–6, 108–9, 111–13, 115–16, 118–21, 125, 131, 152, 156, 195, 199–200, 204, 206–7, 210, 213, 215–16, 223, 228, 229, 239
Straw, Jack 225–27
Sullivan, Bernie 216, 219
Sullivan, Susie 216
Suncokret ('Sunflowers') 12, 14, 30, 66
Sun, The 248
Sunday Mirror, The 91–2
Susan 143
Switzerland 144, 160, 167, 169–70, 182, 186, 213, 219, 227, 239
Talk Radio 142
Teddies for Tragedies 93
Talkback 70
Thaci, Hashim 135, 205, 244
Thierry 29, 42, 44–6, 69, 85, 124

Thornberry, Cedric 53, 64
Times, The 65
Timothy, Christopher 91
Tirana 144, 150, 213, 215, 221, 223–25, 227, 230–31, 234–36, 239, 241
Tito, Josef Broz 10, 39, 220
Today (programme) 61, 212
Tohler, Major 108
Tomkowski, Krysztof 234
Tropoje 146, 148–49, 152, 157, 185, 220–21, 231, 236, **14**
Turner, Karen 12, 142–43, 145, 153
Tuzla 42, 94, 96, 115
UCK (*Ushtria, Clirimatre e Kosoves*) 135, 154
UNICEF 44, 51, 81
United Nation High Commissioner for Refugees (UNHCR) 81, 94, 96, 104, 107, 116, 130, 132, 149, 151, 152, 211, 217, 219, 220, 223, 225, 231, 250, **13**
United Nations (UN) 31, 32, 33, 42, 43, 44, 46, 47, 49, 51, 52, 53, 54, 55, 57, 59, 60, 61, 63, 65, 66, 69, 70, 73, 74, 82, 83, 86, 88, 94, 95, 101, 103, 104, 105, 109, 110, 111, 112, 113, 115, 116, 117, 118, 121, 123, 125, 127, 128, 130, 133, 149, 211, 220, 225, 232, 236, 243, 250, 251, **6, 7**
United Nations Civil Police (UNICIPOL) 46, 48
United Nations Human Rights Commission 134
United Nations Protection Force (UNPROFOR) 42, 43, 48, 51, 57, 64, 74, 78–9, 81, 108, 116, 118
Valbona 149, 222

Variety Club 89, 95
Vatcher, Sean 24, 28–9, 44, 50, 84–5, 124, 136, **1, 2**
Veterans for Peace 94–5, 115
Vitez 43, 87, 108, 127–28, 132
Vllasi, Azem 202–3
Vlora 213
Vojvodina 10
Walshe, Betty 136
War Child, charity 72
Webster, Collette 21, 24, 28, 29–30, 38, 44–5, 72, 82, 83–8, 124, 136, **1**
Weir, Stewart 91–2, 101
West Mostar 44–5, 47, 50, 61, 64, 76, 83–4, 131, 248
Wheatley, Jenny 143, 145, 146, 150, 211
White Hill Hospital (Bijeli–Brijeg) 27, 35, 36, 42, 50, 76, 86, 248
White Roads project 113, 123
White, Robin 127
Wilkinson, Ray 130–31
Williams, Colonel Peter 108, 127
Wilson, Richard 89, 90
Witness 212
Wood CBE, Anne 142
Young, Val 91
Yugoslav Red Cross 135, 136, 139, 184–85
Yugoslavia 10, 19, 34, 77, 195, 208
Zagreb 27, 35, 60, 64, 66, 72, 84–8, 93, 107, 121, 123, 125
Žena BiH 131, 133, 246
Zenica 94, 96, 107, 115, 121
Zepca 42
Zogu, Ahmed (King Zog) 149
Zoya 196–201, 205, 209
Zukić, Senad 115, 133
Zymberi, Isa 142

11/12

MALPAS